Sociological Lives

AMERICAN SOCIOLOGICAL ASSOCIATION PRESIDENTIAL SERIES

Volumes in this series are edited by successive presidents of the American Sociological Association and are based upon sessions at the Annual Meeting of the organization. Volumes in this series are listed below.

PETER M. BLAU
Approaches to the Study of Social Structure (1975)

LEWIS A. COSER and OTTO N. LARSEN
The Uses of Controversy in Sociology (1976)

J. MILTON YINGER
Major Social Issues: A Multidisciplinary View (1978)

The above three volumes are no longer in print.

AMOS H. HAWLEY
Societal Growth: Processes and Implications (1979)

HUBERT M. BLALOCK
Sociological Theory and Research: A Critical Approach (1980)

The above two volumes are available from The Free Press.

ALICE S. ROSSI
Gender and the Life Course (1985)

The above volume is available from Aldine Publishing Company.

JAMES F. SHORT, Jr.
The Social Fabric: Dimensions and Issues (1986)

MATILDA WHITE RILEY
in association with
BETTINA J. HUBER and BETH B. HESS
**Social Structures and Human Lives:
Social Change and the Life Course, Volume 1** (1988)

MATILDA WHITE RILEY
Sociological Lives: Social Change and the Life Course, Volume 2 (1988)

The above three volumes are available from Sage Publications.

Editor
Matilda White Riley

**Social Change and the Life Course,
Volume 2**

Sociological Lives

89- 303

American Sociological Association Presidential Series

 SAGE PUBLICATIONS
The Publishers of Professional Social Science
Newbury Park   Beverly Hills   London   New Delhi

For

JOHN W. RILEY, Jr.

who, save for the happy accident of marriage,
would have been an author in this book

Copyright © 1988 by Sage Publications, Inc.

All rights reserved. No part of this book may be reproduced or utilized in any form or by any means, electronic or mechanical, including photocopying, recording, or by any information storage and retrieval system, without permission in writing from the publisher.

For information address:

SAGE Publications, Inc.
2111 West Hillcrest Drive
Newbury Park, California 91320

SAGE Publications Inc.
275 South Beverly Drive
Beverly Hills
California 90212

SAGE Publications Ltd.
28 Banner Street
London EC1Y 8QE
England

SAGE PUBLICATIONS India Pvt. Ltd.
M-32 Market
Greater Kailash I
New Delhi 110 048 India

Printed in the United States of America
Library of Congress Cataloging-in-Publication Data

Main entry under title:

Social change and the life course / edited by Matilda White Riley in
   association with Bettina J. Huber, Beth B. Hess.
      p. cm. — (American Sociological Association presidential
   series)
      Selected papers from the 1986 Annual Meeting of the American
   Sociological Association, held in New York.
      Includes bibliographies and indexes.
      Contents: v. 1.   Social structures and human lives — v.
   2. Sociological lives.
      ISBN 0-8039-3287-1 (v. 1).   ISBN 0-8039-3288-X (pbk. : v. 1).
   ISBN 0-8039-3285-5 (v. 2).   ISBN 0-8039-3286-3 (pbk. : v. 2)
      1. Sociology—Congresses.   2. Aging—Social aspects—Congresses.
   3. Life cycle, Human—Social aspects—Congresses.   4. Social change-
   Congresses.   I. Riley, Matilda White. 1911-   .   II. Huber,
   Bettina J.   III. Hess, Beth B., 1928-   .   IV. American Sociological
   Association. Meeting (1986 : New York, N.Y.) V. Series.
   301—dc19   87-37658
                                                                  CIP

FIRST PRINTING 1988

Contents

EPILOGUE

About the Authors

HUBERT M. BLALOCK, Jr., is Professor of Sociology and Adjunct Professor of Political Science at the University of Washington in Seattle. His research interests are in applied statistics, causal modeling, theory construction, conceptualization and measurement, race relations, and, most recently, power and conflict processes. His most recent books are *Conceptualization and Measurement in the Social Sciences* (Sage, 1982) and *Basic Dilemmas in the Social Sciences* (Sage, 1984), and he is currently working on a book dealing with power and conflict processes.

LEWIS A. COSER, a former President of the American Sociological Association, is Professor Emeritus of Sociology at the State University of New York at Stony Brook and Adjunct Professor of Sociology at Boston College. His ASA Presidential volume on *The Uses of Controversy in Sociology* was published in 1976 and his book of essays titled *A Handful of Thistles and Other Essays* is published by Transaction Books, 1988.

ROSABETH MOSS KANTER is the Class of 1960 Professor of Business Administration, Harvard Business School. She received her Ph.D. in 1967 in Sociology (Michigan) and has been awarded nine honorary doctorates. She is a member of several editorial boards and boards of directors and a member of the Massachusetts Governor's Commission on Employee Involvement. She cofounded Goodmeasure, Inc., an organizational consulting firm, and serves as Chairman. She is author of many books and articles on organizational change and corporate entrepreneurship including the prize winning *Men and Women of the Corporation* (1977) and *The Change Masters: Innovation and Entrepreneurship in the American Corporation* (1983).

ROBERT K. MERTON is University Professor Emeritus at Columbia University; Adjunct Professor at the Rockefeller University; Resident Scholar, Russell Sage Foundation; and *pro tem* George Sarton Professor of the History of Science, University of Ghent (Belgium). These affiliations reflect his continuing interest in theoretical sociology and in the sociology, history, and philosophy of science. His books include *Science, Technology and Society in 17th-Century England* (1938, 1970); *Mass Persuasion* (1946); *Social Theory and Social Structure* (1949, 1957, 1968); *On the Shoulders of Giants* (1965, 1985); *The Sociology of Science: Theoretical & Empirical*

Investigations (1973); *Sociological Ambivalence* (1976); *Social Research &
the Practicing Professions* (1982); and *Sociological Ideas and Social Facts*
(forthcoming).

BERNICE L. NEUGARTEN currently is Professor of Human Development and
Social Policy at Northwestern University, and also Professor of Sociology
there. Following her earlier career at the University of Chicago, she is
returning there in 1988 as a Distinguished Scholar. She has published widely
in the areas of adult development and aging, the sociology of age, and social
policy. Her principal books include *Personality in Middle and Late Life*
(1964); *Middle Age and Aging* (1968); and *Age or Need? Public Policies for
Older People* (1982). She received the Brookdale Award in 1982, and the
Sandoz International Prize in 1987, both for her research in gerontology.

MATILDA WHITE RILEY is Associate Director for Behavioral and Social
Research (National Institute on Aging, National Institutes of Health), and
Professor Emerita of Sociology at Rutgers University and Bowdoin College.
She is a member of the American Academy of Arts and Sciences and the
Institute of Medicine (National Academy of Sciences). She has received an
honorary LHD from Rutgers and the Common Wealth Award in Sociology.
Her publications include *Sociological Research* (two volumes), *Aging and
Society* (three volumes), *Aging from Birth to Death* (two volumes), *Sociological Studies in Scale Analysis*, and numerous articles on mass communications, socialization, intergenerational relationships, research methods, and
other topics.

ALICE S. ROSSI is Harriet Martineau Professor of Sociology, Social and
Demographic Research Institute, University of Massachusetts (Amherst).
Recent publications include coediting (with Jane Lancaster, Jeanne Altman,
and Lonnie Sherrod) of *Parenting Across the Lifespan: Biosocial Dimensions*
(Aldine de Gruyter, 1987); *Gender and the Life Course* (Aldine, 1985), and
Feminists in Politics (Academic Press, 1983). Current research interests are in
intergenerational relations, sex and gender, and biosocial science.

WILLIAM H. SEWELL is Vilas Research Professor of Sociology and Chancellor
Emeritus of the University of Wisconsin. He is a past President of the
American Sociological Association. His research interests are in social
stratification, social psychology, quantitative methods and rural sociology.
During the last 25 years, much of his research attention has been directed to
social and psychological factors in the educational and occupational aspirations and achievements of a large cohort of Wisconsin high school graduates
which have been reported in several books and numerous articles. He is
currently working on a book with Robert and Taissa Hauser that will report
the aspirations and achievements of this cohort at mid-life. Throughout his

career, he has served on numerous research advisory committees of the Social Science Research Council, the Ford Foundation, the National Institutes of Health, the National Science Foundation, and the National Research Council.

THEDA SKOCPOL is Professor of Sociology at Harvard University, and was previously Professor of Sociology and Political Science at the University of Chicago. She is the author of *States and Social Revolutions* (Cambridge University Press, 1979), cowinner of the 1980 American Sociological Association Award for a Distinguished Contribution to Scholarship, and winner of the 1979 C. Wright Mills Award of the Society for the Study of Social Problems. Her edited books are *Vision and Method in Historical Sociology* (Cambridge University Press, 1984); *Bringing the State Back In* (Cambridge University Press, 1985); and *The Politics of Social Policy in the United States* (Princeton University Press, 1988). Her current research focuses on public policies in the United States in cross-national and historical perspective.

CHARLES VERT WILLIE, former President of the Eastern Sociological Society and a past member of the Council and the Executive Office and Budget Committee of the American Sociological Association, is Professor of Education and Urban Studies, Graduate School of Education, Harvard University. He has been a Vice President and Chair of the Department of Sociology at Syracuse University and a board member of the Social Science Research Council. His most recent books are *Effective Education* (1987), *Five Black Scholars* (1986), *Black and White Families* (1985), and *Race, Ethnicity, and Socioeconomic Status* (1983).

WILLIAM JULIUS WILSON is the Lucy Flower Distinguished Service Professor of Sociology and Public Policy, and former Chairman of the Department of Sociology, at the University of Chicago. He was a fellow (1981-1982) at the Center for Advanced Study in the Behavioral Sciences. He is author of numerous publications including *Power, Racism, and Privilege* (1973, 1976); *The Declining Significance of Race* (1978, 1980); and *The Truly Disadvantaged: The Inner City, The Underclass, and Public Policy* (1987). He is currently directing a large research project, "Poverty, Joblessness, and Family Structure in the Inner City." In June of 1987, he was named a MacArthur Prize Fellow.

Preface

THIS SMALL BOOK provides large glimpses into the sociology of sociology. Its authors, in autobiographical accounts of their own experiences, deal with varied aspects of the theme of the 1986 Annual Meeting of the American Sociological Association: the interplay between social structures and human lives. As a companion piece to Volume 1, this second volume contains the papers from the plenary sessions at that meeting. It opens with Robert Merton's elucidation of the concept of sociological autobiography, and closes with a penetrating commentary by Charles Willie that draws on his own sociological life. Added to these papers as Chapter 2 are my observations on the links between these essays and the program theme, along with some autobiographical recollections of my own. As a glance at the Table of Contents suggests, the collection touches on many aspects of the intellectual development of sociology and the history of its structural arrangements.

In preparing papers, contributors were invited by me as the 1986 President of the Association to consider the sociological meaning of the annual meeting theme, which had been announced in the January 1985 *Footnotes* as follows:

It is a sociological truism that social structures and human lives are inextricably linked. People grow up and grow old, not in laboratories, but in a matrix of groups, networks, institutions, and communities. People's experiences and positions in these social structures influence their attitudes, behaviors, physical and psychological functioning—indeed, all aspects of their lives. At the same time, social structures are shaped by people's changing lives.

The 1986 program is designed to reflect three recent emphases in sociology which bear on this truism:

1. *The dynamic nature of social structures and human lives.* Just as all people, irrespective of sex, age, socioeconomic status, or ethnicity, are continually growing older and changing biologically, psychologically, and socially, so too neither the society nor the culture in which they live remains unchanged. Sociologists increasingly use analytic strategies acknowledging the centrality of change in both social structures and human lives.

2. *The interplay between structural changes and aging (or human development).* Life-course patterns are affected by the social, cultural, and environmental changes to which people are exposed and also by the character of the cohort to which they belong. Similarly, the changed experiences of individuals and cohorts lead to large-scale change in social and cultural structures.

3. *The increasing relevance of work in neighboring disciplines.* Sociological studies of changing social structure, individual aging, and the influence of each on the other are in the mainstream of sociology; but they are also broadly informed by recent studies in anthropology, economics, history, political science, psychology, biology, and other fields.

Eight sociologists were invited to explore this theme, using their own very different lives as foils. They were asked to emphasize intellectual developments rather than scholarly achievements, and perhaps also to say something about the future of the discipline. Rather than presenting rounded autobiographies in the usual sense, they were requested to tell something of how their own sociological lives have been influenced by changing social structures and how, in turn, their lives have influenced these structures.

These authors and the commentators included in this volume are uniquely qualified to address the 1986 program theme. They are widely diversified in background, early history, interests, and types of sociological work; thus their lives are variously located in the structure of sociology. Moreover, they differ in age—or more precisely in date of entry into sociology; thus their lives are variously located in the history of sociology. Together with other members of these successive cohorts, their experience is marked by societal and intellectual trends that span nearly a century. Thus their collective lives illustrate the rich diversity of contemporary sociology.

To be sure, a mere eleven sociologists, all told, can scarcely do more than illustrate this diversity. Necessarily, there are gaps in the array. Voices are heard from several university centers (Columbia, Chicago, Washington, Wisconsin), but not others (contemporary Michigan, Berkeley, North Carolina, or Harvard in the heyday of Social Relations). Only a handful of sociological fields, perspectives, and ideologies could be included. Among the omissions are those sociologists who were attending the concurrent meetings of the International Sociological Association. A notable omission is John W. Riley, Jr., recipient of the ASA's Distinguished Career Award for the Practice of Sociology, who might have told us how academic achievement can lead to sociological contributions to opinion and military research and to the resolution of social issues facing corporations and foundations. Though pressed on universalistic grounds to participate, he declined on particularistic grounds: because he is my husband. (My only appropriate rejoinder is to dedicate this book to him!)

Quite openly, then, the book suffers from obvious biases because the number of contributors is so limited. It is also biased by the "patterned distortions and omissions" to which sociological autobiography is subject, as Merton points out. Nevertheless, the introspection and retrospection of sociological autobiography also give us rare access to inner experience. And, in the words of one of the essayists, "sociologists are uniquely qualified to stand apart from societal and intellectual trends, to appraise them, and thereby to give shape to future trends."

This book is directed primarily to sociologists, both novices and initiates. It should intrigue both disciples and opponents of particular contributors or the schools of thought they represent. It should captivate those interested in otherwise hidden and often overlooked features of the intellectual history of sociology. At the same time, it should interest readers from other disciplines, and those sophisticated lay readers who simply enjoy the delights of autobiography.

For help in planning the program leading to this book, I am indebted to Robert K. Merton and to the members of the 1986 ASA Program Committee, most especially John Meyer and Anne Foner. For assistance in editing, I thank Bettina J. Huber and Beth B. Hess, my Associate Editors for the first of these two volumes. And for advice, assistance, guidance, and forbearance at every stage of the long process of planning, editing, and publishing, I thank my husband and lifelong colleague, John W. Riley, Jr.

—Matilda White Riley

Part I

Introduction

1

Some Thoughts on the Concept of Sociological Autobiography

Robert K. Merton

THE PROSPECT OF having eight colleagues tell of "their sociological lives in changing social structures" raises at once the not uninteresting question: Can we identify attributes distinctive of what we shall agree to call "sociological autobiography" that mark it off as a genre from other kinds of autobiography that have appeared over the centuries since at least the Renaissance? (Or as some have argued—for instance, the Göttingen scholar, Georg Misch, in his classic volumes, the *History of Autobiography in Antiquity,* 1950—as they have appeared over the millennia.)

In musing on this question for the short socially expected duration allowed me, I bypass a more general question. Are the art and craft of autobiography apt to be practiced differently by those variously located in the social and cultural structure: by politician, novelist, sociologist, psychologist, industrialist, and Hollywood celebrity; by prophet, priest, agnostic, and atheist; by men and women; by the young, not-so-young, and comparatively old; and so on through the list of socially differentiated narrators of their own lives and times? Instead, I limit myself to a few observations on the comparative advantages and disadvantages of autobiography and biography and then focus on the notion of a distinctively sociological autobiography. I do so analytically, not empirically. Mindful of though not entirely persuaded by Karl Popper's warnings of the perils of induction, I do not try to infer attributes of sociological autobiography inductively by systematically examining the capsule accounts in this volume or the recent spate of book-length accounts by Charles Page, George Homans, Reinhard Bendix, Don Martindale, and others, or the surprisingly small number of intellectual autobiographies by sociologists all told since they—that is to say, we—first acquired a public identity in the last century. To be sure, Herbert Spencer gave us two volumes of autobiography and Lester Ward, six. Just as we are legatees of Pitirim Sorokin's (1963) *A Long Journey* and Robert MacIver's *As a Tale That is Told* (which, as a longtime colleague of them both, I can attest ring descriptively true and analytically latent). But Marx, Durkheim, Weber, Simmel, W. I. Thomas, and Talcott Parsons are among the many more who have left us nothing by way of autobiography—although the vast Marx-Engels correspondence provides some compensation.

The sociological autobiography utilizes sociological perspectives, ideas, concepts, findings, and analytical procedures to construct and to interpret the narrative text that purports to tell one's own history within the context of the larger history of one's times. Compared with sociological biography, it enjoys the same advantages and suffers the same disadvantages as other forms of autobiography. Put in terms of a workaday sociological concept, auto-biographers are the ultimate participants in a dual participant-observer role, having privileged access—in some respects, monopolistic access—to their own inner experience. Biographers of self can introspect and retrospect in ways that others cannot do for them. That advantage is coupled with disadvantages. As we know, introspection and individual memory (as well as collective memory) are subject to patterned distortions and omissions. Those hazards are probably compounded in the sustained introspections and long-term memory drawn upon to reconstruct long stretches of one's past.

Sometimes, it seems, excessively long stretches. As Virginia Woolf (1976) noted derivatively, in her long-unpublished autobiographical writings, *Moments of Being*, there can come a time when one has forgotten far more of significance to an autobiography than one has remembered. (The specific reference was to Lady Strachey, mother of the unruly biographer Lytton, whose "Recollections of a Long Life" were condensed into ten pages or so.) Or again, the prolific Heinrich Böll, whose novels and stories were published in 45 languages and issued in some 25 million copies, could only manage, in the absence of diary and journal, an autobiographic fragment of 82 pages which announces that "not one title, not one author, not one book that I held in my hand has remained in my memory."

Still, like biographers, autobiographers can have a measure of control over possible tricks of memory and errors of observation. They too can utilize the historical resource of documents: those often uncalculated evidences of what one did, felt, and thought, and of what one failed to do, feel, and think. In effect, the remembered past then becomes transformed into a series of hypotheses to be checked, so far as they can be, by aggregated documents and testimonies of others.

In reflecting on the sociological autobiography as a distinctive form, I find it impossible to avoid drawing on a paper of mine, "Insiders and Outsiders: A Chapter in the Sociology of Knowledge"(1972). For if the autobiographer has the advantage of being the ultimate Insider, the biographer has the counterpart advantage of more readily being the distanced Outsider. If the one has privileged or monopolistic access to portions and aspects of the inner life, the other more easily achieves the required distance and candor. I would propose that in concept—not of course necessarily in practice—the truly sociological autobiography combines the complementary advantages of both Insider and Outsider while minimizing the disadvantages of each.

On still rare occasion, the complementary perspectives of Insider and Outsider can be combined through disciplined collaboration. Witness a condensed prototypical case of the biography of an episode in the history of biology. Here, the biological scientist Joshua Lederberg, who 40 years before had made the consequential discovery of genetic recombination in bacteria, collaborated with the sociologist of science, Harriet Zuckerman, to examine that discovery as a possible case of what was analytically defined as a "postmature scientific discovery": one that was technically achievable earlier with methods then available; expressible in terms understandable by scientists then at work in the field; and capable of having its salient implications appreciated at the earlier time. In this joint inquiry (*Nature*, December 1986), the biologist-participant was successively providing personal and public documents to check on personal memories from the perspective of the ultimate Insider while collaborating in the ongoing analysis of the ac- cumulating data with the sociologist-observer working from the perspective of the Outsider. Each collaborator internalized much of what the other brought to the collaboration. The sociologist learned a good deal of the biology involved as well as its history; the biologist learned a good deal about the sociological questions involved and how one might go about answering them. This composite of highly personal materials and analytical distance did much to enable exploration of the seemingly self-deprecating hypothesis that one's own scientific discovery, declared by those judges in Stockholm to warrant The Prize, might have been made quite some time before. Collabora- tions of this kind could make for a much larger and more instructive corpus of sociological autobiography.

Among other things, then, the sociological autobiography is a personal exercise—a self-exemplifying exercise—in the sociology of scientific knowl- edge. The constructed personal text tells of the interplay between the active agent and the social structure, the interplay between one's sequences of status-sets and role-sets on the one hand and one's intellectual development on the other, with its succession of theoretical commitments, foci of scientific attention, planned or serendipitous choices of problems and choices of strategic research sites for their investigation. Tacitly or explicitly, it draws upon such concepts in the sociology of science as Derek de Solla Price's "invisible colleges," Ludwik Fleck's "thought styles" and "thought collectives," and, to go no further, Thomas Kuhn's "paradigms" and "exemplars" and Gerald Holton's "thematic analysis." The narratives and their interpretations tell of reference groups and reference individuals, the significant others that helped shape the changing character of thought and inquiry. Tacitly or explicitly, they tell of accumulations of advantage and of disadvantage and of self-fulfilling prophecies, both social and individual, in the domain of developing knowledge. And yet again, tacitly or explicitly, they take note of how dedicated commitment to one or another theoretical orientation or mode of research practice can lead to the self-isolating neglect of alternatives or to civil and, on occasion, to uncivil wars between contending thought collectives.

Not least in this truncated inventory, full-fledged sociological auto-biographers relate their intellectual development both to changing social and cognitive micro-environments close at hand and to the encompassing macro-environments provided by the larger society and culture (on the concept of such micro-environments, see Merton, 1979, pp. 82-94). Put in terms of the thematics of this volume, such accounts bear witness that one's runs of experience and foci of interest, one's accomplishments and failures, were in no small part a function of the historical moment at which one has entered the field. Neophytes coming into the domain of sociology at comparable ages but in different age cohorts—say, of the 1920s, 1940s, 1960s, and 1980s—have plainly entered into appreciably different historical contexts. The then current state of the disciplinary art differs from the rest as does the larger social and cultural environment. As a result, the initial and later experience of newcomers to the discipline in the different periods is bound to differ significantly.

After that last observation, I find myself lapsing into a brief retrospect. It puts me irresistibly in mind of the first annual meeting of this Association that I happened to attend. That was in the late 1920s. My treacherous memory estimates—without my having consulted the records—the *total* attendance at that national meeting in Washington at some 200—less than a quarter of our number in this one plenary session. In those primitive, sparsely populated days, and thanks to my mentor at Temple University, George E. Simpson, a 17-year-old sophomore like myself could get to meet—even to talk with—the likes of a Robert E. Park, W. I. Thomas, William F. Ogburn, and E. A. Ross. He could also listen, most consequentially for him, to the inadvertently recruiting sociological voice of the then University of Minnesota scholar, Pitirim Alexandrovich Sorokin, this several years before Sorokin was called to found the Department of Sociology at Harvard. I suspect that under-graduates attending these densely populated meetings—especially those attending for the first time—find it rather more difficult to have a reasonably similar experience. And in complementary turn we might ask: How many youngsters can any one of us lingering oldsters manage to cope with? As we sociologists have been known to suggest, numbers, density, and organizational complexity do make a difference to the character of human experience.

A final word. It will be noticed that this bare sketch of some attributes of the sociological autobiography is less a condensed description than a step toward an elucidated concept. It is rather more a normative concept than a summary of a frequent sociocultural phenomenon. In that sense, not all autobiographies by sociologists qualify as sociological autobiography just as not all sociological autobiography is written by credentialed sociologists. In reading the set of autobiographic accounts in this volume, however, we can sense how and how far the texts, constructed of introspection, retrospection, and interpretation, have been shaped by the sociological consciousness of their authors, and that consciousness, in turn, by the structural contexts in which they found themselves. Those short accounts must condense much into little space. Still, it only requires an attentive sociological eye to see what is being said between the lines as well as on them and to interpolate for our reading selves what the social constraints of allowable space have required the authors to neglect or delete. Perhaps the same attentive readers will do much the same with these brief observations on the concept of sociological autobiography.

References

MacIver, Robert M. 1968. *As a Tale That Is Told: The Autobiography of R. M. MacIver.* Chicago: University of Chicago Press.

Merton, Robert K. 1972. "Insiders and Outsiders: A Chapter in the Sociology of Knowledge." *American Journal of Sociology* 77:9-47.

———. 1979. *The Sociology of Science: An Episodic Memoir.* Carbondale: Southern Illinois University Press.

Misch, Georg. 1950. *A History of Autobiography in Antiquity* (2 vols.). London: Routledge & Kegan Paul.

Sorokin, Pitirim A. 1963. *A Long Journey: The Autobiography of Pitirim A. Sorokin.* New Haven, CT: College and University Press.

Woolf, Virginia. 1976. *Moments of Being: Unpublished Autobiographical Writings.* Edited by Jeanne Schulkind. New York: Harcourt Brace Jovanovich.

Zuckerman, Harriet and Joshua Lederberg. 1986. "Postmature Scientific Discovery?" *Nature* (December 18) No. 6098:629-631.

2

Notes on the Influence
of Sociological Lives

Matilda White Riley

> One generation passeth away, and another generation cometh; but the earth abideth for ever.
>
> ECCLESIASTES 1:4

The interplay between society (with its social structures) and the succession of generations (or cohorts[1]) of individual lives is the theme of this book. Like the earth itself, societies endure, but not without change. As social structures change, the lives of individuals embedded within them are also altered. And, in turn, these altered lives produce further changes in society. This theme, at least as old as the Scriptures, is often taken for granted. Yet its meanings are perennially new.

AUTHOR'S NOTE: *With appreciation for editorial advice and suggestion to Anne Foner, Beth B. Hess, Bettina J. Huber, John Meyer, and John W. Riley, Jr.*

1. In the technical language of this book, the venerable term "generation" is reserved for its kinship meaning. The neologism "cohort" is used when the reference, as here, is to people born (or entering a particular system) at a given time.

On rereading the autobiographical essays in this book, I am struck anew by the meanings that sociological lives hold for the development of sociology. The variety of these narratives is dramatic demonstration of the dialectical nature of the interplay between changing social structures and changing lives. Each continually influences the other. The connecting link is provided by the cohort succession of lives: while social structures are changing, one set of sociologists is continually replacing its predecessors. Thus cohort succession determines the historical intervals during which particular sociologists live out their socially structured lives. (Here, and throughout this essay, I make use of the analytical framework set forth in Chapter 2 of *Social Structures and Human Lives*, Volume 1 of *Social Change and the Life Course*, the companion volume to this one, to which readers may wish to refer.)

In their autobiographical accounts, contributors to this volume provide abundant and fascinating details on the two-way directions of the interplay between social structures and human lives. In *one direction*, their accounts illustrate the influence on their individual experience and intellectual development exerted by the particular social structures in which their lives are implanted. They show how early background affected later decisions and attitudes. For example:

Lewis Coser—Moving in an "upper-middle class society" in pre-World War I Berlin, "I soon developed an acute sense of injustice."

Rosabeth Kanter—"As the grandchild of immigrants, why couldn't people like me do anything we wanted to do?"

Theda Skocpol—"As an upwardly mobile mid-Westerner," a child of the "uppity" generation of the 1960s, I had "the chutzpah to undertake the virtually impossible."

As the authors attest, their educational history, treatment by mentors, and interchanges with peers all affected them at strategic points in their lives. For example:

Alice Rossi—Like parents, "our intellectual mentors often seem bigger than life," and their standards of excellence become "internalized" for continuing future use.

As Robert Merton puts it in elucidating the concept of sociological autobiography in his opening essay for this book, their experience and intellectual development is in part a function of "the changing social and cognitive micro-environments close at hand and . . . the encompassing macro-environments provided by the larger society and culture." In one way or another, as Charles Willie shows in the Epilogue to this volume, each of the eight essays exemplifies the potential influence of social structure on sociological lives.

The Influence of Sociological Lives

At the same time, there is a reciprocal direction in the interplay between structures and lives: The lifetime experiences and intellectual development of individuals also help to shape the surrounding structures. The sociologists included in this volume are not only influenced; they and their peers are themselves "influentials," to borrow another of Merton's terms. Their lives have significant consequences for both sociology and society. The clues they provide here contribute to understanding a largely neglected sociological domain: how structural changes evolve from the lives of successive cohorts of individuals, and most particularly from the lives and work of individuals who are leaders in their cohorts. My rereading prompts me to focus here on this other direction of the interplay between structures and lives: that is, on the *nature and operation of the influence of sociological lives* on social and intellectual structures in sociology and in society.

Clearly, the power of sociological influence depends on the mesh of the attributes of particular lives and the opportunities afforded at the time by the social structure. The following essays shed light on certain aspects of this mesh. Through the process of reconstructing diverse sociological lives, the several authors reflect a wide range of variability in access to influence, not only because of their differing locations in society, but also because of the differing historical eras in which members of their cohorts made critical choices.

To be sure, the essays can tell little about the implications for sociological influence of differing *personal capacities* or differential *statuses* in the world of sociology, because all authors are similarly active participants in the profession, and all have achieved high status and visibility in the discipline. Even about *age*, or career stage of greatest influence, the essays can provide few clues, because none of the authors has yet completed his or her life course. The essays do tell a great deal about the implications of *cohort membership*, however, because cohorts from four decades of this century are represented. The birth dates of the eight sociologists contributing autobiographies to this volume range from 1909 to 1947 though, for some, entrance into sociology is poorly indexed by date of birth. I shall dwell on the differing social structures encountered by members of these successive cohorts during the intervals of history spanned by their respective lives. I shall cite a few of the many clues in these essays that suggest how the "potential for sociological influence" may be facilitated or thwarted by the particular "channels of influence" that, as society changes, become open or closed to individual sociologists at the different stages of their lives.

In examining the influence of sociological lives, one can but wish for still fuller accounts of still more lives. For example, from the few essays in this book we often cannot compare individuals from different cohorts who participate in the same period of history, but at different ages. Nor can we compare individuals from different cohorts who at similar ages participated in different historical periods. Hence I shall take occasional note of other lives and other structures not represented in these essays. Moreover, I shall not hesitate to draw on recollections[2] from the joint lives of John and Matilda Riley, which have been intertwined for well over half a century of marriage and colleagueship. Often collaborating as sociologists, our scholarship has spanned the life course: We first published empirically based articles on contraception; then sequentially on children, on adolescents, on mid-life careers; then on old age and on death; and now we plan to turn back to leisure, the topic which, in our earliest and most idealistic years, we had dreamed of one day being "mature" enough to tackle!

My comments on the power of sociological lives are divided into three parts illustrating, first, sociologists as influentials in the interplay between structure and lives; second, domains of sociological influence; and third, influences on a developing field, using the sociology of age as one instance. A connecting thread in the search for clues to the operation of sociological influence is cohort flow, which is the dynamic link between changing lives and changing structures, locating individuals in time and space.

SOCIOLOGISTS AS INFLUENTIALS

We are all aware of the work of the eight sociologists included in this volume, all of whom are indeed influentials. They themselves—because of modesty or insensitivity to the underlying principle—are often hesitant to discuss this influence. For example, Rosabeth Kanter—claiming that, since Max Weber, sociological attention has shifted from the individual as a driving force to classes of people and social patterns—looks for "some larger institutional patterns that my own career might reflect." Yet the fact clearly emerges that she believes we should "never accept reality, but continually try to reshape it to include the best of human aspirations," and she manifests this belief in her life course to date and in her writings. William J. Wilson, to take a contrasting example, is explicit about the interplay between social and scholarly trends and his own intellectual growth. He dramatizes the ways in which this growth is not merely a passive reflection of structural change and academic controversy, but also a powerfully active force in influencing both sociological thought and public policy. But what is the nature of this "sociological influence" and how does it operate? What "channels of influence" open or close as the social structure changes? What can block the channels and how are barriers removed? How do lives of sociologists in successive cohorts mesh with the changing channels of opportunity? This set

2. For bibliographical references, see sources cited in Chapter 2 of *Social Structures and Human Lives* (Volume 1 of *Social Change and the Life Course*).

of essays, which weave together richly detailed examples of powerful lives, helps to specify such questions. Without providing clear answers, the essays present numerous clues to the ways in which sociological influence operates. Several of these clues can be grouped here to suggest how channels of influence are affected by the historical period when they are experienced at particular life stages by individuals in given cohorts, and by contemporary definitions of gender-based and minority-based roles.

Cohort Differences and Sociological Influence

That all of the contours of each person's life and work, including chronological age and stage of career and family development, are linked to history, is well illustrated in Alice Rossi's autobiography. Her essay, among others, reminds us that, while individuals in successive cohorts are growing older, the historical milieu is changing and with it the opportunities for sociological influence.

The discussion by Rosabeth Kanter illustrates specifically the significance of cohort membership, which guides individual lives through structural changes and opportunities during designated intervals of historical time. Kanter draws a parallel between phases of discontinuity at both the level of the changing society and the level of the unfolding individual career. Noting that the resurgence of modern sociology took place at a time of political and economic revolution, Kanter identifies three phases of societal turmoil beginning around 1960 that again gave sociology a temporary ascendancy: "utopian possibilities," "opposition and estrangement," and "tentative integration." She proposes that these three phases correspond to phases in the lives of sociologists and others in her cohort as they moved from youthful hope, to cynicism about the ability of institutions to change, to a merger of hope and cynicism, as institutions, though imperfectible, nonetheless afford possibilities for reform.

This neat parallelism suggests that the life-course phases of Kanter and others in her cohort were uniquely synchronized with the social changes of that period. These individuals began their work careers when youthful hope was the order of the day and "aged" until they approached the third societal phase of tentative integration. Thus for the members of this cohort there was a distinct mesh between individual lives and historical forces that opened channels of opportunity for sociological influence.

An intriguing question posed by Kanter's account is as follows: Does the parallelism between lives and changing structures hold for members of other cohorts as well? What about those in earlier cohorts, with their differing experiences and ideologies, who were further along in their careers before they faced the "utopian possibilities" of the 1960s? Or members of recent cohorts who now, as they enter their careers, confront not the first but the third phase of societal discontinuity? That is, do the contours of lives in different cohorts mesh equally well with the historical trends and the channels of opportunity of the particular time period?

Such questions merit proper examination through systematic comparison of lives in a succession of cohorts, a task far beyond the reach of this book. But the questions can be formulated and addressed, if only indirectly, from scattered clues throughout these autobiographies. Thus Kanter herself may provide one clue in suggesting that cohort members now young, even though seemingly conservative, may actually be following the life-course contours characterizing Kanter's own cohort because they are shifting "to embrace the utopian and the oppositional agendas of the 1960s and 1970s." During many time intervals, however, the social changes that provide open channels of influence for members of one cohort can also block these channels for coexisting members of other cohorts who are at other stages of their lives. (For the sociologist of age, these questions touch on the significant principle of "asynchrony" between the rhythm of the human life course and the course of social change, which has less clear rhythm or periodicity, as described in Chapter 2 of *Social Structures and Human Lives*, Volume 1 of *Social Change and the Life Course.*)

Ascribed Differences and Sociological Influence

As several essays illustrate, the opportunities for influence encountered by particular cohorts depend to a considerable degree upon the prevalent attitudes toward ascribed characteristics. Gender and race receive particular attention here. Alice Rossi describes how gender differences in the "shape" of an academic career were far greater for her cohort during the 1950s (she herself was "off time") than for any cohort before or since. Males were favored educationally by the World War II GI Bill. In occupations, men secured the top positions; while in academia, women were relegated to assistantships, not because of tight job markets, but because of sex discrimination and antinepotism rules. Thus for women at that time the channels of influence were largely blocked. Most women acquiesced in these arrangements, by lowering their aspirations and often withdrawing entirely from the labor force to raise children.

My own life history as a woman is instructive. Coming from the 1911 birth cohort, which was marked by gender inequality, I managed to find, albeit inadvertently, a series of professional opportunities. In my early years, sex discrimination was taken for granted; to advance, an enterprising woman had to find her own way around the obstacles. When a publisher refused to put my name on the book (on gliding and soaring!) that I had written during a college vacation "because no one will read a book written by a girl," I changed my name from Matilda to Mat, and the book sold quite well. When I sought a job to help support us during my husband's graduate studies, the professor who wanted to appoint me for the only available teaching assistantship was turned down by his dean because "as a woman she will not continue a career." Thereupon, through a stroke of good fortune, my summer vacation experiences in market research and my knowledge of foreign languages qualified me for the first research assistantship in the newly formed Harvard Department of Sociology, where I organized a team for analyzing all the European Le Play studies of family budgets. By the time—many years later—that I considered further graduate study, I was already so immersed in sociology as to have become a full professor.

In those days, gender inequalities were simply not regarded as inequities— perhaps one reason why some women in those earliest cohorts, such as Bernice Neugarten or me, were able to lead our lives as individuals, not as members of a class of individuals; only later, when the gender distinction was more articulately discussed and resisted, did it become a more conscious and visible target for sociological influence. Neugarten, for example, does "not recall a single instance in which the fact that I was a woman made any difference in my education or in my work career." On the whole, I too was generally undaunted by sex inequalities. Nevertheless, I remember one dreadful exception: the years when I attempted to be a full-time housewife. A woman was expected to choose either marriage or a career—not both—and, in my innocence, I had chosen marriage. (Alice Rossi too speaks of her early "innocence" on the position of women.) Yet, I was so utterly unprepared for the shift from student to housewife that only by the help of my supportive husband was I spared deep depression. Even then, I laid the blame on my own weakness, not on the strict gender-based constraints.

It was only in the 1960s, as one of a small number of women on the graduate faculty at Rutgers, that I took up the cudgels for women students, because they were deprived of equal opportunities for fellowships; and for women faculty members with very young children, because their careers were jeopardized by strict enforcement of tenure requirements. I note this change in my own involvement with women's issues only to mark an instance of similarity—rather than difference—in cohort response to a social change, a response that redirected the course of sociological influence. The influx of women into the labor force and graduate schools, culminating in the women's movements of the 1960s, tended to galvanize women from every cohort and at every age.

In this instance, then, it was *not* cohort membership, age, or stage of life that affected the influence of particular sociologists. Rather it was the *emergence of a social issue* that drew the attention of sociologists to new foci of influence: both to gender-based policies and to gender as a major domain of sociological inquiry. Thus Alice Rossi, in a more recent cohort than mine, turned to the sociological study of gender after a personal experience of sex discrimination; and in the most recent cohort, Theda Skocpol reports that she now recognizes "that women's movements and gender relations are . . .

absolutely central to the formation of modern welfare states." In making her future plans, she hopes to "join the many others in our discipline who are already drawing on the travails of changing gender relations to enrich the sociological imagination."

Just as gender barriers have prompted sociologists to exert influence to break them down, the long-standing struggle against racial barriers has taken on new vigor in the last decades. Here too, several essays in this volume suggest how individual sociologists exert influence in response to particular historical situations. Tad Blalock tells how his substantial work in race relations was initially stimulated by his "genuine culture shock" over the ethnocentrism of American sailors who mistreated Chinese war victims in the mid-1940s. William Julius Wilson tells how the course of his intellectual life shifted away from a "concentration on the logic of social inquiry [which] could not be sustained in a period dominated by Black protest." Describing his widely honored career, he shows "how changing social structures influenced the direction of my scholarship, ultimately leading to the writing of *The Declining Significance of Race*"; and how in turn "the post-publication debate on the book helped to shape my subsequent intellectual development and change my aspirations for the future of sociology." These future aspirations include not only enhancing sociology's "substantive and method-ological imaginations" through research, but also drawing serious policy and media attention to central issues of our time. In effect, Wilson's life demonstrates how sociological influence, when effective, can breed further influence.

DOMAINS OF SOCIOLOGICAL INFLUENCE

The availability to individual scholars of channels of influence is affected not only by their location within changing social structures, but also by the exigencies of disciplinary development. Scattered examples from four domains of the discipline begin to contribute to a fuller understanding of the nature and operation of sociological influence.

Methodology

(1) In *methodology*, whether channels of opportunity are open or closed to particular cohorts depends in part on the *state of the art* at the time, and in part also on the *goals and interests of the discipline*. In my own experience in the very early 1930s, I remember calculating by hand literally hundreds of square roots to aid Pitirim Sorokin in the monumental task of classifying and counting, according to his categories of meaning, many thousands of works of art, wars, revolutions, economic conditions, scientific and technical develop-ments, and *all* the historical figures in the *Encyclopedia Britannica*! Sorokin

and his assistants, working without benefit of modern sampling or computers, were not focused on methodological development; but the lack of such methods caused a major diversion of time and talent away from his central theoretical and substantive objectives.

If Sorokin's ambitious enterprise lacked an appropriate methodology, this was not the case for William Sewell, who not only found fertile soil for the development of quantitative methodology but also exercised profound influence on this development. Sewell and his associates have made the Wisconsin Longitudinal Study a model for other researchers. The power of its influence is indicated by the long list of publications emanating from its 25 years of data gathering and by the various national and local research projects modeled after it. Sewell describes the opportunities of the 1960s and 1970s that fostered this accomplishment, and they are worth recapitulating here as highly relevant to my concern with the operation of sociological influence:

(a) The *state of the art* was ready for this development and for those who would emulate it: The mathematical statistical models for analysis and the necessary computer hardware were available.

(b) *Organizational arrangements* had been set up for research colleagues, including students, to work together as teams.

(c) Institutional structures for the *funding of social science research* had been established.

(d) There was sustained and extensive *interest* throughout sociology in social psychology and especially in social mobility and status attainment as an individual process. That is, Sewell's lifelong work could be fully effective in its influence because it met a *felt need* at the right moment in the history of American sociology.

It should be noted in passing that Sewell's contributions relate specifically to one type of method, longitudinal analysis, and are thus especially suited to research on individual lives. The unique advantages of the method for such objectives as life-course analysis can become disadvantages, however, if inappropriately applied, as in the analysis of social systems. Unfortunately, this powerful approach is all too often inappropriately used, which alerts us to quite a different aspect of sociological influence: To yield positive effects, influence requires judicious *responses from the persons influenced.* After all, those being influenced (though not under scrutiny here) are as crucial to the process as the influentials are.

In contrast to Sewell's experience, the very different effort by Tad Blalock to bring theory and method together found little response during the 1950s and 1960s. He complains that "mathematical modelling as a form of theorizing was entirely foreign" to his sociological contemporaries, although he does cite such exceptions as Paul Lazarsfeld and "perhaps a handful of others." In actuality, he might have cited many others; clearly, one obstacle blocking his broader influence at that time was *inadequate communication* among sociological "schools." In my own small segment of the field, for example, there was no communication with Blalock until considerably later. Much like Freed Bales at Harvard at that time, I too was struggling with the use of mathematical models for theorizing about small group interaction. But the concept of groups as systems, as opposed to aggregated individuals, was largely illusory for most quantitative methodologists of the 1950s. (Paul Lazarsfeld once confessed privately that he had spent one long night attempting to derive our social system findings through random combinations of information about *individuals*.)

The polar opposition between theory and methodology (both quantitative and qualitative) still persists and Blalock, now joined by other kindred spirits, continues to struggle with it. Indeed, as he says, these disputes "have tended to occupy my attention in much of my later work," and his American Sociological Association (ASA) Presidential volume (1980) brought together a considerable number of essays under the title *Sociological Theory and Research*. One might describe the impact of Blalock's influence as delayed, as constituting a "lag in cumulation" of scientific work. One small example of his continuing influence is the concern in research today on "age, cohort, and period" with what Blalock, in studying mobility, originally formulated as the "identification problem."

As methodology becomes more catholic in its scope, we find concern in the following essays with combining micro-level and macro-level data; and with combining quantitative, qualitative, and macro-historical approaches (see Skocpol, Wilson). In my own experience, this catholicity approximates more nearly the wide range of sociological methods with which I was familiar in the 1950s and 1960s. Varieties of methods correspond to the differing theoretical approaches from which Lewis Coser selects for elucidation of different empirical problems. And thoughtful matching of method and theory can infuse sociological meaning into research at any system level and in any historical period.

Interdisciplinary Domains

(2) In *interdisciplinary domains*, channels of influence are sometimes blocked by resistance from within the core of the discipline itself. Among attempts to draw relevant interdisciplinary perspectives or materials into sociology, Alice Rossi's autobiography reflects one segment of the historical experience. She recounts how, during her graduate student years at Columbia in the 1950s, Robert Merton was combining cultural-historical with psychological and biological "levels." Rossi traces the roots of her own later attempts to integrate biological and social constructs to her early sharing in the "intellectual ferment of thinking across academic disciplines that was taking place at Harvard, Michigan, and Yale." Her ASA Presidential volume, *Gender and the Life Course* (1985), highlights these interdisciplinary perspec-

tives. Her efforts comport with my own, and those of other students of age, who view aging and human development as an interaction among biological, psychological, and social processes.

Many such interdisciplinary efforts meet with stubborn resistance from within sociology (or other disciplines), however, as the early fate of Social Relations at Harvard makes abundantly clear, as does the midcentury failure of joint departments of social psychology at Michigan, Columbia, and elsewhere. It is apparently in research activities, where the focus is on a common goal, that interdisciplinary work may be most influential in enriching sociology. Thus, for example, Wilson's research on race relations synthesizes the efforts of scholars from several disciplines.

Bernice Neugarten's autobiographical essay describes yet another instance of interdisciplinary development that involves sociology but transcends it. Not only did Neugarten play a major role in creating a completely new program of Human Development at Chicago, she has also built an entire career in this new area, and has used her knowledge to make major contributions to public policy, as by advocating a "focus, not on age, but on more relevant dimensions of human needs, human competencies, and human diversity." It is noteworthy that Neugarten has accomplished this outside the boundaries of sociology or any other single discipline. One wonders under what conditions interdisciplinary work, which draws on outside fields, can similarly feed directly into sociology rather than diffusing sociological influence outward.

Nonacademic Domains

(3) In *nonacademic domains*, as in interdisciplinary domains, the channels of influence run in both directions. Many sociologists, regardless of their occupational bases, use sociological tools in nonacademic settings and, in turn, bring the results of this work back into sociology. Here again, the opportunities for sociological influence have varied markedly over the century.

In the domain of *business and industry* today, Rosabeth Kanter demonstrates "the importance of connecting sociological work to the urgent concerns of society." Like Amitai Etzioni and other sociologists currently at business schools, her influence is exercised through teaching tomorrow's corporate and government leaders, working with corporations, and publishing widely read books.

Much earlier in the century, the relative importance of business to sociology was even greater. In my own experience in market research, when I was joined by Paul Lazarsfeld on his first visit to this country as a Rockefeller Fellow in the 1930s, he found market research in some respects more advanced than academic research. In those Depression years, outside the government it was in large part market research that provided funds for inquiring sociological minds to develop new methods of cross-section surveys, intensive interviewing and observation, panel studies, probability sampling, small group interactions, and much else that has since become the stuff of sociological research. Influential research centers such as the Bureau of Applied Social Research at Columbia and its counterparts elsewhere that were operated primarily by and for sociologists drew much of their support from business. This early experience has informed subsequent work by sociologist members of these cohorts. As just two examples, Paul Lazarsfeld published, as his ASA Presidential volume (1967), a wide range of essays under the title *The Uses of Sociology*; and John Riley, shifting his career from the university to the insurance industry whose business is people rather than products, led the way in applying sociological principles to corporate affairs. Today sociology, if not invariably respected, is utilized throughout the business world, just as knowledge and approaches developed in business and industry have become essential to sociology.

Opportunities for sociological influence in the domain of *military research*, to take another example, have varied with the occurrence of wars. World War II is unique in this century in the extent of multifaceted sociological involvement. The fundamental influence on scientific development of this work is indicated in the range of sociologists, many of them still leaders today, who contributed to the four-volume compendium *The American Soldier* edited by Samuel Stouffer and others (1949-1950). In the present volume, Blalock traces the roots of his sociological career to his postwar experiences in the Navy. And Sewell describes the importance for his later work of participation in the research on the effects of strategic bombing on the morale of Japanese civilians.

In the Korean War, where channels of sociological influence were narrower, John Riley's experience is akin to that of earlier studies of civilian and military populations under the severe stresses of war. Just as, during the World War II invasion of Normandy, he had studied French attitudes toward the Allies, in Korea, Riley participated in surveys for use in advising the generals in the field. The Korean research was equally useful in informing scholars about Communist methods of sovietizing populations under their control. Although the Vietnam War may have dampened interest in military sociology, a recrudescence of sociological analysis of the impact of war on human lives is apparent in the essays by Karl Ulrich Mayer and by Elder and Clipp in *Social Structures and Human Lives* (Volume 1 of *Social Change and the Life Course*).

In the domain of *journalism*, the life of Lewis Coser is, as he says, "a double career." Since emigrating from Germany and following his wife, Rose, into graduate school at Columbia, Coser has published for some 35 years the journal *Dissent*, which he cofounded. Although appreciative of the work of Talcott Parsons, Coser has emphasized conflict in reaction to its neglect by the functionalists; and his volume in the ASA Presidential Series (1976, edited with Otto Larsen) is titled *The Uses of Controversy in Sociology*. As he says, "Throughout all these years, I have cultivated a kind of double vision, a dual set of premises of pure sociological analysis and impure social and moral partisanship."

These few illustrations of the potential significance to sociology of nonacademic domains should serve as bellwethers for "sociological practice," which now constitutes a formal section in the American Sociological Association. There are time-honored precedents for sociologists to apply disciplinary perspectives and knowledge in many nonacademic public and private domains, to use these domains as sites for research, and to bring back into the discipline new empirical findings, new research methods, and new conceptual formulations. Today, in a rapidly changing world, the pressing question is how to identify the appropriate channels of opportunity for exercising sociological influence both on policy and on the development of the discipline.

The Organization of Sociological Research

(4) Finally, the *organization of sociological research* is a domain in which numerous sociologists have exerted significant leadership. Earlier in the century, for example, pioneering efforts by Conrad and Irene Taeuber, which drew support from the U.S. Bureau of the Census and Princeton's Office of Population Research, provided extensive bases of demographic data for use in sociological research. As an example from the essays in this volume, William Sewell has devoted major efforts during his half century as a sociologist to enlarging the scale, scope, and funding of research and graduate training. His strong influence made itself felt in the dramatic transformation of institutional structures at his own university, Wisconsin, and in the organization of scientific research at the national level. The changes at Wisconsin, and comparable changes in other university centers, though taken for granted by new cohorts entering the field, can be fully appreciated by those of us already at work in the 1930s when, as Sewell puts it:

A lone scholar, with the assistance of a student or two, would undertake a research project with very limited funding, obtain information on a small non-probability sample, employ simple counting or cross-tabular procedures in the analysis of the data, write up the results, and hope to get an article or monograph published in one of the then limited outlets for sociological research studies.

The times were ripe for Sewell to exert this influence; and the consequence was to expand enormously the channels of continuing influence for many subsequent cohorts of sociologists.

INFLUENCES ON A DEVELOPING FIELD

My search for clues to the operation of sociological influence, then, preliminary as it is, affords suggestive insights. Thus whether or not channels of influence are accessible during the lifetimes of particular sociologists seems to depend on broad social and intellectual trends and structural changes. Changes affecting the flow of influence include those in the state of the art and the organization of research; in the effectiveness of communication; and, perhaps most important, in the goals and interests of the discipline. In sociology, some of these goals and interests seem to derive from trends in thought; others from emergence of immediate social problems, disruptions, or controversies; and still others from ideologies and values paramount at the time. Sometimes adherence to vested ideas and concerns produces outright resistance to new influences. Sometimes influences from sociology diffuse outward to other disciplines or to policies and practices. Moreover, channels blocked at one time may be opened at a later time, producing a "lag" in the cumulation of scientific work.

As one other phase of my ruminations in this chapter, I am prompted to ask whether similar indications of the operation of sociological influence also appear during the development of a special field. The sociology of age, with which I am currently most familiar, affords a useful instance for analysis.

One might have expected this field to develop early in the history of sociology. After all, aging and cohort flow are powerful and universal processes, and the roles and institutions of every society are structured to accommodate people who differ in age. Yet, systematic sociological thinking and research about age have been slow to take shape, which leads to the intriguing question: Why has age only recently begun to attract sustained sociological attention? What can be learned about sociological influence from the attempts to develop this field?

Early Intellectual Strands

In the past, many sociologists have written about age. Yet, in those earlier years, their works were not cumulative. They did not immediately evoke a coherent theory or produce an integrated body of research. Why not? What produced the "lag in cumulation of influence"? Consider a few of the early contributions:

As early as the second decade of this century (1928), Mannheim alerted sociologists to the importance of studying "generations," tantamount to the concept of "cohort" as it is used in this book. Like social class, Mannheim's generation provides a "location" in society, from which the person derives a unique configuration of predispositions to thought and action. These predispositions, as embodied in successive generations of actors, then become the "stuff" of social change.

Norman Ryder (1964, 1965) specified and elaborated Mannheim's concepts, showed how social change is facilitated by the continual replacement of former cohorts by new ones, and demonstrated through his own research the power of cohort analysis.

Pitirim Sorokin (1947) spoke of age as one of the major bases of social organization, shaping the structure of groups and social systems, molding the characteristics and behaviors of individuals, channeling fundamental social processes and even the course of history.

Leonard Cain (1964) synthesized the writings of several sociologists, and described aging processes as involving "successive statuses" in family, religious, political, economic, legal, educational, welfare, and other institutional spheres.[3]

Such ideas clearly provided building blocks for a sociology of age. Yet their significant contributions have lain largely dormant in the mainstream of sociology. Perhaps if their proponents had written sociological auto-biographies, we might be able to read between the lines to discover why their incipient efforts were temporarily thwarted, or what channels of sociological influence were blocked.

In the absence of such accounts, we can only speculate, following the clues in the essays in this volume, that the *discipline was not ready*. Few conceptual tools were available to deal with the thorny problems of dynamic social systems. The most commonly used methodological approaches were less adapted to analyses of dynamic systems than to cross-section surveys of populations, to longitudinal studies of individual lives, or to examination of cause-effect relationships. Hence scholars inspired by the early works on age often faltered, and few concerted efforts emerged that could galvanize disciplinary attention. Even today, when bold conceptual and methodological efforts are finally underway, significant research accomplishments are still scattered as the discipline has been preoccupied with other concerns. The companion volume to this one, *Social Structures and Human Lives*, shows that many aspects of the sociology of age remain "areas of promise." Age has not generated the social issues that Charles Willie describes as an "abiding and stimulating force in the careers of many sociologists." Major *concerns of the discipline* with class, race, and, more recently, gender have overshadowed attention to age as another crucial basis of stratification.

Some Current Obstacles

Among the obstacles still impeding the development of the sociology of age are *problems of communication*. These problems are complex, because the flow of influence involves not only influentials and the persons being

---

3. References can be found in Riley, Foner, and Waring (1988), cited in Chapter 2 of *Social Structures and Human Lives* (Volume 1 of *Social Change and the Life Course*).

influenced, but also the surrounding networks and social systems. The experiences of a group of scholars with whom I have worked for two decades on age illustrate the difficulties: conceptual confusion and misinterpretation, as well as inadequacy of influence networks and failures of diffusion of influence outside of sociology to other disciplines.

In the early 1970s, we began to forge an integrated analytical framework, combining our own ideas with the several early intellectual strands as illustrated above. We found that, while many of the components for a sociology of age were in place, and each has had specific influences on sociological work, they had not been incorporated into an integrated whole. Some intellectual strands referred to lives or to cohorts composed of lives. Others referred to age-based structures. Ryder, who most nearly integrated these two, did not emphasize the importance of the roles and values institutionalized in the social structures that give sociological meaning to the demographic patterns. Moreover, the asynchrony between lives and structures, with its attendant strains and pressures, went unnoticed.

Our attempts at a new synthesis involved parsimony in selecting only those sociological concepts most essential for analyzing this complex area. Nevertheless, the inherent complexity is still confounded by *terminological confusion*, as exemplified by just two of the concepts involved.

One is "cohort," a term we chose in order to avoid the ambiguous meanings of "generation." Common sense seems to dictate use of a technical term in such a case. Although many scholars have adopted this usage, however, others (not always inadvertently) have persisted in using in scientific discourse such expressions as the "generation born in the 1920s" or the "cohort of grandparents." Even simple confusions between time period and lineage can constitute barriers to communication.

The other concept is "age stratification." Here the consequences are more serious. By introducing this term, we unsuspectingly *caused* ambiguity. The intended connotation was that of a dynamic social system, consisting of age structures and of individuals moving through these structures. (We used the analogy of a school system, where grades are populated by students of differing ages, and individuals move upward in the age-graded structure as they grow older.) We sought to aid communication through the parallelism between age stratification and class stratification, which we conceived as distinct but cross-cutting systems. The latent consequence, however, is that for all too many sociologists we managed to obfuscate the distinction between age and class—another instance of *misdirected sociological influence*.

Such terminological confusion can lead to *conceptual confusion*, often with unfortunate implications for the flow of influence because communication is obstructed and misinterpretation impedes understanding and further scientific development. In the instance of "age stratification," the confusion between age systems and class systems has, on occasion, introduced new difficulties into the developing field because, in some of the research on class, inferences about structure are made from population distributions by class, rather than from direct measures of structure. Yet the sociology of age requires a fundamental distinction between age as a characteristic of *people* and age as an element in the structure of *roles* (whether called positions, statuses, or role-sets and status-sets)—as age, or some surrogate for age, is used as a criterion for role entry and exit and role performance. In the sociology of age, questions of central interest concern "mismatches" between person and role resulting from age-based failures of socialization or allocation, or from undersupply or oversupply of roles appropriate to people of particular ages.

Emerging Interests

While problems of communication remain stubborn, broad changes in the social structure are underway that may bring age-related issues to the center of sociological concern, and thus open new channels of influence for students of age. For example, as the baby boom cohort has moved through society producing dislocations in one age stratum after another, Joan Waring's concept of "disordered cohort flow" is evoking fresh response after a "lag in cumulation of influence." And as the population ages (a process that Bernice Neugarten discusses in this book), an array of new issues is arising that creates a need for broader sociological understanding of age. There are striking problems of "structural lag" in the age structure, because few useful or esteemed roles are available for the mounting numbers of long-lived older people. And we have only begun to face the dilemmas of allocation of scarce resources between old and young. For example, Samuel Preston (see *Social Structures and Human Lives*, Volume 1 of *Social Change and the Life Course*) explores problems of "intergenerational equity" stemming from the diversion of federal welfare funds away from programs that assist children to programs that aid the elderly. Among very old people, though many are vigorous and competent, others generate extreme demands on our inadequate facilities for health care, raising ethical questions about rationing of costly medical procedures or about euthanasia. Thus the *controversial issues, potential conflicts,* or *inequities* of today may revitalize the influence of those sociologists who studied age many years ago.

A FEW CONCLUSIONS

The autobiographical essays presented in this book, as Merton says in his introduction, can be seen as an "exercise in the sociology of scientific knowledge." A mere exercise can scarcely provide a rigorous history of the influence of sociological lives.

One severe limitation is that there are only eight autobiographies in the volume and all are too brief. They lack complementary autobiographies from other times and places. They cannot touch on the many earlier channels of influence provided by such sources as family studies at Minnesota; industrial and organization research or qualitative studies at Indiana, Cornell, or Yale; work on ecology or occupations at Chicago; symbolic interactionism or ethnomethodology at Berkeley; policy studies at Stanford; or the pathways to demographic analysis at Princeton. This list could go on and on and still remain merely illustrative.

Perhaps more important, this small set of autobiographies necessarily excludes the significant numbers of sociologists, many of them beyond reach of the great university networks, whose influence is less visible within the discipline. The large body of "invisible influentials" makes use of channels that proliferate throughout sociology and society. Thus they affect policies and structures through participation in affairs, local as well as national and international. They imbue students and others with the unique "sociological perspective." This perspective, which we sociologists take largely for granted, constitutes a new dimension of thought affecting other scholarly disciplines, and a new approach to practice affecting law, medicine, business, teaching, social work, and other professional fields.

Moreover, apart from all these omissions, this set of autobiographies is without benefit of the analytical distance of Merton's "disciplined collaboration." The intent of the authors in this volume is simply to reconstruct selected segments of sociological history from their own experience or that of their colleagues and associates.

Yet in this reconstruction, their autobiographies point to some of the ways in which sociologists, in pursuing their individual lives, have themselves been influentials. They describe channels of influence open at strategic points in their careers, and identify obstacles blocking other channels. Implicit in their accounts are scattered clues to how a sociologist performs the role of influential. Thus there are occasional comments on their motivation to introduce innovative ideas, encouragement from colleagues, relationships to particular channels of influence, interruptions caused by historical or personal events, accomplishments and failures, and the like. Collectively, the essays begin to show how sociologists living at particular moments in history have been influencing social policies, practices, and the shape of social structures; and how they have been influencing the development of sociology, its content and goals, and its intellectual and organizational arrangements. Perhaps the concept of "the influence of sociological lives," like the concept of "sociological autobiography," may enhance our understanding of the interplay between social structures and human lives.

Part II

Reflections of Eight Sociologists

3

Growing Up and Older in Sociology
1940-1990

Alice S. Rossi

THE TOPIC WE ARE CHARGED to discuss is more often pursued in private musings than dealt with systematically on a public occasion. Most of our work requires a distancing of the self from the subjects of our investigation, while on this occasion we are asked to examine the connections between the social structures in which we have grown up, trained, and worked and our own personal and intellectual lives. I am now 64, and had my first encounter with sociology in 1941, so this backward look is a very long one indeed. And because the two variables of most enduring interest to me—age and gender— have undergone tumultuous changes over the past several decades, in the manner in which the social sciences deal with them, and in the everyday world we inhabit, I am faced with a formidable task.

It is relatively easy to chart the changes that have taken place over the years in a sociological specialty or in the intellectual interests of an individual sociologist, because both leave a paper trail of published, dated work. It is far more difficult to take a retrospective look at the inner development of one's own motivations and thoughts, and to specify what influenced a shift of substantive interest or of theoretical perspective. The temptation is to remain on a cool rational level that discounts the influence of personal experience or political commitment, while in moments of honest introspection we might all acknowledge such influence. Age and gender being so central to personal life, those of us who deal with them professionally are keenly aware of the connections between private experience and professional thought.

In an exercise focused on oneself in relation to social structure, one cannot differentiate cause and effect with the neat time sequencing of, say, a path analysis. The connecting links between cause and effect in a personal life emerge very slowly. On the other hand, the process of writing is itself a way of discovering *sequence* in the twists and turns of a lifetime of work and living. Eudora Welty, commenting upon her life as a creative writer, put it well:

> Like distant landmarks you are approaching, cause and effect begin to align themselves, draw closer together. Experiences too indefinite of outline . . . to be recognized . . . connect and are identified as a larger shape. And suddenly a light is thrown back, as when your train makes a curve, showing that there has been a mountain of meaning rising behind you on the way you've come, is rising there still, proven now through retrospect [Welty, 1983, p. 90].

I encountered this "mountain of meaning" several times while preparing this essay: Often what seemed to be disparate, independent developments in my professional work and personal life turned out to have a vital connection. A self-conscious effort to link social structure to personal experience and intellectual concerns facilitates such "mountain of meaning" insights. I hope to share a few of them in what follows.

To apply a sociology of knowledge perspective to one's own life and work requires a preliminary sketch of the basic contours of that life, to link chronological age and stage of family and career development to historical context. This is precisely what life-course analysts aim to do. Unlike a prior effort at such a life overview, in *The Seasons of a Woman's Life* (Rossi, 1983b), my emphasis here will be more heavily on the professional and intellectual aspects of this history.

MAJOR CONTOURS OF
PERSONAL AND PROFESSIONAL LIFE

As a "tooling up" exercise, I sketched the major characteristics of my life in the three primary areas of family, politics, and profession, each in terms of five decades, from my twenties through my sixties (as far as I have lived them). I have included "politics" because it has had important influences upon and connections with my professional work.

One of those "mountains of meaning" insights resulted from this exercise: that is, how "off time" (to use Bernice Neugarten's telling concept) my life has been in all three of these domains, and it is this "late timing" that reflects a major structural influence upon the shape my life and thought have taken. I earned my Ph.D. in 1957, at the age of 35. I began my current, second marriage at 29. My three children were born when I was between 33 and 38 years of age. I held my first tenure-track appointment at the age of 47. And I only became politically active in any significant way past the age of 40. The same late development has characterized my professional work, as shown in the decade sketches that follow:

Twenties (1942-1951). Most of my twenties was spent attending school— Brooklyn College for a B.A. and Columbia University for graduate work in sociology—with an interruption of four years of employment and travel as an army wife during World War II. Like many young people when the war began, I married at 19, and then joined the host of others after the war in getting a divorce, at 28.

Thirties (1952-1961). During my thirties, I earned the doctorate, remarried, gave birth to three children, and held several appointments as a Research Associate—at Cornell, Harvard, and the University of Chicago. When I turned 40, however, I had published only four papers and no books, although I had written over 1000 pages in the form of research monographs and reports in connection with my research appointments, some of which were folded into the published work of the principal investigators.

Had I not already internalized a self-image as a marginal woman who went her own way in life, I might have thrown in the sponge upon reading Harvey Lehman's book, *Age and Achievement* (1953) in my early forties. Not being aware at the time of my reading that his methods had been found wanting, I was stunned by his suggestion that the age at which peak creative contributions are made had been historically the late twenties for those in the sciences and mathematics, and the mid- to late thirties for those in such fields as philosophy and music. The social sciences fell between, with peak creativity in the early thirties. But I had accomplished relatively little by the age of 40.

Forties (1962-1971). I realize now, with the benefit of hindsight, that 1962 represented a turning point in my life in many ways. It was not, however, passing the then dreaded fortieth birthday that made 1962 significant; rather it was a jolting experience of sex discrimination that was the precipitant: I was fired by the principal investigator of a kinship study I had designed, supervised the fieldwork for, and was happily analyzing at the time my draft of a proposal for continued support was funded by the National Science Foundation. I was "let go" within days of receiving word of the grant's approval, when the principal investigator decided the study was a good thing he wished to keep to himself. In those years, there was no legal recourse. A law school professor told me the absence of any documentation that I was informally the co-principal investigator rather than just an employee on the project left little chance of successful legal action, while the social science dean simply told me the anthropologist was "valuable university property" while I, as a mere research associate, was "expendable." This was, of course, structural discrimination against women, for most young men in academe were assistant professors; it was predominantly women who were the "expendable" research associates.

The "burn" left from this experience of discrimination provided the stimulus for a first venture into a sociological study of gender, and a first publication on sex equality in 1964 (Rossi, 1964). That essay in turn stimulated a hard backward look at my own innocence since adolescence where the position of women or the relations between the sexes were concerned. The innocence is surprising in light of having been involved in radical politics in college, but like many left-leaning students in those years, such politics concerned the structure of the economy, the plight of workers in the Depression, and international relations, not closer-to-home issues affecting family and work roles of a professional woman. I had never thought to question why Mirra Komarovsky was at Barnard College and all my graduate professors at Columbia University were men. In a seminar led by Kingsley Davis and Robert Merton on the sociology of the professions, I wrote a paper on the social-demographic backgrounds of members of the U.S. Congress over a span of 50 years, never once even posing the question of why so few women were members of that legislative body.

Nor did I realize at the time how representative Columbia was in the small proportion of women among the graduate students. The department in those years was not very selective in its admissions policy, with the consequence that the huge number of entering graduate students were largely men drawing on GI benefits to support their graduate education, while the female minority had to pay their own way. Only years later, when the position of women in higher education and the professions became of professional concern to me (Rossi & Calderwood, 1973), did I realize that, when I entered graduate school, women were only 10% of those who would earn doctoral degrees. In contrast, in 1983, women earned 34% of the Ph.D.s granted in the United States (National Research Council, 1984).

The post-Sputnik years of the early 1960s sparked a great deal of federal concern for scientific talent: It was desire to combat the threat of the Soviet Union preempting the United States in space technology that prompted federal concern for the "untapped reservoir of womanpower," the metaphor then used to refer to the female labor reserve. I became a beneficiary of this federal concern, first by joining the staff of the National Opinion Research Center at the University of Chicago, then designing a follow-up survey of college graduates' occupational aspirations and the transition from school to the workplace, and, in 1964, by being granted a career development award for five years from the National Institutes of Health. Freed from working on studies designed by others, I had the luxury of time to reeducate myself, and to read in fields other than sociology, mostly with an emphasis on sex and gender. My institutional sponsor for the NIH award was the Committee on

Human Development at the University of Chicago, and I realize, in retrospect, how indebted I am to my colleagues there, in particular Bernice Neugarten and Robert Hess, for alerting me to the importance of gender differences in adult development. In any event, I ended the decade of my forties with some 25 papers written, and a first book published (Rossi, 1970).

In 1969, I decided not to apply for a second five-year career award, but to seek an academic appointment instead. Johns Hopkins University, which had served as the umbrella institution for the second half of the NIH career award, was not willing to provide such an appointment, suggesting that were I to obtain NIH money I could have an appointment as a research professor, but if I wished to join the faculty without such an award I could only expect an appointment as a lecturer. So I left Johns Hopkins for Goucher College, where I held my first tenure-track appointment, as an associate professor, at the age of 47—"off time" yet again.

The 1960s were also the decade in which I became politically active on gender issues, first on abortion law reform in Illinois, then as one of the founders of the National Organization for Women (in 1966), the Women's Caucus in American Sociological Association (in 1969), and the Sociologists for Women in Society (in 1970). In 1970, I also accepted an appointment as Chair of the reactivated Committee W on the status of women in academe in the American Association of University Professors, a chair previously held by John Dewey in the 1920s.

The *sequence* of these events is significant, for they show a pattern I was to follow several times in later years: a personal experience—in this instance being cheated of a study I was passionately invested in—led to both a shift in intellectual concerns and political action. When I became involved in political efforts to get abortion out of the penal code in Illinois in the early 1960s, I also did a study of public attitudes toward abortion (Rossi, 1966), by inserting six items in an NORC amalgam survey that provided a first anchor point for use by subsequent cohorts of scholars and public opinion researchers in charting changes in abortion attitudes, items that continue to be used after twenty years. So too, it was my appointment by President Carter to the Commission on International Women's Year that led to my study of the impact of participation in the national women's conference upon political attitudes and aspirations of the delegates, a panel study reported in the 1983 book, *Feminists in Politics* (Rossi, 1983a).

Returning now to the decades overview:

Fifties (1972-1981). The five years I spent at a women's college were enormously productive years. Despite teaching seven different courses each year, the ambience of a small liberal arts college was highly conducive to indulging my interests in a wider array of disciplines than sociology. A faculty under 100 on a small campus meant easy access to colleagues in political science, English, American Studies, and psychology, where I found kindred spirits. I have little doubt that had I remained at Johns Hopkins, I would never have indulged my passion for historical and biographic analysis that bore fruit in the book on John Stuart Mill and Harriet Taylor Mill in 1970, and *The Feminist Papers* in 1973. These excursions into historical and biographic analyses provided the background for the later study of contemporary feminist activists: Having struggled with the inadequacy of archival material for any but the conspicuous leaders of the nineteenth-century women's movement, I thought it important to do better by future historians by conducting a large-scale survey of the hundreds of political activists elected in each of the fifty states to serve as delegates to the first national women's conference in our history.

With 15 years of a marginal existence on the periphery of male-dominant elite universities behind me and, before that, only male mentors at Columbia, nothing could have been more confidence-inspiring than serving on a faculty half of whom were women, with a woman academic dean, and many other women chairing their departments, as I did mine. And it was a joy to be in a classroom again with bright and enthusiastic women students to teach.

That new level of self-confidence, with a supportive network of colleagues at work, and a husband willing to share the trials of managing a complex household with three teenagers experimenting with vegetarianism, Afros, sex, and drugs, were the ingredients that made it possible to carry a great many political and professional responsibilities. The transition from Baltimore to Amherst in 1974 notwithstanding, I wrote 32 papers and published five books during my fifties.

Sixties (1982-). Since turning 60 in 1982, I have written only 6 papers, but published three books, am happily analyzing a new data set under a grant from the National Institute on Aging, and look forward to a first-ever collaboration with my husband in a book based on our findings. Beyond that, ideas are stirring for further research and at least two other books. Barring ill health or a radical shift of interest, I cannot imagine calling a halt to the excitement of doing research and writing for years to come. Perhaps this is one of the advantages of an "off-time" life pattern: Just as I finished schooling, reared children, attained tenure, and published at an older age than most of my cohort, so too I may "wind down" and retire at an older age as well. It is comforting to know that my mother is alive, well, and independent at 87, and that a grandmother lived to 96!

There is an aspect of "late timing" that had not occurred to me before, one of those "mountain of meaning" insights referred to earlier: it encourages being in closer touch with people younger than yourself who are at comparable family and career stages. Most of the parents of my children's friends were people 10 years younger than I, while my professional colleagues had children considerably older than mine. During the 1970s, I often felt closer in values to students than to my more "teaching-jaded" colleagues, perhaps because of a close identification with our children's experiences in and reactions to the world around them. For years, I could not understand colleagues who commented that students seem to get younger every year; even at 64, I still encounter students older than my own children, and perhaps as a consequence they do not seem particularly "young" to me.

The age-status discordance has other positive consequences. You are defined by others and come to view yourself in *marginal* terms, for you are difficult to "place" in an age-stratified system. That marginality in turn encourages a fresh perspective. Although the "reason" for my having spent a decade or more as a research associate was rooted in antinepotism rules in academe, it had the positive consequence of bringing a high level of enthusiasm to teaching when I turned professor in my late forties. In fact, I learned to hide that enthusiasm from colleagues my own age who had been in classrooms for twenty years because it seemed to embarrass them, but the combination of the enthusiasm of a novice teacher and the personal maturity that accompanies chronological age clearly attracted and held my under-graduate students in Baltimore.

The social marginality accompanying age-status discordance also does something to one's thinking: you feel less inhibited from striking out into new turf, taking chances, exploring new areas of knowledge. I have experienced this during the past decade, where the biological sciences and demography are concerned. I no longer feel any anticipatory excitement when a new issue of the *American Sociological Review* or the *American Journal of Sociology* arrives in the mail to match what I feel in opening a recent issue of *Population and Development Review* or a journal on endocrinology.

The general point here, of course, is that being "off time" in family and career development may complicate relations with those one's own age but enrich relations with those older and younger than oneself, at the same time it contributes a twist of social and intellectual marginality that stokes curiosity and exploration and curbs the impulse to comfortable but dull complacency.

GENDER AND COHORT DIFFERENCES IN THE "SHAPE" OF AN ACADEMIC CAREER

The shape of my own career is profoundly different from that being experienced by young women sociologists in the 1980s, and the gender differences in my cohort are far greater than any before or since the 1950s. Those of us born in the 1920s, whose childhood and adolescence were spent in the Depression, are familiar to almost all sociologists as a result of Glen Elder's study of our cohort (Elder, 1974). Like the daughters in his families who underwent downward mobility during the Depression, I had a heavy dose of domestic training and carried numerous household responsibilities to ease the burdens carried by my mother. While embittered by the dashing of their youthful hopes, the women in my family also showed enormous strength and ingenuity in coping with economic hardship, while the men slipped into escapist reading, alcoholism, or early death. It is a background conducive to the conviction that hard work and some employment had better be expected if you are a woman, but not that your occupational aspirations should be particularly high, because you plan for "contingency" rather than continuous employment.

For the sons of the Depression who served in World War II, the postwar era brought many opportunities in an expanding economy. Although I had withdrawn from school for four years as they had, once they returned and earned their degrees, their future was assured: With the great expansion of higher education, particularly in public institutions, jobs, tenure and promotion were readily attained, more than compensating for the time lost due to military service. For women of my cohort, that time was not made up, for many remained ABDs, found niches as research associates in laboratories and social research institutes, or simply withdrew from any professional work for a decade or more.

The vast pouring of federal funds into academic research provided many of those research associate jobs for the women, while it additionally facilitated the career advancement of men. Not only did men have wives at home to rear their children, maintain their households, and manage their social affairs, but at their offices, they had an unprecedented array of services as well, with secretaries, large numbers of graduate students, research assistants, and research associates to facilitate their professional work, far in excess of that experienced by their own mentors before World War II.

Note, too, that we were few in number in terms of birth cohort size and number of advanced degree holders. In the whole of the 1950s, some 84,000 doctoral degrees were earned in the United States. This was more than double the number granted in the preceding decade of the 1940s (30,000), but there was ample room for them in the expanding academic market. The men of my cohort in turn contributed, as teachers and mentors, to another doubling of the number of doctorates earned in the 1960s (164,000) and the 1970s (297,000). At the present rate of doctorate production, the 1980s will show a modest rise followed by stabilization, with an estimated 310,000 doctorates for the decade (National Research Council, 1984). I estimate that by 1990, a full *two-thirds* of all the doctorate degrees ever granted in the United States will have been granted since 1970!

It should be noted, however, that not all fields show a plateau or decrease in doctoral production: The humanities have shown a dramatic decline every year since 1973; engineering and the physical sciences reached a peak of doctoral production in 1971, and have declined and stabilized in the years since. Only the social sciences and education reached a peak as late as 1975, and they have retained the same high level each year since. It is little wonder that recent degree earners in sociology have difficulty gaining entry to academic positions, and, when they do, they have to meet far higher standards of productivity and excellence than those who now pass judgment on their credentials had to meet a few decades ago. With the crest of institutional expansion behind us, we are producing a larger number of new Ph.D.-holding sociologists than new retirees.

It was clearly not a tight job market that restricted the professional opportunities of women in my cohort, but a combination of sex discrimination, antinepotism rules, lower aspirations, and a contingency orientation toward employment while children were young. The impact of interrupted employment histories upon professional achievement can be seen in a study of my cohort of women graduate students at Columbia University. Eli Ginzberg and his associates (Ginzberg et al., 1966; Ginzberg & Yohalem, 1966) sampled a top category of women who were graduate students at Columbia University between 1945 and 1951—women who had held a university fellowship for at least a year, in an era when such fellowships were very rare and teaching assistantships almost nonexistent at a private university like Columbia. When they were surveyed some 12 to 18 years later, the achievement level of the women who had "broken" work histories since graduate school was dramatically lower than those with "continuous" histories: Only 17% of those with interrupted work histories were judged to have "good" or "high" achievement levels in their fields, compared to 64% of those with continuous work histories (Ginzberg et al., 1966, p. 100).

I have tried, with only partial success, to explain why I departed from the modal profile of women in my cohort of graduate students in having a very short break in employment history despite family responsibilities. Even during the four years during which my children were born in the late 1950s in Chicago, I worked part-time, either teaching sociology courses in evening sessions or holding half-day research jobs, and, from the time my youngest was two, I have been employed full-time. Some long-standing quirk of personality was no doubt involved: a favorite song in my adolescence had a phrase "don't fence me in" that resonated in my head for years, tapping a persistent desire for independence and a preference for "being in charge" of things. It did not sit well with me to be an economic dependent instead of a cobreadwinner.

The roots of this independent bent go deep: As a child I had been close to a widowed paternal grandmother who ran a complex household of three adult children and six boarders, a feat she accomplished with finesse and a firm matriarchal hand. In my own maternal extended kin household, there was a pronounced dominance by my father and grandfather, but also three unmarried aunts and a softhearted uncle doing interesting things, and my grandfather was accessible and tender in relationship to me, however much he barked commands to his daughters. And, as firstborn and favored child, my father encouraged the belief that I could do anything I set out to do. Fathers often encouraged aspirations in their daughters that they dampened in their wives, for the reason, I suspect, that they would not have to live with the *consequences* of an ambitious daughter as they would of an ambitious wife.

From puberty to midway through college, my aspirations were to be a writer and poet, and there were ample models of women as English teachers, novelists, and poets to emulate. With the shift of goal from writer to sociologist, and entry into graduate school, all my mentors were men, but they were perhaps unique in their encouragement of and confidence in me. While they did not then hire women to become colleagues of theirs, they were highly supportive mentors and sponsors to me and those women students I knew who worked with them, such as Rose Coser, Zena Blau, and Suzanne Keller.

Radical politics in the 1930s, like new left circles of the 1970s, espoused an ideological commitment to sex equality that was rarely manifested in the actual relations between men and women. But there were sufficient examples of couples who served as models of reciprocated admiration and of comradely partnership to rub off on many of us, my husband and I among them. Residues of those earlier political beliefs remained after the war when we returned to academe. To some degree, my willingness to go against the social norms by working while the children were preschoolers was rooted in the high expectations my mentors and my husband held for me. Their high expectations in turn reflected their left of center political orientation.

Of course, none of us in the early 1950s dealt with the structural and psychological constraints imposed on men and women alike in living an egalitarian life-style; that awaited the feminist agenda of two decades later. Indeed, it is still unresolved, to judge by the travail experienced by young adults in the late 1980s in juggling the competing demands of family and profession in a way that sustains gender equity in a relationship (e.g., Johnson & Johnson, 1980). Nor is there any evidence that countries like Sweden (Bohen, 1984; Haas, 1980) or the People's Republic of China (Rossi, 1984) have solved these issues either.

MENTORS AND SPONSORS:
RESIDUAL INFLUENCES

Let me turn now to the specific people who have served as my major intellectual mentors, and the extent to which they have influenced my work in subsequent years. The first sociologist I ever encountered was Louis Schneider in my sophomore year at Brooklyn College. Schneider was then an advanced graduate student at Columbia, whose intellectual interests dominated even an introductory course. That I was an easy prey to his influence stems from the fact that he introduced the course by reading poems and challenging us to identify the social characteristics of the poets, the time and place in which they lived. This pedagogic technique forced the realization that my fascination as an English major was as much in the sociology of literature as in the creation and interpretation of a poem or short story. When he went on to introduce us to Freud, Veblen, and Weber, my excitement grew to such an extent that I changed my major to sociology before the semester ended. It was surely Schneider's own enthusiasm that led to my volunteering to give an oral report on one of the books he assigned: Weber's *Protestant Ethic*. Can you imagine giving such an assignment to a student in an introductory course today?

Like parents from the perspective of a small child, our intellectual mentors often seem "bigger than life." But unlike parents who take on a more human scale when we in turn become parents, our mentors often remain oversized in our memory. How much more this is the case when your mentors are people like Robert Merton, Paul Lazarsfeld, Kingsley Davis, and C. Wright Mills, I leave to you to imagine. I understood this analogy between parent and mentor even back then in 1950, where Kingsley Davis was concerned, for a very special reason: Kingsley Davis looked physically so like my father at a younger age that, despite my gangling height, I often felt my feet did not quite reach the floor when I sat across the desk from him! Not only did he loom larger than life, but I felt smaller than I was.

In retrospect, I believe most Columbia-trained sociologists of that period would concede having been influenced by each of these four men, even if they had only audited one of their courses. But during our actual years in residence, we tended to sort ourselves out into one or another of their spheres of influence. Even in their subsequent work, one associates James Coleman, Peter Rossi, Allen Barton, and Morris Rosenberg with Paul Lazarsfeld; and Lewis and Rose Coser, Peter and Zena Blau, Suzanne Keller, Alvin Gouldner, and Norman Kaplan with Robert Merton.

Like only a few others, I had the pleasure, pain, and privilege of working with both men at close range, as both teaching and research assistant to Robert Merton, including a collaboration on a paper on reference group theory (Merton & Kitt, 1950), and as a student of Paul Lazarsfeld in a research workshop on the 1948 Elmira voting study and as his research assistant on a project exploring the potential influences between history and sociology. Between the two of them, these mentors provided standards of excellence hard for anyone to reach. Despite the intervening 35 years, I sense an *internalized Merton* when it comes to analytic linkages between disparate-seeming phenomena or to clarity and grace of writing style, and an *internalized Lazarsfeld* when it comes to elegance and simplicity of problem formulation and measurement of complex constructs. Many of us who had these men as mentors have struggled to hone and blend the skills of these two master craftsmen of our discipline in theory, writing, method, and analysis. I continue to do so.

Sociology has undergone dramatic changes in the past thirty years, though far more so in the area of methods of data analysis than of theory. Our students can still derive great intellectual benefit from reading Merton's classic essay on "Social Structure and Anomie" or his study of science in seventeenth-century England, but they would find the data analysis in Lazarsfeld's empirical studies quite elementary. Though always with a great lag, I have periodically tried to keep abreast of new techniques with the help of a Lazarsfeld student, Peter Rossi, to whom I am fortunate to have daily access. At a critical point in my own statistical retooling a decade ago, I also benefited by more direct lineal descendants, because, for one summer, while they were still undergraduates, I had my own son, Peter Eric, an econometrician, and Paul's son, Robert Lazarsfeld, a mathematician, as research assistants. That my study of menstrual and day-of-week mood fluctuations had any degree of statistical sophistication is due largely to their contributions (Rossi & Rossi, 1977). Without their help, it is unlikely the data analysis would have involved fitting a polynomial curve to daily mood ratings, or that the regression analysis would have used the Durbin-Watson statistic to estimate the coefficient of autocorrelation.

My indebtedness to Robert Merton is more direct and continuous, without the intermediaries of my spouse and our two sons as in the case of Paul Lazarsfeld. While reading Merton's published work is itself enormously rewarding, it is no substitute for the week-to-week exposure to his lectures, or close collaboration in exploring an idea and carrying it through revisions to a paper he defined as ready for publication. He persuaded me for all time that nothing short of five or six drafts of a manuscript is likely to yield a polished product. And, in my experience, he is equaled only by Irving Howe as a stylistic editor.

During my early years as a graduate student at Columbia, I did not question the prevailing belief in many sociological circles that one needed only other social facts to explain social facts. That "chutzpah" was congenial to a discipline still carving out a place for itself in the intellectual firmament. But my love of literature and history, and new fascination with anthropology, guided my stealing across campus, almost with the feeling of being a traitor to sociology, to attend lectures by Ruth Benedict and Lionel Trilling. In the sociology department, theory was grand, macro-theory, with very little concern for theory-testing with precise empirical evidence. Merton stood to one side of this prejudice, not only in being concerned about building crossable bridges between theory and empirical research, but through an effort he was engaged in then, and on which I assisted for a time, which he called "levels analysis." Sharing the intellectual ferment of thinking across the academic disciplines that was taking place at Harvard, Michigan, and Yale,

Merton distinguished among four levels that placed sociological variables in a broader context, with a cultural-historical level to one side and psychological and biological levels on the other. He argued that a really outstanding piece of scholarship would embrace all four levels, which few social science studies achieved. It was also a schema that permitted us to identity with some precision what was "lacking" when we read and assessed published work. My research task was to locate studies that embraced at least three of these levels, and to ferret out how studies restricted to one level might be reinterpreted if any other level were added to their design.

The topic was among the most fascinating I had encountered at that point in my sociological studies, because it gave promise of a kind of synthesis that would permit escape from the narrow confines in which sociology was then structured, through building bridges to history on the one side, and the biological and psychological sciences on the other. In a brilliant series of lectures, Merton explored these ideas, indulging his delight in the play of ideas. In a semester during which I served as his assistant, he became ill, and I gave a lecture of my own devising, using the variable of Age to demonstrate how differently it is interpreted when one moves from the cultural to the sociological to the psychological and physiological levels of analysis. This was 1950, long before the concept of "cohort" had diffused from demography into common sociological parlance and even longer before "generation" acquired its recent confinement to family and lineage analysis.

It may sound incredible, but until preparing this paper, I had never associated my own long-standing interests in interdisciplinary work in the social sciences, and more recent interest in biosocial science, with that early "levels analysis" project I participated in as Merton's apprentice. Nor did I acknowledge it in my dissertation, drafted only a few years later, though it was highly relevant to the topic I was exploring: what I then called *generational* differences in the Soviet Union, though we would now label them *cohort* differences. The data came from questionnaires and life histories with Soviet émigrés after World War II, and my analytic task was to compare and analyze the respects in which the younger Soviet émigrés (born, reared, and schooled under the Soviet regime) differed from the older Soviet émigrés whose early lives were spent before the Soviets came to power. Throughout the analysis, I struggled with the knotty interpretive problem of differentiating between age differences due to cohort and period influences, and those due to maturational change in adult development, and I did so with none of the concepts of cohort, period, time of measurement, and aging effects that were to be refined in life span and life-course analysis a decade or more later.

My current research is on intergenerational relations between parents and adult children in a life-course framework. It is a cross-sectional survey with personal interviews with a random sample of households in the greater Boston metropolitan area, with supplemental telephone interviews with spinoff samples of some of the parents and adult children of respondents who were personally interviewed. While the cross-sectional design enables me to analyze the extent to which parents and their adult children hold similar or different views of each other and the relationship between them, and to trace differences among the parents and the adult children across the life course, it still leaves the interpretive problem of differentiating between cohort and maturational effects.

I am frank to admit that my interest is greater in maturational effects of aging than in age differences that reflect cohort differences. It is understandable that sociologists have strong interests in cohort and period effects in the study of social structures and human behavior, as it is that many developmental psychologists wish to refute any deterministic model of aging as programmed senescence. But there is a danger that aging as a maturational phenomenon will be left to the biomedical specialties as a consequence. Perhaps, as Lonnie Sherrod and Bert Brim have suggested (Sherrod & Brim, 1986), we are in a period of overreacting to earlier deterministic models of adult development and aging by taking an overly optimistic view of the human organism and our developmental potential for plasticity or "reserve capacities." I wish to strike a better balance, however difficult with cross-sectional data, by allowing the brute facts of metabolic, sexual, and physical changes—and not merely role changes along the life course or cohort differences in educational attainment—to play a role in my interpretation of findings.

This current project also brings together other previously quite separate threads from the past. I had been a sideline skeptic of Peter Rossi's factorial survey method (Rossi & Nock, 1982) for quite some time, but that skepticism faded when I addressed the question of how to measure normative obligations toward kin. I had no measurement problem where consensual, functional, or associational solidarity were concerned, but on normative obligations to kin, I found it difficult to decide which kin types to include, which to exclude. Should I include affinal kin or restrict the study to consanguineal kin? What depth and range of the kindred should I tap in order to detect where the boundaries of felt obligation were located? Does it make a difference if a kinperson is married, unmarried, or widowed?

Without realizing it, I was "discovering" Peter Rossi's method de novo, because the vignette technique permits you to specify *all* these various relationships; to include nonkin such as friends, neighbors, and ex-spouses as well as affinal and consanguineal kin; and to specify marital status and gender of each kin type in the vignettes. The result is a design that includes 74 levels of kin and nonkin, four trauma and three celebratory occasions as levels of the situational dimension, and two ratings (one on financial aid, the other on social and emotional comfort) of the degree of obligation felt toward the person described in the vignette.

While the use of the vignette approach to kin norms greatly enriches the study, to my benefit and delight, the personal interviews contain a wealth of interesting substantive variables for the individual level of the vignette analysis, a benefit and delight to the "other Rossi," because most previous factorial survey analyses were limited to a few basic social demographic characteristics of respondents. The result is an exciting venture into research collaboration, our first in more than thirty years, and an opportunity for me to explore both age and gender as axes in family and kinship relationships. With the benefit of hindsight encouraged by this retrospective essay, I see what was not clear before: the continuity represented by having grown up in a three-generation household, being off time in adult development, having been exposed to Merton's ideas about levels of analysis, my own application of them to the age variable in a lecture while a graduate student, the selection of "generations" as a focus for the work I did at the Russian Research Center at Harvard and used for a dissertation, and the reemergence of interest in intergenerational relations in my current project.

LOOKING AHEAD

We were also charged with suggesting something of what we think necessary or likely developments in the specialties in which we work. This could be an invitation to some banal generalizations. I have chosen instead to select two issues for special comment that I consider important in future research on sex, gender, age, and family.

The first issue concerns the finding, often reported in the family literature, that marital satisfaction or happiness or psychological well-being declines after children are born (McLanahan & Adams, 1987), continues to decline through the children's adolescence, and then undergoes an upturn when the children leave home and the couple settles into what has been called the "postparental" or "empty nest" stage (e.g., Rollins & Cannon, 1974; Rollins & Feldman, 1970).

Family sociologists have had trouble interpreting such findings, and their explanations have changed with the times. Analogous to research on the effects of maternal employment on children, which showed *no* negative effects (Nye, 1974; Nye & Hoffman, 1963), sociologists first called for more research, on the surmise that methodological defects prevented demonstrating what "everybody knows" to be true—that is, that children's development will suffer if they do not receive full-time mothering, just as there must be something wrong if children have a negative impact on marriage when the core function of the family is the legitimation of children and their rearing. This line of thinking predicted not increased marital happiness but trauma for women when the empty nest stage was reached, because women were essentially retiring from their major life purpose and doing so twenty or more years before their husbands' retirement. Why, then, were such couples so happy?

More recently, a new cohort of family researchers has proposed a set of explanations of such results. Reflecting the antinatalist ambience of the time, it is now suggested that child rearing is very stressful for small nuclear families, in part because it interrupts or complicates the mother's pursuit of an independent career. Hence the marriage is strained by both the presence of children and the frustration of the woman (Chesler, 1972; Chesler & Goodman, 1976; Gove & Geerken, 1977; Gove & Peterson, 1980; Laws, 1971; Lowenthal & Chiriboga, 1972; McLanahan & Adams, 1987). When the last child leaves the household, the couple experiences a rejuvenation of sexual intimacy, release from the pressures of the second "life cycle squeeze" attending the increased expenses of supporting adolescent children (Oppenheimer, 1982), and women can more single-mindedly pursue outside interests and employment. Should an adult child return home, family relations are strained because the newly happy postparental pair resents the intrusion.

I suggest that a "married adult bias" has led to a neglect of a critical factor differentiating a family before children leave from a family after children leave. Researchers have been so focused on the happiness, satisfaction, and mental health of the parental pair that they have not seen the relevance of change in the children as important to the parents' happiness and personal adjustment. Adolescent children are not just disturbing the peace and quiet of the household and imposing a strain on their parents' budget. They are experiencing a great deal of stress themselves: in the developmental effort to individuate themselves by testing the limits of parental tolerance, in coping with sexual pressures and desires, in dealing with decisions concerning further schooling and occupational choice, all at the same time their peers are undergoing similar stresses and strains. And, as I suggested in a study of the mothers of adolescents (Rossi, 1980a, 1980b), there is an added strain placed on the parent-child relationship if the mothers themselves are coping with their own aging.

In my current study, *retrospective* ratings of the affective quality of the parent-child relationship at the ages of 10, 16, and 25, and (for those older than 25) *current* ratings of the relationship between parents and children, varying in age from under a year to 63, provide a life-course profile that mirrors the curve shown in marital satisfaction studies: a sharp drop in closeness at 16 compared to 10 years of age, followed by a steady increase in closeness as the children enter their twenties. The closeness level then stabilizes at a high plateau for the remaining years of life of the parents in the relationship to daughters, with a slight decline in the case of sons. The same life-course profile is shown when adult children provide the ratings as when parents do.

I suggest that adolescent limit-testing and acting-out behaviors produce stress for parents individually and within their marriage. Parents feel guilty because they think they are responsible, that they have not done a good job of parenting. The most critical and neglected reason for the increased happiness and improved mental health of a postparental couple is the fact that their children are now older, more settled, employed, and parents themselves, and the parents come to feel they did not do such a bad job of parenting after all.

This same interpretation applies to the impact of an adult child returning to the family nest. I hypothesize that what disturbs the parental pair is not the loss of their freedom so much as the reason an adult child returns in the first place. It is not the happy successful child who comes back home but the unhappy child experiencing a failure of some kind: loss of a job, separation or divorce, illness, or incapacitating depression. Under such circumstances, parents again feel vulnerable and guilty, because in a society that places such undue pressure on individual responsibility, parents see failure in a child as partially their failure as parents, rather than the result of social structural forces affecting the lives of their children.

Marriage and parenthood may be conceptually very distinct among sociologists' theoretical constructs, but they are much less so in reality: life is more fluid and interconnected than many theories allow. Indeed, this is a highly appropriate point to underline in a volume on social structure and human lives, because it illustrates the principle that the life of a single individual or of a marital couple can only be fully understood as it is intertwined with the lives of significant others like their children. In those few studies of parental satisfaction, researchers report significant correlations with marital satisfaction (e.g., Chilman, 1979; Goetting, 1986). Furthermore, in an interesting earlier study, Luckey and Bain (1970) compared couples highly satisfied with their marriages with couples very dissatisfied with their marriages and found high levels of parental satisfaction in both groups; they suggest that parental satisfaction is so deeply ingrained in the marital relationship that it perseveres through the decline of marital companionship. Indeed, Veroff et al. report that parental satisfaction is even higher among divorced men and women (though more strongly so for the men) than among married couples (Veroff et al., 1981).

There has clearly been a softening of attitudes toward childlessness, such that the voluntarily childless adult is no longer seen as selfish or maladjusted, and it has also been shown that young, childless, married couples report greater happiness and satisfaction in their marriages than do married couples coping with young children (Houseknecht, 1982; Veevers, 1979). But the long-term consequences of childlessness are not yet clear. Gove and Geerken (1977), using mental health measures rather than marital satisfaction, have reported that childless couples married for less than seven years show better mental health than parents, but after seven years, childless couples have poorer mental health than couples at later stages of child rearing or post-child rearing. Gove and Peterson (1980) suggest that while rearing children may be stressful, parenting may also involve a maturation process that in the long run results in stronger marriages and better mental health. The dividends from investing in child rearing are clearly suggested by the critical importance in old age of the physical, social, and emotional care provided by adult children to their elderly parents.

A general point in these remarks is the importance of keeping in focus the stage of life not only of parents but of children, and viewing parental investment and gratification not simply in the early years of marriage, but in the longer framework of the life course. Most of us pass beyond child rearing, but we do not experience a "postparental" phase of life: That misnomer should be dropped from our vocabulary in family sociology, because the parent-child relationship is a vital one for many more years after children are grown and independent than those invested in direct child rearing (Hagestad, 1984).

The second issue that I have hopes will be treated differently in future than it has in recent research concerns sex and gender. I will be highly selective here, because space limitations preclude developing the argument fully; in addition, I have already urged a biosocial perspective in gender research elsewhere (Rossi, 1977, 1984a, 1986). Despite a very great explosion of research on gender, we are still in a conceptual muddle for the reason that we persist in using only biological sex as the major variable, or at most some measures on sex and gender role attitudes. A more sophisticated approach would be to so operationalize what we take gender to *mean*, that sheer biological sex as a characteristic of our subjects would lose its statistical significance. It is ironic that those who argue most strongly that gender is exclusively a *social construction* have contributed little to substantiate their claim by devising variables that demonstrably remove any significance attached to the variable of gender per se.

I think the 1980s are a prime time to attempt such measures, precisely because social expectations and the social roles of men and women are undergoing dramatic change, and hence we can expect considerable intra-gender variance. We need measures of those social and psychological traits traditionally linked to gender, so that, at an *individual* level, we can explain differences between men and women in terms of these traits. Further, we need direct measures of physique and hormonal levels to provide a model that includes biology, personality traits, attitudes, and whatever sociological variables are now taken to explain gender differences.

Sociologists have balked at the use of psychologists' measures of Masculinity and Femininity out of concern that this suggests some inherent maleness or femaleness rooted in biological sex. What should be dropped, however, is not the constructs themselves, but the labels. If we relabel Masculinity scales as Dominance, and Femininity scales as Expressivity or Affiliation, it reduces resistance to the questions one poses. Note the difference in tone between posing the question: What produces Masculinity in women? compared to What produces Dominance in women? Or What produces Femininity in men? compared to What produces Expressivity in men? With such measures in my own study, I have been able to explore intragender differences in the relations between parents and adult children. To cite just one example: While parents generally give more help to daughters than they do to sons, this difference is reduced somewhat if sons are high in expressivity, and fathers give more help to sons high in expressivity. Since I administered the same instrument to a spinoff sample of the parents of our respondents, I am now analyzing the effects of variance in Expressivity and Dominance in *both* partners to the relationship for the interaction, closeness, and help exchange between them.

Any direct confrontation with the biological contributions to dominance and expressivity as sex-linked traits would require direct measurement of physical characteristics such as height, weight, hormonal levels, and sexual attractiveness. Research along these lines has scarcely begun. I would urge that any sociologist concerned about the relative contributions of biology, socialization, and social norms to gender differences in sexual behavior look up the recent work of Richard Udry and his associates at the Carolina Population Center. In an unprecedented and elegant research design, Udry is studying gender differences in early sexual initiation among adolescents between 12 and 19 years of age. In the larger study, he obtained questionnaire data from the adolescents themselves, on stage of pubertal development, internalized norms and attitudes, and sex experience; and he has parallel information obtained from the closest same-sex and opposite-sex friends of his core sample of adolescents. Direct measures were obtained from the mothers of the adolescents on parental control, other ratings from the interviewers on the adolescent's sexual attractiveness, and, for a subsample of the adolescents, serum hormone assays.

As a result of this design, he is able to separate hormonal from social effects on adolescent sexual behavior. The results show that male initiation of coitus in early adolescence is dominated by motivational hormone effects and social attractiveness, with no effects of social controls or peer sex experience, while female initiation of coitus is dominated by the effects of social controls, with no effects stemming from attractiveness, hormones, or specifically sexual motivation (Udry et al., 1985; Udry & Billy, 1986; Udry, Talbert, & Morris, 1986).

Most sociological researchers have argued that hormones are only relevant in causing pubertal development, which in turn serves as a social signal to society and the individual that age-graded sexual behavior is appropriate and desirable. Ira Reiss argued such a purely social model for sexual initiation and sexual behavior in his Presidential Address to the National Council on Family Relations (Reiss, 1986). Udry shows that a social-psychological model simply does not hold for males: Free testosterone level had a direct effect upon sexual motivation and behavior net of all social and psychological variables.

The significance of Udry's findings is not limited to the topic of early sexual initiation. We know that testosterone is the major androgenic hormone that is linked to aggressive as well as sexual responses. We also know that it takes time for males to learn control over sexual and aggressive responses. Thus, for example, there are high correlations between testosterone level and aggression among young men, but no significant correlations among older men, because the latter's greater social maturation permits higher levels of impulse control (Persky, Smith, & Basu, 1971). But older men are not all "mature," and we know from the growing literature on stress that life pressures can often escalate to the point that our thin veneer of socialized self-control is lost, with the results we see in our prisons, hospitals, shelters for battered wives or homeless men, and treatment centers for child victims of incest.

What we as sociologists need to learn more about and build into our paradigms are the physiological variables that are involved in social behavior and psychological stress in the differences between men and women and between young and old adults. Feelings and thoughts are molecular events in the brain that have chemical consequences. All the chemical juices the body has for "fight" and "flight" responses are involved in circumstances of high stress: blood pressure goes up, cholesterol rises, the stress hormones of adrenalin and noradrenalin are released, muscles contract, arteries tighten, blood sugar rises, brain enzymes are altered, and a host of chemicals—cortisol and insulin along with testosterone and throxine—increase. The body is bathed in chemicals, and people are literally "stewing in their own juices."

Many of these chemical responses are identical in male and female, but this is not the case for testosterone: Although males and females start from the same prepubertal androgen level, as males mature, their androgen levels go up by a factor of 10 to 20; while in females, androgen levels hardly double. Udry and Billy (1986, p. 35) suggest that, as a result, the hormone effects may more readily overwhelm social controls in males than they do in females.

Sociologists have understandably given their greatest attention to social structure, and we will continue to do so. But age and gender are major variables in almost all sociological specialties, hence our paradigms cannot be adequate without building into them cultural meaning, psychological traits, and physiological attributes and processes. I have emphasized the utility of this interdisciplinary paradigm for research on sex and gender, and Matilda Riley has emphasized the utility and the urgency for comparable inter-disciplinary paradigms in the study of age and aging in her Presidential Address, which appears in the companion volume to this one. In a historic period in which there is great social and political stress, and in which social controls have weakened, there is a greater need than ever before for sociologists to pay attention to the workings of that human animal we are when our socialized veneer wears thin.

References

Bohen, H. H. 1984. "Gender Equality in Work and Family: An Elusive Goal."*Journal of Family Issues* 5(2):254-272.

Chesler, P. 1972. *Women and Madness.* New York: Doubleday.

————. and E. J. Goodman. 1976. *Money, Women and Power.* New York: William Morrow.

Chilman, C. S. 1979. "Parent Satisfactions-Dissatisfactions and Their Correlates." *Social Service Review* 53(June):195-213.

Elder, G. H., Jr. 1974. *Children of the Great Depression.* Chicago: University of Chicago Press.

Ginzberg, E. and A. M. Yohalem. 1966. *Educated American Women: Self-Portraits.* New York: Columbia University Press.

Ginzberg, E. et al. 1966. *Life Styles of Educated Women.* New York: Columbia University Press.

Goetting, A. 1986. "Parental Satisfaction: A Review of Research." *Journal of Family Issues* 7(1):83-109.

Gove, W. R. and M. Geerken. 1977. "The Effect of Children and Employment on the Mental Health of Married Men and Women." *Social Forces* 56(1):66-76.

Gove, W. R. and C. Peterson. 1980. "An Update on the Literature on Personal and Marital Adjustment: The Effect of Children and the Employment of Wives." *Marriage and Family Review* 3(3/4):63-96.

Haas, L. 1982. "Parental Sharing of Childcare Tasks in Sweden." *Journal of Family Issues* 3(3):389-412.

Hagestad, G. O. 1984. "The Continuous Bond: A Dynamic, Multi-Generational Perspective on Parent-Child Relations." In *Minnesota Symposium on Child Psychology*, Vol. 17, edited by M. Perlmutter. Hillsdale, NJ: Lawrence Erlbaum.

Houseknecht, S. K., ed. 1982. "Childlessness and the One-Child Family"[Special Issue]. *Journal of Family Issues* 3(4).

Johnson, C. and F. Johnson. 1980. "Parenthood, Marriage and Careers: Situational Constraints and Role Strain." Pp. 143-161 in *Dual-Career Couples*, edited by F. Pepitone-Rockwell. Beverly Hills, CA: Sage.

Laws, J. L. 1971. "A Feminist Review of Marital Adjustment Literature: The Rape of the Locke." *Journal of Marriage and the Family* 33(3):485-516.

Lehman, H. C. 1953. *Age and Achievement.* Princeton, NJ: Princeton University Press.

Lowenthal, M. F. and D. Chiriboga. 1972. "Transition to the Empty Nest: Crisis, Challenge, or Relief?" *Archives of General Psychiatry* 26(1):8-14.

Luckey, E. B. and J. K. Bain. 1970. "Children: A Factor in Marital Satisfaction." *Journal of Marriage and the Family* 32(1):43-44.

McLanahan, S. and J. Adams. 1987. "Parenthood and Psychological Well-Being." Pp. 237-257 in *Annual Review of Sociology*, Vol. 13, edited by W. R. Scott and J. F. Short, Jr. Palo Alto, CA: Annual Reviews.

Merton, R. K. and A. S. Kitt. 1950. "Contributions to the Theory of Reference Group Behavior." Pp. 40-105 in *Continuities in Social Research*, edited by R. K. Merton and P. F. Lazarsfeld. Glencoe, IL: Free Press.

National Research Council. 1984. *Summary Report 1983: Doctorate Recipients from United States Universities.* Washington, DC: National Research Council, Office of Scientific and Engineering Personnel.

Nye, F. I. 1974. "Effects on the Husband-Wife Relationship." In *Working Mothers*, edited by L. W. Hoffman and F. I. Nye. San Francisco: Jossey-Bass.

———. and L. W. Hoffman. 1963. *The Employed Mother in America.* Chicago: Rand McNally.

Oppenheimer, V. K. 1982. *Work and the Family: A Study in Social Demography.* New York: Academic Press.

Persky, H., K. D. Smith, and G. K. Basu. 1971. "Relation of Psychologic Measures of Aggression and Hostility to Testosterone Production in Man." *Psychosomatic Medicine* 33:265-277.

Reiss, I. L. 1986. "A Sociological Journey into Sexuality." *Journal of Marriage and the Family* 48(2):233-242.

Rollins, B. C. and K. L. Cannon. 1974. "Marital Satisfaction over the Family Life Cycle: A Re-Evaluation." *Journal of Marriage and the Family* 36(2):271-282.

Rollins, B. C. and H. Feldman. 1970. "Marital Satisfaction over the Family Cycle." *Journal of Marriage and the Family* 32(1):20-28.

Rossi, A. S. 1964. "Equality Between the Sexes: An Immodest Proposal." *Daedalus* 93(2):607-652.

———. 1966. "Abortion Laws and Their Victims." *Trans-action* 3(6):7-12.

———. ed. 1970. *Essays on Sex Equality by John Stuart Mill and Harriet Taylor Mill.* Chicago: University of Chicago Press.

———. 1973. *The Feminist Papers: From Adams to deBeauvoir.* New York: Columbia University Press.

———. 1977. "A Biosocial Perspective on Parenting." *Daedalus* 106(2):1-31.

———. 1980a. "Aging and Parenthood in the Middle Years." Pp. 137-205 in *Life Span Development and Behavior,* Vol. 3, edited by P. Baltes and O. Brim, Jr. New York: Academic Press.

———. 1980b. "Life Span Theories and Women's Lives." *Signs: Journal of Women in Culture and Society* 6(1):4-32.

———. 1983a. *Feminists in Politics.* New York: Academic Press.

———. 1983b. *Seasons of a Woman's Life.* Amherst, MA: Hamilton Newell.

———. 1984a. "Gender and Parenthood." *American Sociological Review* 49(1):1-18.

———. 1984b. *Sociology and Anthropology in the People's Republic of China: A Report of a Delegation Visit, Feb-March 1984.* Washington, DC: National Academy Press.

———. 1986. "Sex and Gender in an Aging Society." *Daedalus* 115(1):141-169.

———. and A. Calderwood, eds. 1973. *Academic Women on the Move.* New York: Russell Sage.

Rossi, A. S. and P. E. Rossi. 1977. "Body Time and Social Time: Mood Patterns by Menstrual Cycle Phase and Day of the Week." *Social Science Research* 6:273-308.

Rossi, P. H. and S. L. Nock, eds. 1982. *Measuring Social Judgments: The Factorial Survey Approach.* Beverly Hills, CA: Sage.

Safilios-Rothschild, C. 1974. "The Influence of the Wife's Degree of Work Commitment upon Some Aspects of Family Organization and Dynamics." *Journal of Marriage and the Family* 32(4):681-691.

Sherrod, L. R. and O. G. Brim, Jr. 1986. "Epilogue: Retrospective and Prospective Views of Life-Course Research on Human Development." Pp. 557-580 in *Human Development and the Life Course,* edited by A. B. Sorensen, F. E. Weinert, and L. R. Sherrod. Hillsdale, NJ: Lawrence Erlbaum.

Udry, J. R. and J.O.G. Billy. 1986, May 22. "Initiation of Coitus in Early Adolescence." (Unpublished manuscript)

Udry, J. R., J.O.G. Billy, N. M. Morris, T. R. Groff, and M. H. Raj. 1985. "Serum Androgenic Hormones Motivate Sexual Behavior in Adolescent Boys."*Fertility and Sterility* 43(1):90-94.

Udry, J. R., L. M. Talbert, and N. M. Morris. 1986. "Biosocial Foundations for Adolescent Female Sexuality." *Demography* 23(2):217-230.

Veevers, J. E. 1979. "Voluntary Childlessness: A Review of Issues and Evidence." *Marriage and Family Review* 1:1, 3-26.

Veroff, J., E. Douvan, and R. A. Kulka. 1981. *The Inner American: A Self-Portrait from 1956 to 1976.* New York: Basic Books.

Welty, E. 1983. *One Writer's Beginnings.* Cambridge, MA: Harvard University Press.

4

Notes on a Double Career

Lewis A. Coser

THOSE OF YOU who did not know it already will have noticed from my accent that I am not a native son. I was born in Berlin shortly before World War I into a Jewish bourgeois family. I grew up in the exciting, exhilarating but also tormented years of the Weimar Republic. These were years of a great deal of creativity in the arts and in literature, but they were also years that made one aware that we were all living on the edge of a volcano.

As an adolescent I revolted against the stultifying milieu of my family and against the authoritarian life-styles of my banker father. I soon developed an acute sense of injustice when looking at the upper-middle-class society in which I moved. Be it because I learned early about the contempt with which my parents treated their servants or because of more general Oedipal tensions, I turned against the cultural milieu in which I had grown up and turned toward the socialist movement. Like most of the major figures of the Frankfurt School who came from a similar milieu, I was considered the black sheep of the family, but unlike them I was a mediocre high school student. I read a great deal on my own, but hated the rigid school routines and the generally reactionary or proto-Nazi attitudes of my teachers.

Having been active in the socialist student movement, I left the country soon after Hitler came to power and found asylum in Paris. For my first years in Paris I lived a miserable marginal life. Having no work permit, I developed into a jack of all marginal trades, from commercial traveler to private secretary of a Swiss journalist. Most of the time I lived just above starvation level. Only after the Popular Front government came to power in 1936 was I given a work permit and then secured employment with an American brokerage house as, lo and behold, a "statistician."

A year or two after coming to Paris, I decided to become a student at the Sorbonne, which was easy to do because study at French universities then as now was free. With a good knowledge of several languages, and encouraged by a French girl friend who also spoke German, I decided to work for a degree in comparative literature. I did quite well, and after only a year or two one of my professors, Jean Marie Carré, asked me if I had thought about a dissertation topic. I told him that I thought that it might be a good idea to compare the English, French, and German novel in the mid-nineteenth century in terms of the differing social structures of these countries. "La structure sociale," exclaimed the horrified Carré, "c'est de la sociologie, ce n'est pas de la littérature comparée!" So I switched into sociology and have been stuck with it ever since.

In the interwar years French sociology was a rather dreary affair. The field was dominated by former students or collaborators of Durkheim, all of them in the last phase of their teaching careers. Students felt acutely that their teachers represented the tail end of an era, and the courses were largely routine. In addition, we were offered nothing but Durkheimian sociology. Had I not been of German origin, I would probably have remained ignorant of even the major writings of Weber or Simmel. We heard vaguely about brash young men named Raymond Aron and Jean-Paul Sartre, who had studied in Germany and proposed to write on German sociology and philosophy, but their writings were not yet published. There were Marxist student study groups, in which I participated, but the Sorbonne was still quite free from Marxist contamination.

As distinct from most of my German political refugee friends on the Left, I was active in the French socialist movement while also involved in the sectarian politics of the German antifascist exiles. In Paris then and in the United States later, I attempted to be part of several intellectual worlds, never content to be fully part of either.

A day or two after the beginning of the war, a *gendarme* knocked at my door in the early morning and told me to get ready to be interned as an enemy alien. I told him that I had been officially recognized as an antifascist refugee, but the man stated that it was war now, and the government could no longer afford to make fine distinctions between different kinds of *boches*. So I spent a frightening week in an open football stadium together with several thousand other refugees—Jews, political refugees, as well as Nazis—expecting, like everybody else, German air attacks but without the benefit of gas masks, which had been furnished to French nationals only.

After a while we were dispersed to a number of concentration camps in different parts of France and were told that government commissions would soon visit the camps to separate the sheep from the goats. Such commissions came indeed after a while, but they released mainly Nazi businessmen who had good connections in Paris, whereas the likes of us stayed in the camps until the defeat of France, even though we were later classified as *prestataires* (providers of service). We remained closely guarded, dug potatoes or the foundations of a future aircraft factory, and had a thoroughly unpleasant time.

After the German victory I managed, through a variety of stratagems, to get out of the camp in the Vichy zone where I had been imprisoned last, and managed to join some of my friends in a small town, Montauban, which had a socialist mayor who helped us stay alive partly by calling us "Alsatians," so that we could profit from governmental support provided for refugees from Eastern France.

When we began to put out feelers to America to find out the chances of securing American entry visas, we learned that the German quota was oversubscribed for many years to come, but that Eleanor Roosevelt, who had close contacts with refugees from central Europe, had persuaded her husband to issue a few thousand visas for political refugees outside the quota. I was granted such a visa, and, after a somewhat complicated transit through Spain and Portugal, I got on board one of the last Portuguese ships to leave from Lisbon to New York before the outbreak of the war.

My first visit in New York was to the International Relief Committee, which had handled my "case" with admirable effort and unflagging energies. I was introduced to the young woman who had dealt with my case, a fellow refugee, Rose Laub. We soon got married. We celebrated our 45th wedding anniversary a short time ago.

In my first years in New York I worked as a shipping clerk, a hat checker, a freight forwarder, and finally for a variety of official and unofficial government agencies engaged in the war effort. But I also began to write for a number of journals of opinion, such as *Politics* and *The Nation*, and for literary journals, such as *Partisan Review*, as well as for a number of socialist publications. Using the pen name of Louis Clair, I lived a somewhat double life as a left-wing journalist and a government employee at the Office of War Information and elsewhere.

At war's end I had some ambitious ideas of becoming a high-level journalist, a sort of junior left-wing Walter Lippmann. This soon turned out to be a pipe dream, and so, after briefly coediting the socialist magazine *Modern Review*, I decided to return to my old love and become a graduate student in sociology at Columbia. Rose had already preceded me there and I had already met Bob Merton, Bob Lynd, and C. Wright Mills. But soon after I had decided to come to Columbia in the following year, I received a phone call from Nathan Glazer, then a young radical student at Columbia. "Do you know David Riesman?" he asked. When I said I didn't, Glazer told me that

Riesman was a brilliant lawyer, the last law clerk of Justice Brandeis, who, upon the advice of Erich Fromm, had decided to leave the law and become a social scientist. He had just been hired by the College of the University of Chicago and was on a tour in the East to hire bright young men and women for the College. I was naturally very interested even though I had never taught in a college or elsewhere. I met Riesman soon thereafter, and after walking up and down Central Park for several hours, he invited me to join the teaching staff of the College. When asked what I was suppose to teach, Riesman answered: American history. I was speechless and only managed to convey that I thought it was absurd for a person from Berlin, Paris, and London to teach American history in the Midwest. There, so I thought, went a good chance. But only a week or two later I had a call from then Dean of the College, Champion Ward, who said he would like to talk about my prospective job there. When I told him that I had already told David Riesman that I could not accept a teaching job in history, he informed me that I need not worry, somebody else had been shifted from sociology into history and I could teach the basic Social Science II course.

After two years at Chicago, during which I learned much from colleagues such as Riesman, Phil Rieff, Joe Gusfield, and others, I decided to return to New York to become a full-time student at Columbia—where I had already taken some summer courses with such then unknown teachers as Robert Nisbet and Reinhard Bendix.

The atmosphere at Columbia was totally different from what I had known at the Sorbonne. My major teachers, Robert K. Merton and Kingsley Davis, had been students of Parsons at Harvard and, with enormous enthusiasm and zest, initiated their students into the then novel and innovative mode of functional analysis. They, and most of their colleagues, felt that they were about to inaugurate a mode of sociological study that would revolutionize the field. The contrast between the tired professors and routine teachings at the Sorbonne and the Columbia atmosphere was total. I was caught in the enthusiasm as were almost all of my fellow students. In those days at Columbia it was a joy to be alive in a highly exciting intellectual atmosphere.

And yet, even though I was attracted to functional analysis, I could not bring myself to endorse its approach fully. Even though Merton had already developed some pronounced disagreements with Parsons's theorizing, Parsons was nevertheless taken to be the fountainhead of the structural-functional approach. I spent a whole summer reading *The Structure of Social Action*, line by involuted line, and even though I was impressed by the book, which I still consider one of the few seminal works in social theory written in modern America, I could not bring myself to accept what I saw as Parsons's bias in favor of equilibrium, balance, common values, and harmonious adjustment.

Given my existential experience, it seemed to me obvious that social conflict was a fundamental phenomenon on the social scene and that neglect of social conflict was likely to bias sociological theorizing in a conservative direction. It seemed to me that sets of ideas having matured in a stable society were likely to have a character different from views developed in the turmoil of war and revolution in Europe. And so it came to pass that, if I would at times call myself a functionalist analyst, I was always somewhat of a heretic in the functionalist school. When I called my first book, a part of my Columbia dissertation, *The Functions of Social Conflict* (1956), I deliberately highlighted my concomitant allegiance to two divergent modes of sociological thought.

Dual allegiances to divergent sociological traditions continued, so it would seem to me, in my further development within sociology and in general social and political matters. I no longer considered myself a Marxist, yet I was always aware of the great debt that I owed to my early Marxist training. While Durkheim, Weber, and, above all, Simmel, were my most important intellectual fathers among classical sociologists, I was not an orthodox believer in any of their variant approaches. I understood sociological theories as, in the last analysis, tools for the elucidation of empirical problems and, just like a plumber who carries around a tool kit to take care of the differing problems that he would encounter in the course of his work, I needed the help of a variety of sociological approaches in order to address the differing problems that I would face in sociological analysis (see Coser, 1982). What was needed, so I felt, was what Robert K. Merton has called "disciplined eclecticism."

Just as I stood among a variety of sociological traditions, I also supplemented my purely sociological concerns with writings of a critical and moral-political nature. I tried to follow the guidance of Max Weber to keep apart "value-neutral" sociological studies and writings that were critical and politically engaged. In particular, my friend Irving Howe and I founded the journal *Dissent* during the darkest years of the McCarthy nightmare, to dissent from the intolerance and cowardice of so many intellectual spokespersons that marked this dismal episode in American social and cultural life in the early 1950s. We thought then that the journal would probably not last more than a year or two, but it turned out that we would publish it 35 years later. Throughout all these years, I have cultivated a kind of double vision, a dual set of premises of pure sociological analysis and impure social and moral partisanship. It has not always been easy to maintain such a dual vision, and critics may well have been right when they have attempted to show that too often I have strayed into confounding those two realms. But even Weber was not able to keep his intellectual allegiances completely separate. In any case, I have never been uncomfortable with being, to use the terminology of chairman Mao, both pink and expert.

I taught for nearly twenty years at Brandeis University, then a haven for liberal and radical ideas, and I helped build a strong department of sociology there. I then taught for almost twenty years at the State University of New

York at Stony Brook where I contributed to developing a small undergraduate concentration into a leading graduate department. My students in both institutions knew well that, following Max Weber's example, I refused to proselytize my socialist ideas in the classroom. But these students also always knew that I was eager and ready to address them with talks about the history of socialism or the political demands of the hour in informal sessions and extracurricular study groups. I do not think that my colleagues in the American Sociological Association, with whom I served on a variety of committees and councils and as their President, elected me to these offices because of my political stance, but I am happy to say that they also seem not to have been inclined to discount my scholarly contributions because of it.

I learned a great deal from my students such as Arthur Mitzman, Michael Walzer, Gaye Tuchman, Walter Powell, George Becker, and many others. Some of them came to hold political views similar to my own, but others did not.

Most, perhaps all, of my writings have been inspired and motivated by my life experiences. My work on *Greedy Institutions* (Coser, 1974) has profited and was made possible by my experiences in French concentration camps and in the Marxist sects with which I have been involved. My work on social conflict, as I have already shown, grew from my experiences in war-torn and revolutionary Europe. My *Men of Ideas* (1965) grew out of an effort of self-clarification in order to understand the social roots of my life as an independent intellectual. My *Sociology Through Literature* (1972) was an effort to clarify the relation between my early involvement with literary studies and my later involvement with the sociological imagination. My book, *Refugee Scholars in America* (1984), on the fate of these scholars, was written in order to elucidate some of the sources of my experiences in America. I shall not bore you with additional examples beyond saying that almost all of my writings have biographical sources.

Given my existential location, it is not surprising that a large part of my writings have a critical thrust. Again and again, I have defined my own bearings in developing a critical distance from other sets of ideas and winds of doctrine. My late friend Harold Rosenberg once said that intellectuals are people who turn answers into questions, and I have attempted to live up to this calling.

References

Coser, Lewis A. 1956. *The Functions of Social Conflict*. New York: Free Press.
———. 1974. *Greedy Institutions: Patterns of Undivided Commitment*. New York: Free Press.
———. 1965. *Men of Ideas*. New York: Free Press.
———, ed. 1972. *Sociology Through Literature*. Englewood Cliffs, NJ: Prentice-Hall.
———. 1982. "The Uses of Sociological Theory." In *The Future of Sociological Classics*, edited by Buford Rhea. Boston: Allen and Unwin.
———. 1984. *Refugee Scholars in America: Their Impact and Experiences*. New Haven, CT: Yale University Press.

5

Phases of Societal and Sociological Inquiry in an Age of Discontinuity

Rosabeth Moss Kanter

THERE ARE TWO IRONIES in asking sociologists to describe their own careers, even with an institutional perspective in mind. Sociology, first, is comfortable with patterns, not personalities. Since Max Weber, there has been remarkably little attention in sociology to leadership or to the role of the great person in history; instead, we have looked for ever more elegant theoretical or mathematical ways to describe patterns in which individuals as either driving forces or even passive participants play little role other than that of representing a large class. Therefore, to ask a sociologist to talk about herself would inevitably lead her to want, instead, to describe a group or class or a social pattern—but not delve at all into personal matters or purely individual events.

Second, sociology is the quintessential discipline of detachment. It emphasizes skepticism about the true purposes served by what appear to be harmonious social relations—someone must be manipulating the situation in his or her own interests, and sociologists will soon discover who it is. Sociology is the discipline that searches for unintended consequences, for larger purposes or larger impact of behavior of which participants in a situation cannot even be aware. This propensity in the discipline must be why so many sociologists appear more comfortable with the role of critic or gadfly or stripper of pretenses than with decision maker—unlike practitioners of economics, a sister social science. So if we assume that it takes a detached outsider who can see the total pattern, even a skilled participant observer who "goes native" for a time, how can mere individuals, even skilled sociologists, be expected to describe their own careers with any degree of scientific accuracy?

Aware of, and somewhat intrigued by, these two ironies, I will respond by avoiding talking about myself and looking for some larger institutional patterns that my own career might reflect. But I do this with the humility of one who knows the ultimate intellectual impossibility of such a task.

I entered graduate school in sociology in 1964, at a time when sociology was booming. American sociology was booming because America was at the beginning of what Peter Drucker so aptly termed an "age of discontinuity," an age that began to flower about 1960 and probably will be with us through the 1990s. An age of discontinuity is one in which change is occurring at an unprecedented rate, and old social relations are being redefined, and old categories and limits are being broken and reshaped. It is these particular historical times that create the greatest opportunity for sociological break-throughs, for sociologists or their intellectual fellows are searching for terms to describe the changes that are going on, at the same time that those very changes are helping make social institutions more transparent and therefore more accessible to sociological study.

The best sociology, I feel, arises to reveal disjunction, uncover inequities, explain clashes of ideas and values. Indeed, the birth of modern sociology took place at a time of revolution—both political and economic. And it was recent political and economic turmoil that gave sociology a temporary ascendancy from about 1965 to 1975, even if we do not have something quite as dramatic as a full "revolution" in the move to what Daniel Bell termed the postindustrial society and others call the information age or the service society.

There are many signs that something different began to happen around 1960. Six phenomena are particularly noteworthy

• A wave of new technology, some of it seeded in the extensive research launched during World War II, but not coming to full fruition in terms of its impact on society until the 1960s. This technology included atomic and nuclear energy, and the associated horror at some of the potential of this technology; birth control pills; jet engines; and computers. (To see how recent the latter technology is, recall that Digital Equipment Corporation, leader in minicomputers, one of the first stages in miniaturizing the technology to make it more readily available, was not founded until 1955, and Xerox Corporation did not become important until the early 1960s.)

• Globalization of markets, aided by advances in transportation and communications as well as by the rise to economic prominence of Japan and

West Germany, who had finally rebuilt their industrial capacity after their defeat in World War II.

• A wave of government regulation aimed at protecting human values in the midst of technological change and internationalization, including most importantly civil rights and environmental protection.

• The first of the baby boom generation coming of age, creating a youth bulge in the population and new attitudes from a generation rather primarily mythical (and in some cases real) 1950s suburbia.

• Post-Sputnik active funding of higher education, which put more of that very generation into colleges.

• And slightly later, an unpatriotic, unpopular war covered by television and opposed by students, giving them a taste for protest, participation, and entrepreneurship—the heady power of being in charge.

In this context, there was ample material for sociologists to write about and ample change for sociologists to participate in and observe.

I propose that ages of discontinuity are punctuated by three principle phases: a period of utopian possibilities, a period of opposition and estrangement, and a period of tentative integration. (Any resemblance to Hegelian dialectics is fully intended.) These three phases may also correspond to aspects of the life course—moving from youthful hope (the period of utopian possibilities) to cynicism about the actual ability of institutions to deliver on the hope (the period of opposition and estrangement) to the merger of hope and cynicism through an acceptance of the imperfectability of institutions but the possibilities that exist in any case for reform (the period of tentative integration). I do not want to suggest that these are completely separable, nor that they unfold in linear fashion (as opposed to successive iterations), nor that subsequent periods are "higher" or more mature than previous ones as stage theories often assume. But it is interesting to note the possibility for this dialectical rhythm occurring both at a societal level during periods of rapid change and at an individual level as careers unfold.

During the period of utopian possibilities that began with John F. Kennedy's presidency in the 1960s we were promised—literally—the moon. It did not seem farfetched to envision, to dream about, entirely new possibilities for the design of social institutions. Some of these hearken back to earlier historical periods (for example, the nineteenth-century utopian communities); some rejected technology and the consequences it produced in the form of pollution and destruction; some embraced the new technology as an opportunity.

I began my career as a sociologist as one of many people interested in the frontiers of social organization, in the limits of organization design, in the possibility of creating frameworks for social life that would satisfy utopian longings. The collective form was one of those end points of social organization, and the society was rich with experiments in variations of it.

Furthermore, the idea appealed to people perhaps too young to know that one must "accept reality," as one's elders were always saying. I say that cynically, rather than positively, for I believed that we should never accept reality, but continually try to reshape it to include the best of human aspirations.

But it would also be fair to say that there was a degree of naïveté in the social experimentation, a writing off both of the potentially repressive and totalitarian potential of certain kinds of communities (which I pointed to in my chapter on Synanon in *Commitment and Community*—Kanter, 1972— and was later manifested in Jonestown) and of the difficulties of doing practical things like earning a living. Hoping for a communal existence did not make power inequities go away nor did declaring equality between the sexes as a matter of ideological principle make sex role differentiation go away in American communes and Israeli kibbutzim without attention to the practical details of such institutional arrangements as child care, the ratio of men and women in particular occupations, and opportunities for learning certain skills.

While I was learning what makes people committed, with commitment theory an important by-product of my work, I was also learning what makes certain kinds of social arrangements difficult, if not impossible, to sustain; and what makes them highly limited as models for the rest of society.

While some were exploring utopian possibilities, others were engaged in confrontation. Protest against the Vietnam War reached a crescendo in the late 1960s, but the theme of estrangement went far beyond that. In the very midst of antiwar protests, women were also discovering that they could not join their male counterparts as full colleagues (Kanter, 1977). The same utopian belief that anything is possible and that the limits lie only in our imagination led women to believe that the new sexual freedom (in part engendered by the birth control pill) would be translated into the ability to take on any kind of role in society. So a woman's movement was born on top of an antiwar movement, ultimately going far beyond it to form lasting organizations dedicated to equality for women and making incremental progress—limited, but at least discernible progress—in reaching the goal.

If issues of commitment seem appropriate to a period of utopian possibilities, then issues of power best fit a period of opposition and estrangement. The power of institutions or organizational arrangements to shape people's fate and control their behavior, the power of one social group over another social group—all of these are grist for the sociological mill. While these have always been important concerns in the discipline, they take on an important kind of urgency when they fit the actual events unfolding in the immediate world around the sociologist.

For me, the particular sense of urgency came from an unusual direction. As a firm believer in utopian possibilities, as one whose background as grandchild of immigrants seemed to reinforce the American dream of upward mobility by dint of one's own effort, it was very difficult for me to accept the legitimacy of the organizational and interpersonal barriers placed in the path of advancement for women. Why couldn't people like me do anything we wanted to do? Furthermore, it was a source of great personal irritation that the major explanations advanced in the society for the failure of women to do as well as men in the public realm were largely psychological, blaming the *victim* rather than the victimizers. These explanations (from fear of success to propensity for mothering) simply did not fit with either more personal observations or the messages received from participation in the period of utopian possibilities during the age of discontinuity.

Thus I translated my abiding interest in social organization—the one continuing thread in my work of the last twenty years—to an investigation of the barriers that seem to inhibit women that had nothing to do with individual or psychological limits but could be attributed to organizational design instead. Knowing that organizations were human creations—a knowledge that would only be reinforced by observation of a period of utopian possibilities—I found it easier to see the flaws in those designs than perhaps would have been possible without the age of discontinuity making old assumptions questionable and institutions more transparent to our view. Limited opportunity and power, a series of images built into organizational roles, and the dynamics of tokenism were the structural problems that limited success for both women and men. Clearly, the flaws in the design of the modern corporate bureaucracy were exposed, just at the time when the institution itself was under attack (for poor productivity, suppression of human potential, rigidity, and blindness to its environment) and beginning to change.

Next came a third phase. A tentative, if uneasy, integration seems to have followed from the periods of utopian dreaming and opposition and estrangement. What both the dreamers and the opponents had in common was a turning away from any belief that mainstream institutions could satisfy the aspirations they held and a distrust in leadership to marshal the new forces of technology in constructive rather than destructive ways. But the next development in the unfolding of the age of discontinuity seemed to be the merging of hope and cynicism in the rise of both dreamers and cynics themselves to positions of leadership in which they began to seek reform of mainstream institutions from inside (Kanter, 1983).

Sheer aging of cohorts played a role. Jerry Rubin became a famous symbol of the "yippie" protester turned "yuppie" stockbroker, but there are many more examples. Writers and editors for radical publications such as *Mother Jones* and *Working Papers for a New Society* now staff *Inc.* magazine, a magazine dedicated to entrepreneurial success in business. Such writers endorse a platform that embraces economic growth while preserving social justice.

Furthermore, society began to change as the youth bulge moved into adulthood and went to work. Many of the values of youth movements of the 1960s have been brought to the workplace as their adherents moved on from the college campus to the workplace. In particular, the search for meaning in work and the belief in rights in the organization were carried to adult employment, as I demonstrated in a 1978 article in a *Daedalus* issue devoted to an examination of a new America. (Parenthetically, it was difficult to get that argument accepted by certain establishment scholars when I first advanced it in 1977, although this is rapidly becoming conventional wisdom almost ten years later.) Some of the concepts that dominated youth movements—such as participation, the fact that work could be play—are now being held out to corporate executives as models of what the most progressive businesses do and as a factor in their financial success. The dreamers were ready to embrace this and turn some of their utopian hopes to establishing corporations built around such values. Apple Computer is perhaps one of the most visible examples of this, but many more abound.

Cynics, opponents, and critics remain highly skeptical about these as other than a new form of manipulation or control, but regardless of their distrust, it is increasingly an empirical fact that such models exist. One can remain skeptical about the motives of those who benefit the most, but one cannot deny that they exist. With this tentative integration, however, the age of discontinuity is itself being transformed into an age of incorporation of change in the guise of reform—again, reform that may be considered modest by many standards but still reflects an attempt to bring into conjunction again forces of change that were disturbing the institutional framework. The new issues have been identified, and now attention has shifted to repairing (rather than rethinking) institutional arrangements to allow them to continue under new conditions. As this occurs, the boom in sociology as a leading discipline to help one understand the disjunctions is clearly over. The interest in the social sciences that was so great in the late 1960s and early 1970s has been replaced by an interest in technical tools that will allow people to enter—and run— mainstream institutions.

I note these trends. I observe them without applauding them. But the apparent conservatism of today's youth and the citizenry in general masks how much the society has already shifted to embrace the utopian and the oppositional agendas of the 1960s and 1970s. As studies of many of those MBA and related programs show, we should not assume that the fact that people want to join the business world means that they uncritically embrace the way its institutions are organized, or at least the legacy of those institutions from the 1950s and 1960s. Instead, they hold out very different expectations for what those institutions will become—expectations that match the reforms of what I am calling the period of tentative integration.

There are a number of critical shifts beginning to occur in organizations, as a result of internal and external pressures, that represent responses to the utopian hopes and oppositional criticisms aimed at corporations and other large work organizations. New questions are being raised: Do we need as many layers of the hierarchy? Do we need managers at all, if more professionalized employees manage their own work? How should people be paid, if organizations seek new ideas rather than maintenance of the status quo? Is there any justification for the current definition of pay grades, especially if it results in gross inequities between men and women? Can older organizations revitalize themselves by setting up new ventures in new areas— and, if they do, can they tolerate the disparities in management styles? Can labor and management redefine their traditional adversarial roles?

At the same time, changes in the regulatory environment and in industry structure are causing many organizations in many sectors to go through a difficult period of refocusing their goals and redesigning their structures as they attempt to deal with the changes. Financial institutions, health care organizations, and telephone companies are among those most dramatically engaged in a process of redefinition and restructuring to deal with major change in their environments.

My own recent research has been an attempt to document the possibility— or the limits—of change or reform in establishment institutions such as the large corporation. This is now an arena in which a great deal of unease still exists and experimentation is beginning to go on, and thus, intellectually, it represents an opportunity to test the limits of hope as well as the possibilities for correcting the concerns that arise from opposition and estrangement. In *The Change Masters*, I attempted to document the ways in which the age of discontinuity was beginning to affect major corporations and the difference between those new breed corporations that arose out of the values of the new era and the rigid, stagnating nature of those corporations rooted in old assumptions. I tried to show how, in some corporations, the conditions that disempowered people and limited opportunity—the core of the critique in *Men and Women of the Corporation*—were replaced by other kinds of organizational arrangements that were more empowering. But I also began to show that the development of new forms was itself accompanied by new dilemmas—such as dilemmas of managing the expectations and hopes engendered by greater employee participation.

My next book will be about these organizational dilemmas—about the importance of organizational change to realize a vision of a society with a sound economy that also realizes human values, but also about the impossibility of realizing all of the ideals and all of the expectations that people now bring to the workplace. At the 1985 ASA meeting, I pointed to the tensions and contradictions involved as organizations struggle to implement more participative and more entrepreneurial practices (Kanter, 1987). Thus I am returning to a concern with the limits of institutions as well as with their possibilities. I am also involved in attempts to reformulate the agenda of the Democratic party to incorporate what has been learned in states like Massachusetts that have successfully managed an economic transition from old to new industry, via innovation, while taking action to spread the fruits of that transition to the people. There is, again, rich material for a sociologist in the documentation of such a transition.

My overall conclusion from this brief attempt to find larger patterns in my own career is the importance of connecting sociological work to the urgent concerns of the society. It is not so much a matter of being relevant—although relevance is certainly a ticket to employment. Indeed, I have always preferred the attempt to pursue lasting value to the attempt to pursue relevance, in part because of an awareness of how quickly fads and fashions change in this society. But I think that the greatest potential for important sociological insights comes from studying questions that arise in fact because society, or some important subsection of it, is changing. In the process of change, in the midst of crisis, in the midst of awareness of problems, it is possible to see what otherwise would be invisible, to uncover what otherwise would be hidden, because it would be taken for granted. I accept the common definition of sociology as a discipline that makes the familiar strange. But I also think there's an important role for sociology in making the strange familiar—that is helping make people understand what is new and different, what is emerging, what is changing.

References

Kanter, Rosabeth Moss. 1972. *Commitment and Community: Communes and Utopias in Sociological Perspective*. Cambridge, MA: Harvard University Press.

———. 1977. *Men and Women of the Corporation*. New York: Basic Books.

———. 1978. "Work in a New America." *Daedalus: Journal of the American Academy of Arts and Sciences* [Special Issue] (Winter):47-78.

———. 1983. *The Change Masters: Innovation for Productivity In the American Corporation*. New York: Simon & Schuster.

———. 1987. "The New Workforce Meets the Changing Workplace: Strains, Dilemmas, and Contradictions in Attempts to Implement Participative and Entrepreneurial Management." In *Working*, edited by Kai T. Erikson. New Haven, CT: Yale University Press.

6

Academic Controversy and Intellectual Growth

William Julius Wilson

IN 1978, at the 73rd annual meeting of the American Sociological Association in San Francisco, my book, *The Declining Significance of Race* (1978; 2nd edition, 1980) was denounced by the Association of Black Sociologists. In a widely circulated statement,[1] the black sociologists expressed outrage "over the misrepresentation of the black experience" and concern that the book "was considered sufficiently factual to merit the Spivack award from the American Sociological Association." The number of people who actually read this statement, however, was small in comparison to the audience generated when the book and the controversy surrounding it were the focus of a cover-page story in the *New York Times Sunday Magazine*, two featured stories in the *Washington Post*, op-ed-page articles and syndicated columns in the *New York Times*, the *Wall Street Journal, Washington Post, Chicago Tribune*, and several discussions in the national electronic media. When a controversial scholarly work receives this kind of attention, how does it affect an author's intellectual development? We shall see.

---

1. The statement has been reprinted in two books by black sociologists; *Footnotes* of the American Sociological Association; *The Amsterdam News*, a black newspaper published in New York; and the black journal *Freedom Ways*.

For this session, we have been asked "to stand back from our own work to consider the sociological meaning of the theme: the interplay between changing social structures (including opportunities, norms, sanctions, etc.)" and our "developing lives as sociologists, as each influences the other."[2] In the process of such consideration, we were encouraged to state our "own aspirations and efforts toward the future of sociology." I would like to do this by showing how changing social structures influenced the direction of my scholarship, ultimately leading to the writing of *The Declining Significance of Race*. I would then like to reflect on how the postpublication debate of the book helped to shape my subsequent intellectual development and change my aspirations for the future of sociology.

Before beginning, however, I ought to comment briefly on Pierre Bourdieu's (1986) warning about biographical illusions.[3] Bourdieu argues that, in order to understand adequately an autobiographical or biographical trajectory, it is necessary to construct the successive states of the field in which it has unfolded, that is, the set of objective relations that link the subject under consideration to all other subjects facing a similar space of possibilities. This provides a theoretical basis for conclusions that are made, and is a requisite for any rigorous assessment of the particular choices an individual makes considering the space of possibilities he or she confronts. It also reduces the tendency to select, identify, or interpret certain significant events in accordance with an ideology that the autobiographer or biographer happens to hold at a given moment. Unfortunately, I shall not be able to follow Bourdieu's instruction, and I am fully aware that my own subjective view of the social world may have resulted in the selection of particular events for discussion in this essay. But this does not necessarily mean that the relations I draw are untrue. It only alerts you to possible selective attention to certain events that I deem significant in my own intellectual and personal life. Let us now turn to those events.

THE BLACK PROTEST MOVEMENT AND THE DEVELOPMENT OF THEORETICAL INTERESTS IN THE FIELD OF RACE RELATIONS

Unlike many who enter a field of specialization on the basis of graduate training, I did not pursue race and ethnic relations as a major field of study in

---

2. Compare Matilda Riley's Chapter 2 in *Social Structure and Human Lives* (the first volume of *Social Change and the Life Course*), where she develops some of those ideas.

3. I am indebted to Loic J.D. Wacquant for calling to my attention and translating this article.

graduate school at Washington State University—my graduate study focused on theory and the philosophy of the social sciences and my doctoral dissertation was an exercise in theory construction. Indeed, the title of the paper I presented as part of my first job interview was "Formalization and Stages of Theoretical Development," my first four publications all dealt with the logic of sociological inquiry, and the subject of my first book proposal was the context of discovery versus the context of validation. My concentration on the logic of sociological inquiry could not, however, be sustained in a period dominated by events in the black protest movement.

In my last two years as a graduate student in the mid-1960s, I—like most blacks—was caught up in the spirit of the Civil Rights Revolution and was encouraged by the changes in social structure that led to increasing opportunities for black Americans. I also followed with intense interest the ghetto riots in Watts, Newark, and Detroit. And although at this point I had not developed a serious academic interest in the field of race and ethnic relations, my intellectual curiosity for the subject, fed by the escalating racial protest and my sense of the changing social structure for blacks in America, was rising so rapidly that by the time I accepted my first full-time academic job as Assistant Professor of Sociology at the University of Massachusetts, Amherst, in the fall of 1965, I had firmly decided to develop a field of specialization in that area.

What struck me as I became acquainted with the literature on race and ethnic relations in the late 1960s was the incredibly uneven quality of the scholarship. I read some classic works such as Myrdal's (1944) *An American Dilemma*, Park's (1950) *Race and Culture*, Frazier's (1949) *The Negro in the United States*, and Weber's ([1922] 1968) theoretical writings on ethnic relations in *Economy and Society*. I also read some excellent contemporary works. But a good deal of the scholarship in the 1960s was ideologically driven and laden with polemics and rhetoric. The most serious problem with the 1960s literature on race and ethnic relations, in my judgment, however, was the paucity of comprehensive theoretical formulations. With the exception of the influential works of scholars such as Robin Williams (1947), Hubert Blalock (1967), Milton Gordon (1964), and Stanley Lieberson (1961), much of the writings on race and ethnic relations were written as if theory had no relevance to the field. There was also the problem of the paucity of cross-cultural and historical research, except for the stimulating scholarship of R. A. Schermerhorn (1964) and Pierre van den Berghe (1967).

My concerns about the lack of theoretical, historical, and cross-cultural studies in the field of race relations ultimately led to the writing of a book (*Power, Racism and Privilege: Race Relations in Theoretical and Sociohistorical Perspectives*) published by Macmillan in 1973 and by Free Press in a paperback version in 1976. This study presents a comprehensive theoretical framework that is applied to race relations in the United States and the Republic of South Africa. By the time the book was in press and much too late to retrieve, however, my thinking about the field of race relations in America had already begun to change and I regretted that I not only paid so little attention to the role of class in understanding issues of race, but also that I tended to treat blacks as a monolithic socioeconomic group in most sections of the book. The one notable exception was a brief discussion, in one of the later chapters, of a paper written by Andrew Brimmer (1970), a consulting economist, on the deepening economic schism in the black population. Brimmer's paper reinforced some thoughts I had begun to develop on changing social structures and the differences in personal trajectories of professional blacks, like myself, from those mired in the ghetto. I further elaborated on this theme in a book I edited in late 1973, with Peter Rose and Stanley Rothman, on black and white perceptions of race relations in America for Oxford University Press. I was careful to emphasize the need to disaggregate racial statistics and to recognize the importance of both racial and class position in understanding the way that people respond to different situations involving racial interaction. But my views were no further advanced than those of Andrew Brimmer and others who emphasized intraracial differences at that time. It was not until after I moved to Chicago and joined the sociology faculty at the University of Chicago in 1972 that my views on the intersection of class with race in the United States sufficiently crystallized.

THE MOVE TO CHICAGO AND THE
CRYSTALLIZATION OF THE
RACE/CLASS THESIS

My thinking about intraracial divisions in America during the 1970s was in no small measure shaped by my perception of the changing social environments in Chicago's variegated ethnic neighborhoods. At one extreme were the upper-middle-class black professional neighborhoods in parts of the South Side; at the other extreme were the communities of the underclass plagued by long-term joblessness, welfare dependency, and crime in other parts of the South Side and on the West side. The widening gap between the haves and have-nots among blacks that Andrew Brimmer first talked about in the late 1960s would be obvious to any student of urban life who wanted to take the time to drive around the Chicago neighborhoods at different points in time as I did in the early to mid-1970s.

But intragroup differences were not of course confined to black neighborhoods in Chicago, they were even more noticeable in the different white neighborhoods. There were the racially liberal, predominantly white, and largely professional communities in Hyde Park and along the North Side lakefront; but there were also the racially hostile working-class white ethnic neighborhoods on the West and South sides. Unlike in the black community, these patterns were established long before I came to Chicago. What had recently changed, however, and what was evident to me in the early 1970s, was the growing number of inner-city white ethnics who were not only trapped in their neighborhoods because of the high cost of suburban housing, but had become increasingly physically removed from the industries in which they were employed because of the industrial shift to the suburbs and other locations.[4] This situation increased the potential for racial tension as white European ethnics competed with blacks and the rapidly growing Hispanic population for access to and control of the remaining decent schools, housing, and neighborhoods.

But it is one thing to recognize and describe these intragroup differences, and quite another thing to account for their evolution and relate them not only to the problems of intergroup relations, but, more important, to the broader problems of societal organization in America. And it was in this connection that the stimulating intellectual environment of the University of Chicago came into play because it encourages interdisciplinary contact and thereby afforded me the opportunity to confront questions about racial interaction from students of varied disciplinary backgrounds. The net result was a holistic approach to race relations in America that directed the writing, particularly the theoretical writing, of *The Declining Significance of Race*.

The theoretical framework in this book related problems associated with race to the broader issues of societal organization. To study problems of race in terms of societal organization entails not only an investigation of the political, economic, and other institutional dimensions of societal organization that affect intra- and intergroup experiences, but the investigation of technological dimensions as well. And the basic theoretical argument presented in the *The Declining Significance of Race* is that different systems of production in combination with different policies of the state impose different constraints on the structuration of racial group relations by producing dissimilar contexts not only for the manifestation of racial antagonisms but also for racial-group access to rewards and privileges.

I had hoped that my major academic contribution would be to explain racial change by applying this framework to historical developments of race relations in the United States. But there was another contribution I had hoped to make—I wanted to highlight the worsening condition of the black underclass, in both absolute and relative terms, by relating it to the improving position of the black middle class.

4. John Kasarda (1978) has written effectively on this subject.

THE CONTROVERSY AND THE
INITIAL REACTION

The Declining Significance of Race generated an even greater controversy than I had originally anticipated. At the time of publication, heightened awareness of racial issues had been created not only because changing social structures altered many traditional patterns of race relations, but also because the state was inextricably involved in the emerging controversy over affirmative action.

In the initial months following publication of the book, it seemed that critics were so preoccupied with what I had to say about the improving conditions of the black middle class that they virtually ignored my more important arguments about the deteriorating position of the black underclass. The view was often expressed that because blacks from all socioeconomic class backgrounds are suffering there is no need to single out the black poor. And few of these early critics paid attention to my macro-structural arguments.

After the dust had settled, and especially since 1983, however, scholars not only discussed my macro-structural arguments, they, along with journalists and policymakers, devoted far more attention to my arguments about the deteriorating condition of the black underclass—a topic of my current research.

FROM CONTROVERSY TO CURRENT RESEARCH:
UNDERSTANDING THE
PLIGHT OF THE UNDERCLASS

During the controversy over *The Declining Significance of Race*, I committed myself to doing two things: (1) I would address the problems of the ghetto underclass in a comprehensive analysis; and (2) I would spell out, in considerable detail, the policy implications of my work. These two commitments provided direction for my latest book, *The Truly Disadvantaged: The Inner City, The Underclass, and Public Policy*, published in 1987 by the University of Chicago Press. The first commitment grew out of my personal and academic reaction to the early critics' almost total preoccupation with my arguments concerning the black middle class. And it was only after I began writing *The Truly Disadvantaged* that serious scholars were beginning to focus on my previous analysis of the underclass in *The Declining Significance of Race*, particularly those scholars who are working in fields such as urban poverty, social welfare, and public policy.

The second commitment was a reaction to those critics who either labeled me a neoconservative or directly or indirectly tried to associate *The Declining*

Significance of Race with the neoconservative movement. Although I am a social democrat, and probably to the left politically of an overwhelming majority of these critics, and although some of the most positive reviews and discussions of *The Declining Significance of Race* have come from those of the democratic left, the title of my book readily lends itself to an assumption that I am a black conservative. Nonetheless, because I did not spell out the policy implications of *The Declining Significance of Race* in the first edition, it was possible for people to read my arguments selectively and draw policy implications significantly different from those that I would personally draw. Herbert Gans's discussion of the failure of the controversial Moynihan Report to offer policy recommendations is relevant here. Gans (1967, p. 449) states that "the vacuum that is created when no recommendations are attached to a policy proposal can easily be filled by undesirable solutions and the reports' conclusions can be conveniently misinterpreted." In the second edition of *The Declining Significance of Race*, published in 1980, I wrote an epilogue in which the policy implications of my work were underlined in sharp relief, but by then the views of many readers of the first edition had already solidified.

If the idea for the *The Truly Disadvantaged* grew out of the controversy over *The Declining Significance of Race*, does it mean that the former will also generate controversy? It will be controversial. *The Truly Disadvantaged* challenges liberal orthodoxy in analyzing inner-city problems; discusses in candid terms social dislocations of the inner city; establishes a case for moving beyond race-specific policies to ameliorate inner-city social conditions to policies that address the broader problems of societal organization, including economic organization; and advances a social democratic public policy agenda designed to improve the life-chances of truly disadvantaged groups, such as the ghetto underclass, by emphasizing programs to which the more advantaged groups of all races can positively relate.

It should be emphasized, however, that the central theoretical argument of *The Truly Disadvantaged* was inspired not by the debate over *The Declining Significance of Race*, but by travels to inner-city neighborhoods in the city of Chicago in the past several years and my perception of changing social structures in inner-city neighborhoods. Parts of that theory found their way into a controversial and widely read article by Nicholas Lemann on the "Origins of the Underclass," in the June 1986 edition of the *Atlantic Monthly*. Lemann interviewed me in early 1986 and in that conversation I discussed my thesis and gave him a copy of an article that now appears as the first chapter of *The Truly Disadvantaged* and that outlined my theory on the social transformation of the inner city. Also, one of my graduate research assistants, featured in his article, took him around various inner-city neighborhoods. In the first chapter of *The Truly Disadvantaged*, I emphasize that inner-city neighborhoods have undergone a profound social transformation in the last several years as reflected not only in their increasing rates of social dislocation but also in the changing economic class structure of ghetto neighborhoods. I point out that, in previous years, especially prior to 1960, these neighborhoods featured a vertical integration of different income groups as lower-, working-, and middle-class professional black families all resided more or less in the same ghetto neighborhoods. I also state that the very presence of working- and middle-class families enhances the social organization of inner-city neighborhoods. Finally, I note that the movement of middle-class black professionals from the inner city, followed in increasing numbers by working-class blacks, has left behind a much higher concentration of the most disadvantaged segments of the black urban population, the population to which I refer when I speak of the "ghetto underclass."

These ideas were picked up and incorporated by Lemann.[5] Instead of focusing on the changing situational and structural factors that accompanied the black middle- and working-class exodus from the inner city, however, Lemann emphasized the crystallization of a ghetto culture of poverty—claiming that this crystallization was possible only after the so-called black middle-class self-consciously imposed cultural constraints on southern lower-class culture were removed. Indeed, he goes so far as to suggest that

> every aspect of the underclass culture in the ghettos is directly traceable to roots in the South—and not the South of slavery but the South of a generation ago. In fact, there seems to be a strong correlation between underclass status in the North and a family background in the nascent underclass of the sharecropper [Lemann 1986, p. 35].

The last section of the second chapter of *The Truly Disadvantaged* is devoted to explaining why this thesis is incorrect and why the emphasis on a ghetto culture of poverty is misdirected.

The Truly Disadvantaged, however, is not the culmination of my research on the ghetto underclass. I had outlined another research project in the early 1980s that was partly shaped by the ideas developed in that book and that I had planned to begin in 1985. The publication of Charles Murray's (1984) book, *Losing Ground: American Social Policy, 1950-1980*, in 1984 made me realize that this proposed project would have to be much more ambitious than I had originally conceived. Murray argues that social welfare programs far from relieving poverty and welfare, increase them and should be eliminated. This book has had an enormous influence on conservative policymakers. As a *New York Times* editorial (February 3, 1985) put it, it is the Reagan "budget-cutter bible." Yet Murray conducted no actual empirical research. His conclusions are based mainly on an analysis of secondary documents

5. A belated public acknowledgment appeared in the September 1986 issue of *The Atlantic*.

including census documents. Nonetheless, the book has dominated recent public policy discussions on poverty, welfare, and the ghetto underclass.

After *Losing Ground* was published, I realized that my existing research plans on the ghetto underclass would have to be altered if I were to produce a work that would draw sufficient attention both inside and outside of academia to have a real impact. I felt that the study that would have the greatest effect would be one that combined survey, ethnographic, and macro-historical research. I wrote several drafts of a long research proposal that included an initial budget of 1.5 million dollars. Shortly after the project began in October 1985, the research budget climbed to more than 2.5 million thanks to the generous support of foundations such as Ford, Carnegie, Rockefeller, Spencer, Lloyd A. Fry, Joyce, William T. Grant, the Woods Charitable Fund, and support from the Department of Health and Human Services. This mammoth three-year study, titled "Poverty and Family Structure in the Inner City," has included as many as twenty research assistants (ten of whom have conducted ethnographic research in the black, white, Puerto Rican, and Mexican American inner-city neighborhoods), two project administrators, and five coinvestigators.

A LOOK AHEAD:
ASPIRATIONS AND EFFORTS
TOWARD THE FUTURE OF SOCIOLOGY

There are five reasons why "Poverty and Family Structure in the Inner City" differs significantly from what I take to be the typical research projects in sociology. (1) It is interdisciplinary with a team of graduate students and faculty representing various academic disciplines. (2) It combines different methodologies—the quantitative survey method and the more qualitative methods of ethnography and macro-historical research. (3) As suggested by the different methodologies, it combines individual micro-level data with societal macro-level data. (4) Far from focusing on trivial issues, it addresses one of the major domestic social problems in the last half of the twentieth century. (5) It will, therefore, draw the attention of policymakers and the media. Few research projects in sociology accomplish even one of these objectives. And I think that is a problem.

First of all, very little sociological research is interdisciplinary. It is true that we are probably not as insulated as economists, but I think our research projects would be greatly enhanced if they were directed to a broader social science audience and incorporated insights and methodological approaches from other disciplines. For example, the development of the ethnographic design for our research project was greatly influenced by the research techniques of one of our coinvestigators—Raymond Smith, an anthropologist at the University of Chicago. Smith emphasizes the collection of genealogies not only as a means of recording the individual's kin universe, but also of suggesting lines of inquiry on topics of interests to our research. In the course of collecting the genealogical data, we have accumulated information on such tangible matters as the geographic dispersion of kin; the spread of occupations within families; the influence of the kinship and friendship network on aspirations, norms, and behavior; the social context in which kinship and friendship ties are worked out; and the conjugal and childbearing patterns of couples.

Second, very little research in sociology combines different methodologies. We need only to consider studies that relate to the subject of our research project to see the advantages of this approach. We have a few excellent longitudinal and cross-sectional surveys that provide useful information on changes in the family structure, but they were not structured, due to the very nature of the survey technique, to probe symbolic meanings attached to different life situations or pursue over a given period of time possible leads suggested by responses to the survey items. And although ethnographic studies have uncovered many subtle patterns of behavior that are difficult, if not impossible, to ascertain when the more conventional survey techniques are used, they suffer from problems of representativeness in sample design. It is important, therefore, to link these two research strategies. Furthermore, neither survey nor ethnographic data should be interpreted in a vacuum. Often events external to the neighborhoods in which the survey and ethnographic research are being conducted profoundly affect developments within these neighborhoods. And previous developments that shape current behavior are often overlooked. A macro-historical analysis of prior or external events that affect present experiences within these neighborhoods is called for to enhance our interpretation of the survey and ethnographic data, and thereby provide an important link between individual micro-data and societal macro-data.

Third, I do not think it would be unfair to say that a review of many of the articles in our leading journals will reveal a paucity of important research problems. Too often this is seen in articles with elaborate and sophisticated quantitative techniques, but trivial substantive issues. To say that a research problem is important, however, does not mean that it is necessarily topical. By an important problem, I mean research on issues that determine the quality of life or the life chances of a substantial segment of our population. For example, our research on poverty, joblessness, and family structure in the inner city is not only addressing what many regard as one of the most pressing domestic social problems in the last quarter of the twentieth century, it is also providing data on fundamental social structural issues.

Finally, very little sociological research draws the attention of policymakers and the media. Some sociologists feel that this is a good thing because it both insulates the discipline from outside pressures to pursue certain research topics, particularly those that are topical, and protects the discipline from being sanctioned by the state if the research does not support a particular political agenda or ideology. I, on the other hand, view the situation as problematic. More specifically, the more our discipline is ignored by policymakers and the media, the less attention we receive as an academic discipline and therefore the more removed we are from the decision-making arena, the fewer students we attract, and the more difficult it is to receive funding support from private foundations and government agencies. In this connection, our current research in Chicago is being followed closely by policymakers and the media. And I maintain that this is because we are bold enough to address, with an innovative methodology, one of the most important and sensitive social problems of our time.

I am not suggesting that research projects in sociology need to be as ambitious as ours to attract attention. Our budget is over 2.5 million dollars and it would be unrealistic to suggest that many research projects in sociology could attract that kind of support. But my experience in raising money for this project clearly suggests that interesting and important research will be supported *whether it is controversial or not*. We only need to broaden our horizons and increase our substantive and methodological imaginations.

In sum, my aspirations for the future of sociology are that we become more interdisciplinary, combine quantitative and nonquantitative techniques and macro-historical and micro-level data, pursue important and even controversial research topics, and generate research that will be taken seriously by policymakers and the media alike. As the foregoing discussion suggests, these aspirations grow out of my own intellectual experiences, experiences that have been shaped not only by changing social structures but by the lively controversy over *The Declining Significance of Race*.

References

Blalock, Hubert M. 1967. *Toward a Theory of Minority-Group Relations.* New York: John Wiley.

Bourdieu, Pierre. 1986. "L'illusion Biographique." *Actes de la Recherche en Sciences Sociales* 62/63:69-72.

Brimmer, Andrew. 1970. "Economic Progress of Negroes in the United States." Paper read at the Founder's Day Convocation, Tuskegee, Alabama, March 22.

Frazier, Franklin E. 1949. *The Negro in the United States.* New York: Macmillan. (rev. edition, 1957)

Gans, Herbert J. 1967. "The Negro Family: Reflections on the Moynihan Report." Pp. 445-457 in *The Moynihan Report and the Politics of Controversy*, edited by Lee Rainwater and William L. Yancey. Cambridge: M.I.T. Press.

Gordon, Milton M. 1964. *Assimilation in American Life.* New York: Oxford University Press.

Kasarda, John. 1978. "Urbanization, and the Metropolitan Problem." Pp. 27-57 in *Handbook of Contemporary Urban Life*, edited by David Street et al. San Francisco: Jossey-Bass.

Lemann, Nicholas. 1986. "The Origins of the Underclass." *The Atlantic Monthly* 257:31-61.

Lieberson, Stanley. 1961. "A Societal Theory of Race and Ethnic Relations." *American Sociological Review* 26:902-910.

Murray, Charles. 1984. *Losing Ground: American Social Policy, 1950-1980.* New York: Basic Books.

Myrdal, Gunnar. 1944. *An American Dilemma.* New York: Harper.

Park, Robert E. 1950. *Race and Culture.* Glencoe, IL: Free Press.

Rose, Peter, Stanley Rothman, and William Julius Wilson. 1973. *Through Different Eyes.* New York: Oxford University Press.

Schermerhorn, R. A. 1964. "Toward a Theory of Minority Groups." *Phylon* 25:238-246.

van den Berghe, Pierre. 1967. *Race and Racism: A Comparative Perspective.* New York: John Wiley.

Weber, Max. [1922] 1968. *Economy and Society.* New York: Bedminster Press.

Williams, Robin M., Jr. 1947. "The Reduction of Intergroup Tensions." *Social Science Research Council Bulletin* 57.

Wilson, William Julius. 1973. *Power, Racism, and Privilege: Race Relations in Theoretical and Sociohistorical Perspectives.* New York: Macmillan. (2nd edition; New York: Free Press, 1976)

———. 1978. *The Declining Significance of Race: Blacks and Changing American Institutions.* Chicago: University of Chicago Press. (2nd edition, 1980)

———. 1987. *The Truly Disadvantaged: The Inner City, The Underclass, and Public Policy.* Chicago: University of Chicago Press.

7

The Aging Society and My Academic Life

Bernice L. Neugarten

EACH OF US IS addressing the theme of this book, social structures and human lives, from a different perspective, but my perspective may be even more different from the others because I was not formally trained as a sociologist.

If, however, I have not had a formal education in sociology, I have surely had an informal one. In my undergraduate and graduate student days at the University of Chicago, I was influenced by some noted students of society: among them, Herbert Blumer, William Ogburn, Louis Wirth; and later, by sociologists who were my senior colleagues in the Committee on Human Development, including Ernest Burgess, Nelson Foote, Everett C. Hughes, David Riesman, and particularly by Lloyd Warner and Allison Davis, both of whom, although trained as anthropologists, carried out studies of American social class structures and age-grade structures that were as sociological as any I know.

In pondering how best to address the theme, I have elected to comment primarily on a set of changes in academic perspectives and structures that themselves reflect the dramatic change in the age structure of the population—for, historically speaking, it is the attention to aging and the aging society that is the context for viewing my own academic career.

My graduate education took form in what was then a newly created program in the Division of the Social Sciences at the University of Chicago called Human Development. That program is a multidisciplinary one, whose faculty are drawn primarily from anthropology, psychology, and sociology; and whose faculty and students draw upon those disciplines in studying the course of lives and issues of continuity and change from infancy to old age.

This is not the occasion for a conceptual analysis, but it should be said that Human Development is a broader program than those that, in many other universities, are called Developmental or Life-Span Psychology, for while attention is given to changes that occur within the individual, the focus is on the individual-in-society; on the social structures and on the culture as much as on the mind and the psyche. The program centers on processes of socialization, on personal change and social change as they interact throughout life time. The social structures of the society are regarded as fundamental in shaping the individual's experience, but at the same time persons are perceived as proactive, not merely reactive. From this perspective, people can be said to invent their future lives, just as, in the telling and retelling, they reinvent their past lives—as we contributors to this volume are doing here in a highly self-conscious manner.

The Committee on Human Development is the oldest of many interdisciplinary committees at the University of Chicago. It began as the Committee on Child Development, created in 1930 by a group of social scientists and biologists who undertook studies of children and adolescents within the contexts of the family, the school, and the community. By 1940 those interests had widened and studies of older people were also under way. The name was therefore changed from Child Development to Human Development. The first Chairman was Ralph Tyler, later Dean of the Division of Social Sciences at Chicago, and later still, Director of the Center for Advanced Study in the Behavioral Sciences in Palo Alto. Its second Chairman was Robert J. Havighurst, who played the major role in building the curriculum and in planning many of the major research programs for which the Committee became known.

In the late 1940s a course was created called Maturity and Old Age, the first of its kind so far as I can determine. That course was joined with those in childhood and adolescence to form the core sequence for the Ph.D., and together with courses from the supporting disciplines, there was for the first time an interdisciplinary Ph.D. program in place organized around continuity and change across lives from birth to death.

The Committee has flourished over the years, with an active research faculty, a succession of communitywide studies and other large-scale research, and more than 400 Ph.D. graduates. Programs called Human Development have appeared in many other universities, many of them patterned after the one at Chicago. The term "life-span development" was coined later (by others) and has become widely used among developmental psychologists; and the "life-span perspective" is now appearing in many other of the social sciences (Featherman, 1983). Historically speaking, it was first the cultural anthropologists who adopted this perspective, with their studies of age grading and their interests in life histories. It was next the personality psychologists with what they called the studies of lives, and next, as already mentioned, the developmental psychologists. Sociologists, although concerned with individual social mobility and status attainment since Sorokin's work appeared, have only recently come forward with their work on age stratification and the sociology of age—represented in particular by the work of Matilda Riley and her colleagues (Riley, Johnson, and Foner, 1972). A new bridge between sociologists and historians is presently leading to a proliferation of studies of "the life course"—studies of the timing and sequencing of life events and role transitions, focused usually on intercohort comparisons (Neugarten and Hagestad, 1976; Hagestad and Neugarten, 1985). A number of economists have adopted the life-course perspective on their studies of economic and consumer behavior, as have a few political scientists, in studies of political socialization and participation. It is apparent that investigators of many persuasions are now organizing their data and reexamining their theories to reckon with change over the lifetime.

AGING AS AN ACADEMIC FIELD

It was the attention to aging that led historically to the definition of the academic field called Human Development. But the study of aging has also had a vigorous independent development.

At Chicago, social science research in aging began in the early 1940s with relatively large-scale studies undertaken by Ernest Burgess, Robert Havighurst, Ethel Shanas, and others—studies, for example, of work and retirement and of psychosocial adaptations to old age. (It is probably a little-known fact that, as early as 1943, the Social Science Research Council created a subcommittee called Social Adjustment in Old Age, headed by Burgess and Havighurst, to survey what was known about aging and to suggest directions for research. That group issued its report and bibliography in 1946.)

By the end of the 1940s dissertations in aging had begun to appear in Human Development, and a few in Sociology. In subsequent years, the Committee on Human Development became a major center for social science research in aging and a center for training Ph.D.s in this area. For over 20 years I directed a special training program in adult development and aging, first funded in the late 1950s by the National Institute on Mental Health, then through the Program on Adult Development and Aging of the National Institute on Child Health and Human Development when that institute was formed in the early 1960s, then by the National Institute on Aging when that institute was formed in the mid-1970s. During that 20-year period, some 80 Ph.D.s graduated from our special program, almost all of whom are now on university faculties around the country, teaching and carrying out research, with some who are administering multidisciplinary gerontology centers. Insofar as these former students represent a strategic population of teachers and researchers, it can be said fairly that the Chicago program played the leading role in creating the academic field of adult development and aging. The fact that I was the formal director of that training program for those 20 years does not mean that it was all a single-handed effort. There were as many as a dozen faculty in Human Development in some of those years who were committed to research in aging and another dozen in other parts of the university who helped guide dissertations that crosscut their own fields.

In subsequent years, academic programs in aging have appeared in many other universities, some of them doctoral programs in the biological or social sciences, but many more at the master's level in professional areas such as nursing, social work, or public administration. In most instances, aging represents an area of specialization within a degree program in an established department or School, but in a few places a degree called Gerontology is offered at the bachelor's or master's level.

It is understandable that the dramatic increase in life expectancy and the increased proportion of older people in the society should have created the so-called demographic imperative that is having its effects on academia. In the 40 years since the first course was given at Chicago, some 1100 colleges and universities in the country have begun offering courses or special certificates or degree programs in aging. Gerontological societies, scientific and professional, are flourishing in this country and have appeared in more than 50 other countries over the world, all with the express purpose of furthering research and education. There are now some 70 journals in the field, research oriented or practice oriented. It is against this background of aging as a growth industry in academia that my own academic life has taken shape.

MY FORMAL CAREER

The formal outline of my career can be set forth in brief terms. I came from a small town in Nebraska to the University of Chicago; I took an undergraduate degree in English and French literatures, a master's degree in educational psychology, and a Ph.D. in Human Development. (It happens that I was the first person to complete the Ph.D. after the Committee changed its name from Child to Human Development. Presumably this makes me the first fully credentialed Human Developer—an obvious anomaly of labeling, given all the poets and philosophers who through the ages have reflected upon the course of human lives, often in more insightful ways than the social scientists.)

I then spent an eight-year period "out," as it is often ironically referred to, raising two children, doing part-time writing and research jobs, becoming involved in local independent politics, and, with my husband, in organizational efforts aimed at building a racially-integrated community.

In 1951 I returned to the university to join the faculty in Human Development. At my request, I remained on part-time appointment for five years, then moved onto the tenure track, and was tenured four years later. (It happens that I was the first person to be given tenure in Human Development alone—that is, without a joint appointment in another department. Thus, so to speak, Human Development itself was also tenured in this same move—a certain milestone in the changing structure of the Social Sciences at Chicago.)

After another four years I was promoted to professor; and five years later I began a stint as Chairman of the Committee. Altogether I spent 30 years on the faculty at Chicago, then took an early retirement in 1980 and moved to Northwestern University to begin a new academic program called Human Development and Social Policy. (The 30 years at the same institution, plus all my student years there, probably makes me one of the least geographically mobile academics in this country.)

To flesh out this outline a bit: For one thing, although I was paying it little attention for most of the time, this progression of events was unusual for a woman of my birth cohort or my academic cohort. For another thing, it is likely that my research interests in the sociology of age and age-norms that I pursued later in my career stemmed in part from the fact that I was so "off time" in my youth. I was carrying courses in high school when I was 11 years old; and, after high school, I marked time for two years before coming as a teenager into the intellectual excitement and the sometimes buzzing confusion that marked the undergraduate "Hutchins's College" at Chicago in the 1930s. There it was not altogether rare to have a 14- or 15-year-old fellow student among us; and because we met degree requirements by placement tests and comprehensive examinations, not by number of courses or length of residence, academic acceleration was a common pattern. Although I tried to stretch things out, I had a master's degree by the time I was 21 and I looked much too young to find a job as a high school teacher. I was rescued when one of my professors called to offer me an assistantship if I would enter the doctoral program under the Committee on Child Development. Thus I was already one of its students when that committee later changed its name to Human Development.

Things slowed down thereafter, for, after several graduate assistantships, I was approximately on schedule in terms of academic age norms when I finished the Ph.D. at age 27; "late" when I joined the faculty at 35; and in a different sense, "on time" again when, at age 40, I published my first paper on middle age.

RESEARCH AND TEACHING

The substantive or intellectual side of my career is more difficult to summarize. My interest in sociological issues was evident from the first: My dissertation dealt with social class as a determining factor in the friendship patterns of children and adolescents; I taught courses in educational sociology for a brief time; and then collaborated with Robert Havighurst in producing a text in that field titled *Society and Education* (Havighurst and Neugarten, 1957). Some years later, in connection with the Kansas City Studies of Adult Life, I coauthored with Richard P. Coleman a book on the social class structure of Kansas City in the 1950s (Coleman and Neugarten, 1971).

At the same time, I also pursued psychological topics: personality changes in adolescence, a cross-cultural study of moral and emotional development in children of six American Indian tribes, and so on.

It was an accident that led me to concentrate on the study of adult development and aging. A year or two after I returned to the university, the course that I have already mentioned, Maturity and Old Age, needed a teacher. I was invited to give that course and, at the same time, to join the research team that was beginning a communitywide study of middle-aged and aging persons in the metropolitan area of Kansas City. Had it been the course in child development that needed an instructor, I might well have wound up today as a child psychologist. Thus, despite the fact that I was aware that the changing age structure of the population had enormous implications for the society at large, and despite the fact that I might have chosen to enter the field of aging because of it, it was not foresight or planning, but chance that was the major factor. (This unpredicted turn of events in my own career may be one of the reasons for my belief that, in the study of human lives, insufficient attention has been given to the unanticipated and the off-time events, to the discontinuities as well as the continuities [Neugarten, 1969]).

The following six months were spent reading all I could find about personality change in adulthood (there was very little except for Erik Erikson's work) and all the theoretical and empirical work I could find in the social sciences on age, aging, and age structures. In the early 1950s this task could be accomplished in six months. Now one cannot keep up even with the titles, let alone the content of publications, in aging, and the problem has become how to separate the new from the redundant.

I reorganized the course, renamed it Adult Development and Aging, and have given ever-changing versions of the course every year since.

In the next three years, I published my first paper on the psychology of aging, a paper that appeared in a volume titled *Potentialities of Women in the Middle Years* (Gross, 1956). The editor of that volume was ahead of her time, for the book appeared well before any attention was given, in the women's movement of the 1960s and 1970s, to middle-aged and older women. A year afterward I published my first paper written from the societal perspective, a paper on social change and the aging population. My studies have been of these two general categories ever since, a point I will return to in a later section of this essay.

In my forties, most of my publications were reports of empirical studies, often carried out in collaboration with colleagues and graduate students. In my fifties, although I undertook new empirical researches, more of my publications were "think pieces"—essays and review chapters. My fifties were also a period in which more of my time went to administrative roles, and much more to teaching, especially to the one-to-one teaching involved in dissertation supervision. Various kinds of rewards accumulate over the course of a long career, but two were of special significance to me in this period: the first, when in a single year four of my former students authored textbooks in middle age and aging, something I myself have never done; and, second, when I received a national award for graduate teaching.

By my early sixties, I was involved in the policy field. Earlier, much in the pattern typical of academics, I had served on study sections and advisory panels in the National Institutes of Health and in other parts of the Department of Health and Human Services and the Department of Education. But these groups had all been research related. Now I was appointed to the Federal Council on Aging, a 15-person group appointed by the president, with the mandate to report each year to the president and to Congress on the situation of older people, and to make recommendations regarding legislative and executive initiatives. In my three years there, I began to learn about policymaking and politics. Not that the Federal Council on Aging was an important or even visible body, as such things go, but it was a place where an array of major policy issues were studied and debated.

A year later I was appointed a Deputy Chairman of the 1981 White House Conference on Aging—where, amusingly enough, because of a slipup by a staff member, my first inkling of this appointment was when I was asked to appear at the White House to be sworn in—this, without ever having been told that such a post existed, much less ever being asked if I wanted it. Although I was then of the opinion, as I am today, that there was no national need for a White House Conference on Aging, I decided that if that conference were to take place, I would welcome the opportunity to help shape its agenda. I spent a good deal of time in Washington for the next 15 months, planning the organization of the conference and the range of issues to be dealt with; I was then summarily removed when the administration changed in 1981; then a few months later, I was reappointed by that new administration to a different but still visible role in the conference. I have never had any political visibility, so mine is an instance of an academic maintaining the role of an academic. But by now I had learned a good bit more about policymaking and politics. More important, I learned that an academic has something to learn from, but also something to offer to, the policymaking endeavor.

By now, too, I had become convinced that for students in the social sciences—whether in aging or any other related field—it is important that they understand the significance of policy decisions in influencing the course of lives. So, by my early sixties, it seemed natural enough that, building on my own experiences, I should want to organize a new type of doctoral program that would bridge the social sciences and policymaking in the study of lives. Thus I moved from Chicago to Northwestern in 1980, at the persuasion of a new dean there who had been my colleague at Chicago, and who has facilitated the creation of the new graduate program called Human Development and Social Policy—a program in which, not surprisingly, I have been concentrating on policies related to the aging society.

If, then, I entered the field of aging by accident, I have stayed in it by design. And I suppose it can be said that the changing age structure of the society has not only influenced, but has indirectly created the context and the content of my academic life.

THE ISSUE OF GENDER

Because I am a woman—and because we have not yet created a climate in which that fact is insignificant in considering the career of an academic—I should comment here on how changes in societal structures that relate to gender have affected my academic life. It may appear strange to the reader to be told first that my experience in this regard has been singularly atypical for a woman of my cohort—for I do not recall a single instance in which the fact that I was a woman worked to my disadvantage, or to my advantage, in my education or in my research career.

I had encouragement all the way: first from my parents, particularly my father, then from teachers. When I was in high school, the superintendent of schools called me into his office several times to explain that there was a man at the University of Chicago named Robert Maynard Hutchins who had exciting ideas about education and that it was therefore the place I must go. He made no mention of possible difficulties because I was female, nor did I hear any such mention made throughout my student years at Chicago.

In Human Development there were approximately equal numbers of men and women students each year; fellowships were awarded without attention to the sex of the applicant; and there were always women as well as men faculty. (In the program with which I am now associated at Northwestern, we have equal numbers of men and women faculty, but of thirty Ph.D. students, only four are men, a historical change in the sex ratio of graduate students that is appearing in many social science departments throughout the country.) It happens also that among the many students whose dissertation committees I have chaired over the years, there have been—without planning it that way— about equal numbers of men and women.

In another respect, also, Human Development at Chicago was unusual, for beginning in the late 1950s we saw fit, at my suggestion, to admit for the Ph.D. a number of middle-aged women who had been housewives for most of their lives—this at a time when such admissions were rare in top-rated universities. These women proved to be as successful as younger men or women in completing their degrees. In fact, they had one major advantage, for while some had trouble at first in making the transition into the student role, none of them suffered, as did young women students, over sex role conflict—they did not worry that to take a Ph.D. might diminish their femininity, either in their own or other people's minds.

I recall that when I was chairman of Human Development at Chicago in the early 1970s a form letter arrived from the women's caucus of the American Psychological Association, asking me to describe my efforts to hire a woman faculty member, and if those efforts had met with any success. I sent back information about the sex distribution of our faculty, and said that although the wording of their letter seemed to be an instance of the approach to data-gathering that can be characterized as "When did you stop beating your wife?" I was nevertheless strongly supportive of their goals, as I hoped our record in Human Development would show.

Although I was never aware of any obstacles put in my way because I was a woman, still I did not go untouched by the women's movement of the late 1960s and 1970s. The major instance of student protest on the Chicago campus in 1968-1969—and the sit-in that paralyzed much of the university for a few weeks—was triggered by the fact that a young woman faculty member who held a joint appointment in the Committee on Human Development and the Department of Sociology was not reappointed. The student leaders held that it was because she was a woman and because she held radical political views; and they did not waver when it was pointed out that both these facts, particularly the first, had been well known to all those involved in her original appointment.

The student protest was taken very seriously in all parts of the university. I spent much of my time for several months working with a small group of other faculty and students in altering the governance procedures in Human Development to give students a greater role. Probably because I happened to be the only woman in the Council of the University Senate at the time, I was appointed chairman of the first Committee on Women of the University of Chicago. That committee was created as an arm of the council and was given access to all confidential data regarding faculty appointments for both women and men over the years—data regarding recruitment efforts, salaries, promotions—a fact that made our group something of an exception during that period when women faculty groups were organizing on other campuses to protest inequitable treatment and were often dealt with by administrators as outsiders rather than insiders.

Our Committee on Women gathered a great deal of local and national data, and issued a long report that was widely circulated over the country (Committee on University Women, 1970). (This is not the occasion to discuss the findings of that report, but it may be of interest to mention here that the Department of Sociology was one of the departments at Chicago that had never had a tenured woman—a situation that changed, happily enough, as one of the outcomes of our Committee's efforts.)

I was also elected Chairman of the Committee on Human Development in that year—a role that senior faculty members were expected to take turns in filling, but that I had hoped to defer for several more years.

All this affected my scholarly productivity, for I was at the time completing work on three book-length manuscripts, one on the sociology of age, one on middle age, and one on patterns of aging. All this work was laid aside for what I regarded as compelling reasons; but the manuscripts grew cold; and they were never published (some of the research findings appeared later as journal articles). I took comfort some years afterward when a publisher told me that the student movement of the late 1960s had evidently had a similar effect on many other social scientists, for the number of manuscripts he and other publishers received for several years thereafter had been noticeably fewer than before.

It is fair to say, then, that in those years, as the university dealt with the issue of gender and the closely related issue of student empowerment, the changes—whether or not they were far-reaching enough to satisfy many of us—had their effects on my own academic career.

INTELLECTUAL DEVELOPMENT

We contributors to this volume were asked to comment on our intellectual development. I have chosen to do so indirectly, by describing some of my work and some of the interpretations I have placed on the findings.

My pattern of research has been to open up new topic areas rather than to follow a single line of inquiry; to use sometimes qualitative, sometimes quantitative methods; to prefer exploration to replication—in short, to map out some of the landscape of what had earlier been the neglected territory of the second half of life.

As already mentioned, my studies have been of two general types: the first relates to aging persons—to such topics as changes in personality and in age-sex roles, the diversity of patterns of aging, middle-aged parenting and grandparenting, adjustment to retirement, the changing meanings of age to the individual, and the internalized social clock that tells people if they are "on time" in following the social timetables.

The second category relates to the sociology of age from the societal perspective—to such topics as the changing age-status system, age norms as systems of social control, societal implications of the lengthened life span, the relations among age groups and the rise of the young-old age distinctions, as they are embodied in the law, and policy issues related to the aging society.

I have chosen illustrations from that work that I hope will be of most direct interest in the context of the present volume, and that I hope will serve also to indicate how my thinking about these particular topics has developed over time.

Early on, I began to study the life events that in the 1950s were touted, as they still are today, as the significant transitions of middle age. I found that the menopause was a psychological nonevent to most women; that the so-called emptying of the nest—that is, when children grow up and leave home—was not a loss event to mothers or fathers (unless it occurred later than anticipated and therefore signified delayed maturity in the child). We found also that most middle-aged and older people had never experienced—nor had they perceived in others—a mid-life crisis (Neugarten and Datan, 1974). (This, despite the journalists who seized on the term as a revealed truth and treated it as high drama.)

Drawing from my own studies but also from the work of others, I learned that retirement is welcomed by most men if they have adequate income (we knew little about formal retirement in women, for it was then a relatively rare occurrence); that health improves rather than deteriorates after retirement; that most older people have high levels of life satisfaction, and, of equal significance, that in the second half of life, the level of life satisfaction is not related to age. And so on. It became clear that the myths and the negative stereotypes about middle age and old age did not fit the realities. The large majority of older persons, although retired, are vigorous and competent people, active in their families and communities. I called them the "young-old," described them as a new historical phenomenon in postindustrial societies, and suggested that the young-old represent a major resource to the aging societies in which we live, but a resource thus far underutilized (Neugarten, 1974, 1975). The term "old-old" I reserved for that minority of frail older people who need special care and support. I pointed out that the distinction between young-old and old-old was of central importance in policymaking, for the desires and needs of the two groups are very different.

It became clear also, from the work my colleagues and I were doing, that there was no single pattern of social-psychological aging, nor a single pattern of optimal or so-called "successful" aging (Neugarten, Havighurst, and Tobin, 1968). The widely held view that the person who remains active and maintains the social role pattern of middle age is the successful ager—the so-called "activity theory"—and the contrasting view that aging is an inherent and universal process of mutual withdrawal between the individual and the society, and that the successful ager is the person who has disengaged—the so-called "disengagement theory" set forth by Cumming and Henry (1961), and so hotly debated by gerontologists in the 1960s and early 1970s—these are both reductionist theories that do not account for the diversity of patterns.

Not only do people grow old in very different ways, but the range of individual differences becomes greater with the passage of life time. Age therefore becomes a poor predictor of the adult's physical or social or intellectual competence, of the person's needs or capacities. In this sense, as compared to earlier periods in history, age has declined in significance in distinguishing among middle-aged and older people. (In different terms, age turns out to be a very weak variable in multivariable analyses.)

The corollary is that change over adulthood is not "ordered" change, as stage theorists would have it (Neugarten, 1979b), and further, that patterns of adulthood and aging are affected by, but not determined by, early experience. These ideas are not yet altogether popular among developmental psychologists, so some of the papers I have written on these topics have not always been happily received.

As another step in my thinking, I noted that, despite the fact that age is becoming less useful or less relevant in assessing adult competencies and needs, we have witnessed a proliferation of policy decisions and benefit programs in which target groups are defined on the basis of age, a trend particularly evident with regard to older people. At federal, state, and local levels of government, programs are created that provide persons with income, health services, social services, transportation, housing, and special tax benefits on the basis of their age. Much the same is true in the private sector, where civic, educational, and religious bodies create special programs for older people in health care, education, recreation, and other community services. (Thus what social scientists know is one thing; what policymakers do is quite another—not, in itself, a new discovery.)

I pondered this anomaly and in the past few years I have written several policy papers that have made me something of a controversial figure to the special interest groups in aging—in particular, to the so-called "age-advocacy organizations" that, in their efforts to influence government and governmental programs, claim to speak for older people as a group. I have suggested, for instance, that age-entitlement programs be reexamined from the perspective of need entitlement (Neugarten, 1979a, 1982)—a suggestion that is anathema to many persons who have labored long to improve the economic and social status of older people in this country, and who fear that those gains would be reversed if anything so radical were even to be contemplated. I persist, nevertheless, in believing that all of us, young and old, would be well ahead if policymakers would focus not on age, but on more relevant dimensions of human competencies and human needs.

To return to the theme of social science research: On the societal level, it is clear enough that age status and age-stratification systems are themselves dynamic; that age-group definitions, age distinctions, and age norms are constantly altered in concert with other types of social change (Neugarten, 1968; Neugarten & Peterson, 1957; Neugarten, Moore, & Lowe, 1965; Neugarten & Neugarten, 1986; Passuth, Maines, & Neugarten, 1984). And to return to the theme of this volume, both the study of lives and the study of social change must therefore be seen as the constant interweaving of life time, socially defined time, and historical time. It has long been understood that the course of human lives—and, therefore, patterns of aging—are different in different societies, in different subgroups, and at different points in history. Aging, then, is not an immutable process, either in the social or the biological patterning of lives, as the increase in average life expectancy itself has made so clear.

This common knowledge has not always been taken seriously by social science investigators. Some gerontologists searched at first for a common social pattern of aging or for "laws" of change that would be neither culture-bound nor history-bound. Today most would agree that all that can be said for certain on this topic is that people are born, grow up, and die, and that in postindustrial societies most people now grow old before they die. Although we do not yet know the limits of mutability—that is, how much change can be achieved—the new view is that a vast range of positive interventions can be made in patterns of aging. To have laid the basis for changing the climate of opinion in this way has surely been a major contribution of both the social and the biological scientists over the past forty years.

Looking back, I sometimes wonder why it was that many researchers were preoccupied with questions about social and psychological aging that now seem so naive. Perhaps it is only an instance of that for which we social scientists are often criticized—that we elaborate what is common sense. Yet, it often turns out that common sense is not so common; and that to document one version of common sense over another may itself be an important achievement.

A colleague once asked what my personal goal was in studying aging. I laughed and said "To return old people to the human race—to make it clear that they are not a special species, nor creatures from another planet." I think we social science researchers, as a group, have now accomplished that task. We have come to realize that the same general theories regarding the nature of human nature will serve us as well—or as poorly—for older people as for younger.

THE FUTURE

It is unlikely that in the future social scientists will make dramatic theoretical advances in the study of aging. Conceptual ones, yes, as in the conceptualizations of the age-stratification and age-norm systems, and in the perspective that the course of lives and the course of social change are mutually interactive, as the essays in this volume are illustrating. Some of us will develop new conceptual approaches, and others of us will carry out the descriptive and analytic studies that will continue to be important.

Still others of us I hope will take a new direction: To turn matters around, as it were, and to ask not only "How do societal changes influence the lives of older people?" but also "How does the presence of increasing numbers of older people affect the society at large?"

To elaborate on this point: In all parts of the world, societies are undergoing change that is perhaps as fundamental as any in human history, change that comes with the increase in life expectancy and the increasing proportions of older persons in the population. These demographic trends have been dramatic in industrialized countries in the last 80 years; and it is being projected—barring catastrophic famines or wars—that the numbers of older people will increase at as rapid a rate in the developing countries over the next twenty years as in developed countries over the past 80 years.

We have created an aging population, but we do not know much about its effects on our social institutions and social structures. We know, for instance, that the family has become a multigenerational structure, but we know little about patterns of social interaction or economic transfers in the four- or five-generation unit. What is the influence of the changing age distribution on our educational institutions? On systems of medical and social services? On the social structures of communities and the relations among age groups? On our political structures, laws, and legal institutions? On the responsibilities of government for the support of the young and the old? On the meanings of age as a dimension of social organization?

It is not altogether a secret that we students of society have sometimes missed out on some of the big social issues of our times. If, for example, more of us had studied race relations in the 1950s and 1960s, we might not have been so surprised by the form of the civil rights movement in the early 1960s and by the riots that occurred in some of our cities. Some readers may recall Everett Hughes's Presidential address to the American Sociological Association when he asked, "How did it happen that we missed the boat on race relations?" and when he suggested that perhaps it was our own professionalism that had blocked our view.

Another example is our failure, as psychologists and sociologists and anthropologists alike, to give sufficient attention to family patterns and motivations for parenthood, with the result that so many of us were caught by surprise by the baby boom, soon to become the senior boom. Are we now missing the boat on the aging society?

This is not, of course, the first time it has been suggested that we should attend to the social implications of the aging population. A decade ago a colleague and I coedited two publications that dealt with social policy, social ethics, and the aging society (Neugarten & Havighurst, 1976, 1977), but, as long ago as the 1950s, sociologists like Ernest Burgess were pointing to the need to study the impact of older people on the society. Thus far, few of us have heeded that advice.

Things may change. As a straw in the wind, the National Academy of Sciences recently created a short-lived, but nevertheless active Committee on the Aging Society, whose purpose was to stimulate research on this topic in the various parts of the Academy. And the book called *Our Aging Society: Paradox and Promise* (Pifer and Bronte, 1986), a collection of essays written by a varied group of academics, may help create an agenda for empirical research.

It is my hope, then, that social scientists will pursue the questions of how societies, not only populations, grow old, a set of issues that is highly significant for the society in which we live. The issues are significant also for the future of sociology, for their study might lead to new conceptualizations of the nature of social change and, to restate the theme of this volume, to new conceptualizations of the interplay between changing social structures and the course of human lives.

References

Committee on University Women. 1970. *Women in the University of Chicago*. Chicago: University of Chicago.

Coleman, R. P. and Neugarten, B. L. 1971. *Social Status in the City*. San Francisco: Jossey-Bass.

Cumming, E. and W. E. Henry. 1961. *Growing Old*. New York: Basic Books.

Featherman, D. L. 1983. "The Life Span Perspective in Social Science Research." In *Life-Span Development and Behavior*, Vol. 5, edited by P. B. Baltes and O. G. Brim, Jr. New York: Academic Press.

Gross, I. W., ed. 1956. *Potentialities of Women in the Middle Years*. East Lansing: Michigan State University Press.

Hagestad, G. O. and B. L. Neugarten. 1985. "Age and the Life Course." Pp. 35-61 in *Handbook of Aging and the Social Sciences*, edited by B. Binstock and E. Shanas. New York: Van Nostrand Reinhold.

Havighurst, R. J. and Neugarten, B. L. 1957. *Society and Education*. Boston: Allyn & Bacon (2nd ed., 1962; 3rd ed., 1967; 4th ed., 1975).

Neugarten, B. L. 1968. "The Changing Age Status System." Pp. 5-21 in *Middle Age and Aging: A Reader in Social Psychology*, edited by B. L. Neugarten. Chicago: University of Chicago Press.

——. 1969. "Continuities and Discontinuities of Psychological Issues into Adult Life." *Human Development* 12:121-130.

——. 1974. "Age Groups in American Society and the Rise of the Young-Old." *The Annals of the American Academy of Political and Social Sciences*, pp. 187-198.

——. 1975. "The Future and the Young-Old." *Gerontologist* 15(1, Pt. 2):4-9.

——. 1979a. "Policy for the 1980s: Age-Entitlement or Need-Entitlement?" Pp. 48-52 in *National Journal Issues Book, Aging: Agenda for the Eighties*. Washington, DC: Government Research Corporation.

——. 1979b. "Time, Age, and the Life Cycle." *American Journal of Psychiatry* 136(7):887-894.

——, ed. 1982. *Age or Need? Public Policies for Older People*. Beverly Hills, CA: Sage.

——. and N. Datan. 1974. "The Middle Years." Pp. 592-608 in *American Handbook of Psychiatry*, Vol. 1. *The Foundations of Psychiatry*, edited by S. Arieti. New York: Basic Books.

Neugarten, B. L. and G. O. Hagestad. 1976. "Age and the Life Course." Pp. 626-649 in *Handbook of Aging and the Social Sciences*, edited by B. B. Binstock and E. Shanas. New York: Van Nostrand Reinhold.

Neugarten, B. L. and R. J. Havighurst. 1976. *Social Policy, Social Ethics, and the Aging Society* (Report prepared for the National Science Foundation). Washington, DC: Government Printing Office. (Stock #038-000-00299-6; 121 pages)

——. 1977. *Extending the Human Life Span: Social Policy and Social Ethics* (Report prepared for the National Science Foundation). Washington, DC: Government Printing Office. (Stock #038-000-00337-2; 70 pages)

—— and S. S. Tobin. 1968. "Personality and Patterns of Aging." Pp. 173-177 in *Middle Age and Aging: A Reader in Social Psychology*, edited by B. L. Neugarten. Chicago: University of Chicago Press.

Neugarten, B. L., J. W. Moore, and J. G. Lowe. 1965. "Age Norms, Age Constraints, and Adult Socialization." *American Journal of Sociology* 70:710-717. (Reprinted in Neugarten, *Middle Age and Aging*, 1968)

Neugarten, B. L. and D. A. Neugarten. 1986. "The Changing Meanings of Age in the Aging Society." Pp. 33-51 in *Our Aging Society: Paradox and Promise*, edited by A. Pifer and L. Bronte. New York: Norton.

Neugarten, B. L. and W. A. Peterson. 1957. "A Study of the American Age-Grade System." Pp. 497-502 in *Proceedings of the Fourth Congress of the International Association of Gerontology*, Merano, Bolzano, Italy, July 14-19. Vol. 3. *Sociological Division*. Firenze: Mattioli.

Passuth, P. M., D. R. Maines, and B. L. Neugarten. 1984. "Age Norms and Age Constraints Twenty Years Later." Paper presented at the Midwest Sociological Society Meeting, Chicago.

Pifer, A. and L. Bronte, eds. 1986. *Our Aging Society: Paradox and Promise*. New York: Norton.

Riley, M. W., M. E. Johnson, and A. Foner, eds. 1972. *Aging and Society*, Vol. 3. *A Sociology of Age Stratification*. New York: Russell Sage.

8

Socialization to Sociology by Culture Shock

Hubert M. Blalock

OUR BEHAVIORS, AND THOUGHTS, are a joint function of situational factors and our own interpretive processes—a truism of social science if there ever was one! I am a male WASP, raised in an upper-middle-class, heavily Republican, suburb of Hartford, Connecticut, a Mayflower descendent, and graduate of a New England preparatory school and two Ivy League colleges. There was absolutely no question in my mind, and also that of my parents, that I wanted to become a scientist. In junior high school it was chemistry, and in high school physics and math. My weakest subjects were English and social studies, and the most boring by far was history. But because I knew exactly what I was going to do, all that was necessary was to wait it out until I could leave these "lesser subjects" behind me.

As Matilda Riley continually stresses, certain of our experiences are peculiar to the cohorts into which we are born, though, of course, we interpret these experiences in diverse ways. In my case, the first major shock occurred when I was drafted, at age 18, into the Navy in December 1944, after completing a semester at Dartmouth. I was a total misfit in the Navy, from the very first day when our Chief Petty Officer delivered a speech ending with the sentence, "Remember, youse guys, in the Navy you don't think!" I believe I also gained insights into what it must feel like to be a member of a minority group—trapped in a system one detested, having to take orders requiring one to do senseless tasks, and having to salute and defer to officers.

But there were other events that made me comprehend just how sheltered my previous life had been. Shortly after the surrender of Germany, we were shown films of the unbelievable horrors of Dachau and other extermination camps and, for the first time, I began to realize that what I had taken to be highly misleading anti-German propaganda during the war was, in fact, an understatement of what had actually taken place. Then there were the bombings of Hiroshima and Nagasaki. I decided I wanted to get out of the Navy as quickly as possible, and so I quit radar training school and was assigned to ship duty in the Pacific. I was assigned to an LST (landing ship, tank) operating in Shanghai and other Chinese coastal cities.

My first genuine culture shock then occurred as a result of my exposure to a highly anomic situation in the Nationalist China of 1945-1946, where I saw my fellow American sailors behaving at their very worst. The carefully cultivated image of the American GI as caring deeply for the victims of war, poverty, and disease was very much at odds with what I actually experienced. For the first time I came into close contact with shipmates who actually admired Al Capone and who delighted in their nightly fisticuffs (and worse) with the so-called "Gooks." This seamy side of American ethnocentrism was explained away, in my own thoughts, by blaming it all on the tensions of war—no matter that these Chinese had actually been the victims of a prolonged war and had been our allies and not our enemies.

I returned to Dartmouth after my release from the Navy, still determined to major in either physics or mathematics, probably the former. My previous experiences and concerns about the uses to which the sciences were being put began working on me, if only very slowly. One of the major factors influencing my switch from physics into pure mathematics was the atomic bomb and my negative reactions to the science-for-science-sake arguments being advanced, within physics, as a justification for scientists' participation in the development of such a destructive weapon. These arguments took several forms. One was to claim that the products of science are neutral and can be used either for good or evil, but that this is not for scientists to decide. A second justification took the form of arguing that we have to work on the bomb in order to beat the Germans to it. Neither type of rationalization seemed very convincing, at the time, and I decided that I did not want to contribute to the process. Because I was fascinated by theoretical issues in physics and philosophy, however, my retreat from science took the form of deciding to major in mathematics, while only minoring in physics.

Several other experiences contributed to a gradual awareness that there were other things than science to be concerned about. A more intellectual experience, but one that reinforced the "real life" Navy experience, involved a "Great Issues" course required of all seniors at Dartmouth, a course that exposed us to a wide variety of social problem issues. A third experience, immediately after graduation, involved my participation in an interracial Quaker summer work camp in a black area of a midwestern city. I had always had a concern about the treatment of blacks in America—perhaps a Myrdallian white guilt complex—but had had absolutely no prior contact with blacks, except with the proverbial domestic servants who, by day only, populated our middle-class suburb of Hartford.

BECOMING A SOCIOLOGIST

I entered graduate school, at Brown, in mathematics and discovered the meaning of "pure" mathematics, as well as the impact of absolutely horrible teaching. At about that time I began to realize that I did not want to spend my lifetime being quite so pure, and that there was something of an escape from reality in all of this. So I selected sociology, almost sight unseen. Actually, I had had two courses in sociology at Dartmouth, but no other work in social science other than a single course in European history.

I again experienced culture shock on entering sociology, almost as great a one as my traumatic encounters with the Navy and Chinese-American interaction patterns. In retrospect, I can now see that coming into sociology, cold, from two disciplines that have precise terminology, tight reasoning, and well-formulated questions created a number of tensions and frustrations that I continue to experience. My first reaction was that I must be terribly dumb. Students around me *appeared* to understand Parsons's *The Social System (1951)* and were able to use all the big words that I could barely pronounce. They also spoke learnedly of the great European theorists, whose arguments seemed to me almost as opaque as those of a few of the faculty who taught us the required theory courses.

Then I found George Homans's *The Human Group (1950)* and Robin Williams's *The Reduction of Intergroup Tensions (1947)*, both of which had the advantage of being written in plain, simple English! Homans's work also had the appeal, to me, of starting with a few general concepts and building theory by means of explicit propositions linking them. Williams's work not only was in my own field of interest, race relations, but involved a serious effort to collect and interrelate some 100 general propositions. Another pair of chapters that we all read also made a whole lot of sense to me. These were Robert Merton's (1949) classic papers on the bearing of research on theory, and of theory on research, including his appeal for theories of the middle range.

Although I did not find out until several years later that most of my fellow students also did not really understand Parsons or most of the "big words" we were encouraged to use, I gradually felt more at ease with sociology. Having relaxed a bit, I began to take a closer look at what seemed to be going on, what the differences were between physics and sociology, why there was such a gap between, on the one hand, statistics and methods courses, and, on the other, what was called "sociological theory," and why it was so difficult to move from diffuse bodies of literature, as, for example, that in race relations, to more systematic approaches.

These are basically the same concerns that I have today. I suspect that I would not have experienced them anywhere nearly as intensively, and traumatically, had I not made the sudden change of fields and had I known more about the social sciences before I made that critical decision. The phenomenon of culture shock is not only real, but it carries over to disciplinary cultures as well. I think I understand the notion of "Marginal Man," having experienced a special kind of marginality during those formative years.

GAPS, AMBIGUITIES, AND DISPUTES

When I entered sociology I was puzzled, and still am, by a number of rather intense disputes, one of which seemed to imply that there are two distinct entities, theory and research, which are somehow or another linked to qualitative versus quantitative approaches. Theory was taken to be non-quantitative and entirely verbal; research could be either qualitative or quantitative. Statistics courses and discussions of survey research and experimental designs dealt with the quantitative side and were never connected, at least in my mind, with the thing sociologists called "theory."

With the exception of Paul Lazarsfeld and perhaps a handful of others, the notion of mathematical modeling as a form of theorizing was entirely foreign. Indeed, the role of mathematics and of conceptual models (e.g., of the atom) in a science such as physics was largely unappreciated, except possibly through discussions of Weber's notion of the "ideal type." The fact that all theoretical arguments necessarily rest on assumptions was understood, I think, but the importance of making explicitly stated assumptions, in the form of axioms, was largely ignored.

Statistics was taken as something one used in data analysis, but the role of statistical models, as theories, was not really stressed. Data analyses were relatively simple and certainly not capable of handling large numbers of complexities, except by boiling them down, as, for example, through the use of factor analysis. For the most part, multivariate analysis meant cross-tabulations involving no more than one or two simultaneous controls. If more than two variables entered the picture, the most common approach involved the dichotomization of continuous variables into high and low, present or absent, or "yes" and "no" responses.

The few attempts to use mathematical modeling in sociology seemed far too simplistic to me and, of course, to most others. I recall, for example, the results of a disaster model implying that a community should have all fire engines and no telephones, and another modeling effort (by a biological scientist, however) that attempted to link the "average rationality" of a society with the ratio of the length of its boundary to its area (Greece having a very jagged coastline). I reacted very negatively to these and other modeling attempts believing, as I still do, that it will be necessary to handle a very large number of complexities in any such models. It was not until I began to appreciate the flexibility of structural-equation modeling that I had any hopes that such modeling efforts might really be of value.

Things were not quite this extreme, of course, but what seemed to me to be mere caricatures of "opposing" theoretical positions often made them seem this way to students. The tendency to think in terms of something *versus* something else (e.g., theory versus research, case studies versus statistical ones) also tended to sharpen the disputes and, perhaps, helped rival "schools" put down their opponents. All of this seemed very strange to me, although perhaps this is because controversies that took place in physics a century or more ago are now treated in a more matter-of-fact way in undergraduate texts. Anyway, what seemed to me to be needless and poorly defined disputes bothered me considerably, and I'm rather glad that they did so, because they have tended to occupy my attention in much of my later work.

The gap between the "big words" of theorists and the measures or indicators that actually were used in empirical research also disturbed me, and I first turned for answers to the philosophy of science literature on operationalism. I was especially influenced by F.S.C. Northrop's *The Logic of the Sciences and the Humanities* (1947), in which he stressed that there are basically two kinds of concepts, "concepts by postulation" that are theoretically defined and "concepts by intuition" that are used in our actual research operations. There are, in Northrop's view, two distinct "languages" that are related by means of what he termed "epistemic correlations" between the two kinds of concepts. Such epistemic correlations, however, can never be estimated empirically.

Gradually, I began to realize that Northrop's formulation had features in common with a number of rather confusing discussions of various types of "validity" and with current treatments of concepts and their "indicators," as well as the factor analysis literature that was fashionable at that time. It was only somewhat later, when I began reading about structural-equation or causal modeling in the econometrics literature, that I realized that such factor-analysis models were actually special cases of causal models and that measured and unmeasured variables—or Northrop's concepts by intuition and postulation—could be linked by making causal assumptions about their relationships. Such assumptions, like Northrop's epistemic correlations, could not be directly tested, but they could be used to make specific testable predictions about relationships among indicator or measured variables. Factor analysis types of causal models became merely special cases of what I referred to as "auxiliary measurement theories" that, together with one's substantive theories, are always necessary in the scientific enterprise. What I also began to recognize, through the agony of this effort to straighten out my own thinking, is that it takes considerable time to put ideas together, even though after-the-fact linkages seem "obvious."

In retrospect, I believe that the philosophy of science literature coming out of the discipline of philosophy itself has not been as useful to me as work produced by persons from other substantive disciplines who have had basically philosophical interests on the side. I have in mind persons such as Arthur Eddington (an astrophysicist), Herbert Simon, Sewall Wright (a geneticist), Herman Wold (a statistician), Mario Bunge (a physicist), and our own Paul Lazarsfeld. Perhaps there is a lesson in all this. There seems to be a breed of scholar who is intrigued with very general philosophical questions that crosscut disciplines, and who attempts to locate disciplinary problems or issues in a larger context. I believe that it has ultimately been this type of scholar who has had the greatest impact upon my own thinking.

At the time I entered sociology, the great debate over operationalism had somewhat subsided. Lundberg (*Foundations of Sociology*, 1939), on one hand, had very much overstated and oversimplified the case for the importance of measurement, so much so that I became angered and rejected his arguments as too one-sided and extreme. But they remained to plague me, especially whenever I encountered the "big words" or a series of confusing disputes that seemed to involve, primarily, a failure to make clear conceptual distinctions. In my own field, a case in point was the fruitless debate over whether or not the situation of American blacks involved a "true" caste system. Because I was also interested in social power, I quickly became confused by the many, somewhat overlapping discussions of the power concept. Even a concept supposed to be simple, such as "discrimination," gave me troubles, which—as a naive graduate student—I thought I could rather quickly resolve. I am still at it!

The very extensive literature in race relations, and especially that at the macro or societal level, seemed entirely too diffuse to turn into the propositional format so well illustrated by the work of Robin Williams. Indeed, on examination, I discovered that most of his propositions were at the social-psychological level, or perhaps what we would now refer to as the contextual-effects level. One could locate descriptive statements with general implications in the macro literature, though these often had to be reformulated so that they would apply beyond the immediate situation being described. The numbers of distinct concepts or variables appearing in these propositions made it next to impossible to interrelate them, however. One proposition would relate variables X and Y, a second W and Z, and a third U and V. Thus I encountered so many "holes" in the literature that it seemed almost impossible to fill them. Equally disturbing, however, was the tendency for authors to use completely different terminology, so that I could not "add up" the literature in any intellectually satisfying way.

These problems are obviously still with us, but I cannot tell how bothersome they are to others whose exposure to sociology has been much more gradual. I sense that we often take them so much for granted that, before long, they cease to bother us. Whenever I become reasonably satisfied with some portion of our theoretical literature, say within a small segment of race relations, I wonder whether this is merely because my own standards have shifted and my tolerance for ambiguity has become raised. I would like to hope, of course, that we have made genuine progress, but others will have to judge whether or not this is actually the case.

LEARNING ABOUT THE
REWARD SYSTEM

One more shock, or at least surprise, needs to be mentioned, although it is unfortunately not one that is confined to my own cohort or even to sociology. This concerns the lack of tangible rewards for teaching. When I was hired at the University of Michigan, I was asked to take charge of both graduate and undergraduate statistics courses and the undergraduate methods course, and to teach introductory sociology both semesters. In addition, I was given the responsibility for counseling our undergraduate majors. Needless to say, if one takes these responsibilities at all seriously—as I did—there is not a whole lot of time left for research. Nevertheless, I moved along with a research program that I thought to be adequate enough, given my commitment to teaching, to justify my being awarded tenure. About three years along, I began to perceive a need for a statistics text, but it was not until I had actually completed *Social Statistics* (1960) that I learned from one of my junior colleagues that, in the opinion of a key senior colleague, "as a textbook, that won't help much!" I wish I had been told earlier, but in those days we received very little guidance on such matters.

Fortunately, I received a tenure offer from Yale a year before my up-or-out decision had to be made, and so I took the matter to our Chair, who in turn took it to our senior faculty. I was genuinely shocked, and hurt, to learn that my colleagues voted not to keep me on because I had not published enough. At that time I made a private commitment to myself that, if I ever should "make it" via the publication route, I would do what I could to convince others that teaching should be rewarded. I am indeed pleased to see progress within the American Sociological Association in this regard and have started making noises at my own university. But the problem remains with us, especially at our major research universities. It affects even male WASPs, perhaps more so than women or minorities, if only because we cannot claim or rationalize that there has been discrimination against *us*. I continue to regard the academic "system" as being highly defective in this regard but do not believe it will change unless enough of us howl loudly about it. I hear very few such howls, however, especially among the elites of our profession.

SOME PRESENT CONCERNS

My greatest current concern about sociology involves what I perceive to be an increased fractionating of the discipline that has resulted from a tendency to deal with far more social phenomena than we are capable of studying with the intensity and depth required to understand them. We seem to invent new subfields at the drop of a hat, whenever a new dependent variable arises on the horizon. One result is that we have a "Sociology of X" for just about every imaginable X. If we had sufficiently strong theories capable of subsuming these Xs under previously studied ones, this would be fine. But we have a tendency to lose interest in the old Xs after we have applied the standard set of variables to them and have discovered that the proportion of explained variance is not especially high. We are, of course, engaged in turf wars with other social science disciplines for the right to study each of these Xs, and in most instances they do no better than we.

One result of all this is that outsiders continue to characterize our efforts as superficial, naive, biased, or perhaps all three. Another unfortunate outcome is that only a very tiny fraction of us are interested in any given piece of research. In departmental meetings, I hear far too many colleagues in effect arguing that almost everyone else's work is boring and not at all relevant to their own research interests.

I believe that the only way to overcome this problem is to make much more substantial efforts to raise the level of abstraction, every time we plan a research project or report on our empirical research. We need to ask ourselves, continually, "What is the importance of my own research to someone who is not doing any work in this immediate field?" I do not believe a very encouraging answer to such a question can be given unless and until problems are formulated in such a way that they have relevance at least to theories of the middle range, in Merton's sense. I fear that we are moving farther and farther away from a normative system that demands that researchers make such efforts. This applies equally to quantitative and qualitative or case-study research.

Second, I do not see anywhere near as many careful conceptualization efforts as I believe are necessary, given the current confusion and proliferation of sociological concepts. Perhaps this is a cohort effect, or one of pure and simple aging, but it seems to me that the quality of conceptualization attempts was higher in the 1940s and 1950s than it is today. I am constantly surprised, for example, when I ask students in fields with which I have grown unfamiliar to cite serious efforts to conceptualize the important variables in their field. They very often cite literature I was reading when I was a graduate student or that was written by some of my colleagues back in the 1950s.

Along with this inadequate conceptualization goes a lack of attention to measurement comparability, which is, of course, related to the above-noted proliferation of subfields and our tendency to move along to the next interesting problem before we have really sunk our teeth into the older ones. There are all sorts of statistical and mathematical approaches to *measurement*, but I believe our conceptualization efforts lag far behind. And this, of course, means that persons from other disciplines cannot help us to anywhere near the same extent that has occurred in connection with statistical data analysis techniques. In this instance, it is our theoretical side that is not keeping up. My prediction is that, unless greater attention is paid to conceptualization issues, sophisticated data analyses will fail to have the intellectual payoffs that many of us would like to see. In the quantitative arena, it is these measurement-conceptualization issues that constitute a critical roadblock. Perhaps related to this is my perception that our data *collection* procedures, today, seem hardly superior to those practiced in the 1950s. It is in our data *analyses* that we have made the most rapid progress.

Third, as I have become increasingly aware of simultaneous methodological complications that arise from the complexities of the real world with which we are dealing, from imperfections in measurements, and from the tricky kinds of causal relationships that seem to exist among the variables we wish to study, I have become convinced that our research efforts need to be far more ambitious and carefully coordinated. Longitudinal research will become increasingly needed, with observations closely enough spaced to enable us to get a better grasp of temporal sequences and lag periods. Yet we are both underfinanced and too poorly organized to undertake such ambitious research, and this will be all the more true if we continue to spread ourselves too thin. It is time that we moved beyond small-scale, exploratory research in many fields—though it may well be these same data hang-ups that are partly responsible for our tendency to move too quickly to unexplored terrain once we have explained 5% to 10% of the variance with our limited lists of sociological "background" variables. Perhaps we have little control over our sources of funding, but I do believe we could examine more carefully the ways in which we are organized to do research.

Related to all of the above is my final concern. Because most of us entered sociology with the hope that we could, at some point, contribute something of value to a policy area in which we were interested, it is indeed frustrating to have to say that "almost nothing works" or that we are not yet ready to make policy-relevant suggestions. There is then the temptation to make too much of weak relationships and to make a series of highly oversimplified policy recommendations that later may backfire on us.

A dilemma that we continually face is that if we do, indeed, introduce all of the proper notes of caution and indicate that most of the variance is yet to be explained, there will be others who are not so timid. We are certainly in competition with economists, who do not hesitate to get into the policy arena—often with disastrous results. And, if we are to "sell" our proposals, it seems as though exaggerating and overpromising are part of the game.

Physicists have only belatedly discovered that they have been "used" in the arms race and that politicians seldom take their advice. Regardless of how many Nobel laureates or National Academy of Sciences members sign petitions objecting to "Star Wars" research, they have let the nuclear genie out of the bottle. We sociologists need to have similar concerns. If we make a double-barreled suggestion of the form "Do away with program X (and thereby save money) and substitute for it program Y (which will also be costly)," we run the risk that the first part of our proposal will be implemented but not the second. Because a few proponents of almost any position can be found among social scientists, power wielders can always pick and choose among policy recommendations so as to bolster their own positions. And we can easily be misquoted or misrepresented. To assume that, when this occurs, we are merely "unfortunate" is naive.

In defending their participation in the development of the atomic bomb, physicists pointed out that science *can* be used for peaceful or warlike purposes but they did not adequately address questions relating to its *probable* uses. We must be careful not to make the same mistakes. Our genies may be more benign than their nuclear counterparts, and we undoubtedly have multiple genies in each bottle. The trick is to release them in a controlled way, rather than to create genies that drift in the direction of those who, from our perspective, will misuse them. Merely making policy recommendations, then, is not enough.

We are also faced with the problem of remaining intellectually honest about our meager findings and imperfect research, while still having an impact on policy issues that are in immediate need of "answers." We must keep in mind, however, that bad answers can come even from sociologists, and our policy recommendations can be based more on personal or disciplinary biases than on sound research. This is all very frustrating, and I do not pretend to see an easy resolution or any emerging consensus.

References

Blalock, Hubert M. 1960. *Social Statistics*. New York: McGraw-Hill.

Homans, George, C. 1950. *The Human Group*. New York: Harcourt, Brace.

Lundberg, George A. 1939. *Foundations of Sociology*. New York: Macmillan.

Merton, Robert K. 1949. *Social Theory and Social Structure*. Glencoe, IL: Free Press.

Northrop, F.S.C. 1947. *The Logic of the Sciences and the Humanities*. New York: Macmillan.

Parsons, Talcott. 1951. *The Social System*. Glencoe, IL: Free Press.

Williams, Robin M., Jr. 1947. *The Reduction of Intergroup Tensions*. New York: Social Science Research Council.

9

The Changing Institutional
Structure of Sociology
and My Career

William H. Sewell

BECAUSE MY CAREER in sociology spans more than half a century and because definitions of social structure are notoriously vague, I shall limit my discussion to the ways in which the changing institutional structure of American social science in general and sociology in particular have influenced and possibly been influenced by my career. My life as a sociologist has witnessed a great transition from the 1930s to the present in the general orientation of sociology; the training of sociologists; the scale, scope and methods of sociological research; the funding of the sociological enterprise; and the place of sociology and the social sciences in the university and in national affairs. I believe that my career illustrates the impact of these changes and also suggests that they have come about, at least in part, because of the efforts of well-placed and energetic actors. My career illustrates how my

AUTHOR'S NOTE: *I thank William H. Sewell, Jr., for his encouragement and comments on earlier drafts of this essay. I am indebted also to my Wisconsin colleagues Robert M. Hauser, Leon O. Epstein, Fred Harvey Harrington, Warren O. Hagstrom, and Burton R. Fisher for their suggestions and comments, to John Clausen for information on the development of social science in NIMH, and to Matilda and John Riley for editorial suggestions.*

research and intellectual development have been strongly influenced by the changes that I and others were struggling to bring about in our own universities and at the national level. This, of course, could have been equally well illustrated by the careers of other active members of my cohort in sociology.

LIFE BEFORE WISCONSIN

Before discussing my career in sociology, most of which took place at the University of Wisconsin, I should first mention my social origins, thus locating myself in the stratification structure, and I should say something about my educational preparation. I grew up in a middle-class family in a small Michigan community, where my father was the local pharmacist. I was born in 1909, the second of four children and the first son. I worked in my father's drugstore from a very early age until I went away to college. My father taught me responsibility and held me to high standards of performance but praised me for my accomplishments; thus anticipating by forty years David McClelland's prescription for creating high need for achievement. When my sisters and I were ready for high school, our family moved to Jackson, Michigan, a city of 60,000 with excellent schools. There we purchased an established pharmacy that remained in our family for another fifty years. After graduation from high school, I attended Michigan State College (now Michigan State University), graduating in 1933 with a major in sociology and full qualifications for medical school. By the time I finished undergraduate work, I began having doubts about wanting to become a physician so I decided to go to graduate school for a year while I made up my mind. I completed my master's degree in Sociology in 1934, doing an ecological study of delinquency in my home community for a thesis. In the course of this research, I became interested in the quantitative study of social behavior and decided to study at either Chicago or Minnesota for a Ph.D. in Sociology. I was especially interested in the work of Ogburn and Burgess at Chicago and in Chapin's research at Minnesota. I was offered a Teaching Assistantship by Chapin that was adequate to cover my expenses, whereas Chicago responded to my inquiry by saying they would be glad to admit me but they had a policy of giving awards only after a year of study there. I decided to go to Minnesota.

Graduate Study at Minnesota

I arrived in Minneapolis in the fall of 1934 and took up residence in a new dormitory that was reserved for Graduate Assistants. This proved to be most fortunate for my intellectual development because it put me into close contact with an unusually able group of graduate students in the social, biological, and physical sciences. My closest friends were historians, political scientists, economists, and psychologists, most of whom later became well-known scholars. Our informal discussions greatly enlarged my knowledge of these fields and made me aware of the common problems the social sciences share in methods and theory.

I found nothing nearly that exciting about graduate teaching in sociology. The graduate courses were taught exclusively by the tenured faculty, which included F. Stuart Chapin, Wilson W. Wallace in social and cultural change, George Vold, in criminology, Clifford Kirkpatrick, in social psychology and the sociology of the family, and Robert W. Murchie, in rural sociology. Reed Bain, who taught a seminar in social theory, was a Visiting Professor during my first year. Calvin F. Schmid, Joseph Schneider, and Elio Monachesi were Assistant Professors. The number of full-time graduate students, all of whom were Teaching Assistants or part-time Instructors, varied between eight and twelve at any one time. Also, there was an equal number of part-time graduate students, most of whom worked in government agencies. The graduate courses were adequately taught but were not particularly challenging. Only one seminar was taught regularly, Chapin's Sociological Theory and Method. No advanced courses in statistics or measurement were taught in the department. To fill this void, I audited courses in statistics in other departments and, for the most part, read up on statistics on my own. Actually, much of my graduate education came from reading and discussion with faculty members and fellow graduate students. Among the faculty, I found Kirkpatrick to be very stimulating and spent many hours discussing my readings with him. Also, I learned much more than I realized at the time from Chapin, both in his seminar and from the contacts I had with him as my major professor. Although not a well-trained statistician or quantitative methodologist, he had good ideas and was committed to the development of quantitative sociology. As evidence of this, one need only examine his pioneering quantitative studies of social change, his work on the measurement of social status, his sociometric studies, and his ex-post-facto experimental research on the effects of welfare programs on the behavior of clients.

In reality, there was no discernible formal structure to the graduate program at Minnesota at that time. There were no required courses. Students more or less took what they pleased but were advised to take at least one course from each senior professor and to prepare for and take the preliminary examination toward the end of the required three years of residency. The examination was oral and covered whatever the graduate faculty in sociology and representatives of the minor department wished to ask. Much depended on one's general training and ability to perform in what the students defined as a very threatening confrontation with the faculty. Failure was not uncommon.

I was the only student taking the examination that year (1937), so I prepared on my own, reading widely and taking careful notes. I had no trouble with the examination. In fact, I thoroughly enjoyed the experience.

Unlike the present situation in most graduate departments, there were no large research projects on which a graduate student could find employment and probably develop a Ph.D. dissertation. Consequently, it was expected that one would take a position in a college or university and do a dissertation on the job. In my own case, I was offered and accepted an Assistant Professorship at Oklahoma Agricultural and Mechanical College (now Oklahoma State University) by Otis Durant Duncan, whom I had met at Minnesota during my second year there, when he was taking further graduate work. The appointment included half-time research in the Agricultural Experiment Station and half-time teaching in the Sociology Department at a salary of $2800 per year. The only other alternative I had was an Instructorship at a prominent midwestern university with a salary of $1800 and a 12-hour teaching load made up of introductory courses.

In retrospect, Minnesota turned out to be a good place for me, although I found much fault with the department at the time. Its unstructured graduate program encouraged the further development of my sense of independence and permitted me to follow a program that fit my interests and to seek intellectual stimulation from teachers and students in other disciplines. I was made an Instructor during my second year and taught introductory courses independently in general sociology, social psychology, and rural sociology. While there, I developed substantive interests in social psychology and social stratification that have remained my principal concerns over the years. Moreover, I left Minnesota with a firm commitment to the development of a scientific sociology, characterized by a positivist, pragmatic, and quantitative orientation.

The Oklahoma Experience

The structure of the department at Oklahoma A&M was very favorable to my professional development. Duncan had also brought other young men, who were bright and able, into the department. We were given the courses we wanted to teach and were encouraged to develop our own research interests. Soon after I arrived, a colleague, Robert McMillan, and I developed a project proposal on the social correlates of farm tenure status, which was given financial support by the Agricultural Experiment Station. Within a few weeks, we had drafted and pretested an interview schedule. Soon after that we were in the field with a team of interviewers we had trained, and we began interviewing a sample of 800 farmers and their wives. That survey was, to my knowledge, the first rural study to use a sampling design—crude though it was by modern standards. While my colleague was in the field supervising the interviewing, I was already teaching my two first-semester courses, one of which was on research methods in sociology. We had agreed that he would analyze the information on migration and land tenure, and I would be free to analyze the data on the levels of living of farm families. I wanted this division of labor because I was interested in developing a way to measure the socioeconomic status of farm families that would not depend on a detailed analysis of family budgets and consumption.

I had been interested in Chapin's early attempts to devise a "living-room scale" based on the possessions of urban families (Chapin, 1933). The rationale for the Chapin scale was anchored in the differing life-styles of urban families of varying socioeconomic status. Its methodological foundation was suspect, however, because the items were arbitrarily selected, despite the fact that some rather good scaling techniques were available in the existing literature in psychology and educational psychology. I knew about this work from my reading and from my discussions with psychology graduate students and, particularly, with Louis Guttman, whom I had in one of my classes and had helped to recruit into sociology. I was quite certain a scale for the measurement of farm family socioeconomic status could be constructed using appropriate techniques for item selection and weighting and for establishing validity and reliability. With the help of my wife, we coded the 123 items we had included in the interview schedule as indicators of socioeconomic status and punched them on IBM cards. By use of a counting sorter, the state-of-the-art machine technology in the pre-computer days of 1937, we began the long and tedious hours of sorting and item analysis that reduced the scale to the 36 items that best differentiated the socioeconomic status of the farm families in our sample. Using another sample of families, we computed reliability and validity coefficients for the scale. All of this plus some rather elementary factor analysis was done on the counting sorter and required many days to complete—an operation that could be done now in minutes using a modern computer. A dissertation based on this work was accepted for my Ph.D. degree, which was awarded in 1939.

The dissertation was published in a somewhat revised version by the Oklahoma Agricultural Experiment Station in 1940 (Sewell, 1940b). By then, I had given papers on it at several conferences and had published an article briefly describing the scale (Sewell, 1940a). The technical bulletin on the scale was widely distributed and much of my time in the next few years was spent on restandardizing the scale for use in other areas, further reducing its length, and working on various problems related to the measurement of socioeconomic status. All of this work found ready publication. The scale was widely used and I was invited to give seminars and lectures on it at several universities. Probably as a result of this activity, I received several offers from other universities, including the University of Minnesota, all of which were matched or bettered locally. Meanwhile, I had other research under way on demographic and social psychological topics that was published in leading sociological journals during my stay in Oklahoma. In other words, my career was in full swing by the coming of World War II.

The War Years

Like many others faced with the possibility of being drafted and with the feeling that I should do my part, I sought and was given a commission in the U.S. Navy Reserves. I was assigned to duty as a Lieutenant (Junior Grade) in Washington, D.C., in the Research and Statistics Division of the National Headquarters of the Selective Service System as a Navy liaison officer. My experiences in Washington taught me about life in a bureaucratic agency and I resolved never to return to this life after the war, a resolution that I kept despite several tempting offers. On the positive side, I learned something about problems of manpower estimation, allocation, mass data processing, and the need for making quick but adequate statistical estimates.

Throughout my stay in Washington, I worried about the interruption of my academic career. I had no idea when the war would end and feared that it might be years before I could get back to academic life. But two important events that would affect my career happened during that period. First, I accepted an open-ended offer from the University of Wisconsin to join its faculty on my release from military service; and second, I was asked to join a team of social psychologists who were preparing to make a survey of the effects of strategic bombing on the morale of Japanese civilians, once the war was over.

At the end of the war in Europe, but before the surrender of Japan, I was reassigned to the Survey in Japan. Within a few days after the surrender, I was on my way to Tokyo with Raymond V. Bowers to help in further development of the plans for the survey. We were met there by Morris Hansen and Harold Nisselson, our sampling experts, who were finishing the design of the national sample, using techniques they had developed for the U.S. Census. Soon to join us were several other outstanding younger social scientists, some from the various branches of the armed forces and others from universities and government agencies. Among them were David Truman, the political scientist; social psychologists Horace English, Donald Adams, Egerton Ballachey, and Burton Fisher; psychiatrist Alexander Leighton, and anthropologists Conrad Arensberg, Fred Hulse, Jules Henry, and David Aberle. Working in interdisciplinary teams, we completed and pretested a survey instrument and trained our Japanese American interviewers in nondirective interviewing techniques in about a month. Each of us took a team of interviewers into selected sample areas, and we completed interviewing of the 2000 members of the national sample in about two months. On New Year's Day, I returned with the interviews to Washington. Herbert H. Hyman, who had worked on the German survey, and I then went to Swarthmore College, where we developed the code for the interviews and trained psychology students to code them. When the coding was completed, I returned to Washington to join my colleagues and we proceeded with the analysis of the survey data. This is not the place to summarize our many interesting results. But I must report that our most important finding was that, contrary to expectations, the more our Air Force bombed civilians, the greater became their will to resist (U.S. Strategic Bombing Survey, 1947). This was also suggested by the British and German experience. Unfortunately, this finding has been ignored by our political and military leaders in the wars in Korea, Vietnam, and Cambodia.

Before leaving the war years, I should point out that the disruption of my professional career was not nearly as calamitous as I had thought it would be. Although I did not enjoy the bureaucratic experience in the Navy or Selective Service, the Bombing Survey was quite another matter. It was my first experience in interdisciplinary research and I was particularly impressed with the way a group of talented social scientists could effectively pool their efforts and skills in the pursuit of a large-scale scientific research project.

I decided that when I returned to academic life I would do all I could to promote interdisciplinary research and training. I should say also that, over the years, several of my colleagues on the Bombing Survey and I have continued to work together on the promotion of interdisciplinary social science research and training activities.

THE WISCONSIN YEARS

The Social Structure of the University

Before turning to the Wisconsin Years, I need to say something about the University of Wisconsin, where I have been for over forty years. Wisconsin in many ways is the prototypical public land-grant university in its traditions, its organizational structure, and its aims. From the beginning, the university has sought to maintain high levels of scholarship in the natural sciences, social sciences, humanities, and the professions and, whenever possible, to bring the fruits of its scholarship not only to its students but also to the people of the state. It was among the first universities to develop programs of agricultural, engineering, and general extension. From its earliest years, it has been a faculty-controlled institution. With very few exceptions, its presidents/chancellors, and deans have come from the ranks of its scholars rather than from outside. Academic freedom has flourished at Madison—even when it was seriously threatened elsewhere. Out-of-state students, particularly from the New York, New Jersey, and Chicago areas, have constituted more than one-fifth of its undergraduate student body for decades. Originally, many of the brightest of these students came to Wisconsin because they found it difficult to gain admittance to the best private institutions of the East because of their ethnic origins. Their children and grandchildren have followed them to Madison, adding zest to what otherwise might have been a somewhat bucolic student body. In this setting, the university pioneered in the development of the social sciences and, for many years, its social science departments have enjoyed high national ranking. Within the university itself, only the biological sciences have been more prestigious.

Sociology and the Social Sciences

Sociology was introduced very early at Wisconsin (1893) but it was not until E. A. Ross joined the university (1906), following his dismissal from Stanford for criticizing Leland Stanford's business practices, that Wisconsin developed a significant program in sociology. Ross soon brought John L. Gillin, the pioneering criminologist, to the university and, in the following years, added the social psychologist Kimball Young, the social anthropologist Ralph Linton, and Samuel Stouffer in statistics. Ross was also influential in bringing Charles J. Galpin and later John H. Kolb as rural sociologists into the College of Agriculture. Under Ross, Wisconsin became one of the leading graduate training centers in sociology.

When I arrived in 1946, Ross and Gillin were retired but still living in Madison—in fact, Gillin continued to come regularly to his office until the day of his death in 1960. The other luminaries had moved elsewhere, except for Kolb. On my arrival, the sociology professors were Howard Becker in social theory, T.C. McCormick in statistics and demography, Svend Riemer in urban sociology, and George W. Hill and Kolb in rural sociology. Hans Gerth in social theory and social psychology had not yet been granted tenure. Don Martindale was an Instructor, teaching mainly introductory courses. Except for some part-time people, that was the entire faculty in sociology. In that year, Marshall B. Clinard and I came in as tenured professors and John Useem as a Research Associate. It was quite apparent that the sociology faculty, although it had some well-known members, had not kept pace with its national rivals. To make matters worse, the faculty was riven with discord. The university administration was aware of this situation and wanted the sociology program strengthened. I was brought in with the understanding that I would take a leading role in the rebuilding of the program. My original appointment was in Rural Sociology in the College of Agriculture but, like Kolb and Hill, I was also a member of the Sociology Department and served on its executive committee. A major reason for my appointment in Rural Sociology was that I insisted on a half-time research appointment, which was only possible then in the Agricultural Experiment Station.

I learned soon after my arrival that most of the other social science departments also had slipped during the late 1930s and early 1940s, due to the loss of outstanding faculty through death, retirement, and failure to replace adequately those who left for government and academic positions elsewhere. This seems to have been true in other divisions of the university but clearly to a lesser extent.

My Research on Personality and Social Structure

When I came to Wisconsin, I had already planned a research project in the area of personality and social structure. My interest in this area grew directly out of my reading of Linton (1945) and Kardiner (1939, 1945) and others in what came to be known as the "Culture and Personality Movement"(DuBois, 1944; Henry, 1940; Henry and Henry, 1944; Fromm, 1941; Erikson, 1939, 1950; Gorer, 1943, 1948). What these writers shared in varying degrees was the belief that national character or modal personality could be explained by Freudian theories of personality development. The theoretical position held by many psychoanalysts, and by some anthropologists and child development psychologists, was that of Freud's theory of psychosexual development. This theory emphasized the crucial importance of the infant disciplines, particularly breast-feeding, weaning, and toilet training, in determining later personality characteristics and patterns.

I was intrigued by the ideas of the culture and personality school but questioned the Freudian theoretical assumptions and the adequacy of the ethnographic observations that were offered as evidence of their validity. I had discussed these matters with several of my colleagues on the Bombing Survey and began formulating plans for testing the theory in a more empirically sound manner. By the time I got to Madison, I had what I believed was an appropriate design for testing the general theory. This involved deriving a set of specific hypotheses from the theory regarding the influences of particular training practices on the personalities of the children so trained.

The hypotheses were then to be tested by obtaining information from a sample of mothers of young farm children on the specifics of how each had handled the feeding, weaning, and toilet training of her child, and relating these practices to the child's personality traits and patterns, as determined independently by projective and standardized tests of personality once the child entered school. The project was funded by the Agricultural Experiment Station, using state and federal funds. The amount required for the fieldwork and statistical analysis was small by modern standards, somewhere in the neighborhood of $6,000.

The interviewing was done by three women graduate students whom I had trained in nondirective interviewing techniques. I selected the sample and supervised the field interviewers. The testing was done by an experienced clinical psychologist. Relatively simple measures of association were used to test the hypotheses. The principal finding was that none of the training practices or configurations of practices thought to be critical by the Freudians had any relationship to the personalities of the children! An article reporting these findings, "Infant Training and the Personality of the Child" (Sewell, 1952), received a great deal of attention from the social scientific community—in general, acclaim from sociologists and psychologists, and condemnation from psychiatrists and some anthropologists. Several other articles growing out of this study were published, including papers on the design of the research, on social status and patterns of child training, on social status and childhood personality, and on socialization theory and methods (Sewell, 1949, 1956, 1961, 1963; Sewell and Haller, 1956, 1959; Sewell and Mussen, 1952; Sewell, Mussen, and Harris, 1955).

It is difficult to assess the impact of this research. Probably it was a stimulus to sociologists and social psychologists to press forward with the development of the now commonly held view that personality is not fixed in early childhood but rather continues to develop and change throughout the life course, dependent both on individual propensities and on the changing roles that one comes to play in the structured groups in which one participates. It also could be said to illustrate a general model for theory testing in social science (Sewell, 1956). But whatever the contributions of the study, it certainly demonstrates that social science research at Wisconsin, and probably at other universities in the late 1940s, was generally limited to what an individual scholar, working on a small budget, could do. Not only were the funds available small, but the sources were severely limited. If it were not for my appointment in the Agricultural Experiment Station, I doubt that the study could have been done.

The Struggle to Change the Institutional Structure of Social Scientific Research at Wisconsin

The limited funds for scientific social research at Wisconsin were especially vexing to the large cohort of social scientists who had been brought to the university to take over leadership in the social science departments in the mid-1940s. Most of these younger scholars were pre-World War Ph.D.s, who had a strong commitment to the scientific model of social science research. Many of them had already become established in their fields and were impatient to begin their research programs. They were soon confronted by the fact that, although the biological and physical sciences at Wisconsin generally had adequate support for research, there was great need for improvement in research support and facilities for the social sciences. (This view was not shared by our colleagues in the administration.) I became a leader and spokesman for this group, initially as Chair of the Faculty Division of Social

Sciences (1950-1952) and later as Chair of the Social Science Research Committee (1953-1956), which was more or less forced on the top administration by the social science "young Turks" as a mechanism for expanding external and internal support for social science research.

During this period, the Ford Foundation announced basic grants of several hundred thousand dollars to several leading universities to strengthen their behavioral science research programs. Wisconsin was not included in this list, much to the chagrin of the social science faculty and the university administration. The reason given by the Foundation was that Wisconsin had not demonstrated sufficient willingness to extend support for social science research from the considerable funds under its control. These funds were available through the Wisconsin Alumni Research Foundation from patents resulting from university research. This is a very complicated matter, which cannot be detailed here, but the president of the university and the dean of the Graduate School, both eminent biological scientists, and most trustees of the foundation were unalterably opposed to the allocation of any of these funds to the social sciences. Needless to say, they had the strong support of the biological and physical science faculty. Our committee, with the full support of the social science faculty, launched a continuing campaign to change this situation and, although our efforts were supported by a few of the trustees and by several prominent natural scientists, we were not successful. We did succeed, however, in getting the administration to allocate more state and other available funds to social science facilities and research support. But it was not until a decade later, when my successor as chairman of the committee, the noted historian Fred Harvey Harrington, became president of the university, that the Wisconsin Alumni Research Foundation trustees finally and reluctantly changed their policy and made the social sciences eligible for research support. The battle that was waged over the years was not easily won and, to this day, a few of the trustees and natural science faculty remain resentful about the decision, despite the fact that by that time there was a plenitude of funds for the support of research in the natural sciences from government sources. In a very real sense, what was happening at Madison was a microcosm of the struggle of the social sciences against the established sciences, not only for a piece of the funding pie but also for recognition as a legitimate member of the community of sciences. This battle was waged with varying intensity in most of the major research universities and at the national level as well.

The Struggle to Change the Institutional
Structure of Research at the National Level

The struggle for recognition of social science research at the national level has been a long and difficult one. Although advances have been made, the battle is far from won. After World War II, the United States government became committed to world dominance in science and developed the necessary mechanisms for reaching this goal, mainly through research grants to university scientists. Leading social scientists immediately began to lobby for the inclusion of their disciplines in research grant programs. This is best exemplified in the National Science Foundation (NSF), which originally did not include provision for support of social science research. In addition to lobbying, which for some years met with little success, another strategy emerged. This was to gain acceptance through infiltration. This strategy was used effectively first at the National Institutes of Health (NIH), and later at the NSF. Infiltration was not particularly difficult at the NIH because some of its administrators were already convinced that social science research was relevant to health and health care. This was particularly true in the National Institute of Mental Health (NIMH), where John Clausen was appointed Social Science Consultant to the Director in 1948. He soon launched a modest program of social science research on mental health. In this effort, he benefited from the advice of prominent sociologists, including Leonard Cottrell, Jr., Kingsley Davis, H. Warren Dunham, August Hollingshead, Clifford Shaw, and Robin M. Williams, Jr. By the time that Clausen left this position (1951) to become chief of the Laboratory of Socio-Environmental Studies, an important program of social science research grants was in place in the NIMH (Clausen, 1950).[1]

In 1956, I replaced Robin Williams as the only sociologist on the Mental Health Study Section, the body charged with reviewing research proposals. The other members were all psychiatrists and psychologists, some of whom had little appreciation of the potential contribution of sociology to the study of mental health. Immediately I began advocating a broader definition of mental health relevance and the need for greater representation of sociology and anthropology in the study section. The next year, another sociologist and an anthropologist were added to the group. We let it be known that research proposals with mental health relevance from sociologists, social psychologists, and anthropologists would be welcomed. The response was so great that it was necessary to create a Behavioral Science Study Section to evaluate the new proposals. I was asked to chair the new study section during its first three years (1959-1961). The study section was asked to review all social science proposals relevant to mental health other than those in psychiatry and experimental psychology. In the first year of its existence, over 300 research proposals were

---

1. John Clausen has throughout his career contributed to the development of social science in the NIMH, as Chief of the Laboratory of Socioenvironmental Studies, his research and that of his colleagues (Melvin Kohn, Morris Rosenberg, Marian Yarrow and Irving Goffman) won the respect of the social science community but also the support of the psychiatrists at NIMH. Since joining the faculty in Berkeley (1960), he has continued to make scholarly contributions to the sociology of mental health and to serve on NIMH advisory committees.

evaluated, of which 125 were funded. These included several studies that have become classics in their fields. The section continued to be a major source of support for social science projects, until the Reagan administration's insistence on a very restricted definition of mental health relevance crippled it.

I also lobbied for and chaired the new Behavioral Science Training Committee, established by the National Institute of General Medical Sciences in 1963, which provided funds for pre- and postdoctoral training programs to social science departments in medical sociology, research methods, demography, and other areas. This greatly added to the existing opportunities for graduate training in sociology without endangering the existing NIMH training programs. During 1968 to 1970, I served on the NIMH Research Advisory Committee, which was charged with advising the top staff of the Institute on its research programs. I also, for the NIH, was a member of the advisory committee that drew up the plans for the National Institute of Child Health and Human Development (NICHD). In 1973, a large measure of the emphasis on adult development and aging was transferred to the newly established National Institute on Aging (NIA). Today both NICHD and NIA have become major sources of funds for sociological study of human development and for demographic research. Since 1978, under the vigorous leadership of Matilda White Riley, the National Institute on Aging is the major source of research funding for the new sociological focus on the aging process. Thus, for a total of 15 years, working with other social science colleagues and with the help of an increasing number of sociologists, we were able to increase greatly the amount of support for social science research in the National Institutes of Health. In fact, the Institutes have been the major source of support for social science research from the early 1950s to the present.

The problem of gaining support for the social sciences in the NSF was much more difficult. The act establishing the foundation did not provide for a social science program (although earlier drafts of the act had). After concerted efforts had failed to get Congress to remedy this situation, social scientists began to try to convince the Director of the NSF and members of the Science Board to make provision for the support of social science research. The justification for this was that social science research was in the national interest and that the legislation establishing the NSF did not prohibit such funding. Finally, on the recommendation of the director, the Science Board approved a limited program of research and fellowship support in areas of convergence of the natural and social sciences, including anthropology, demography, mathematical social science, experimental psychology, economic geography and the history, philosophy, and sociology of science.

In 1953, Harry Alpert, an experienced sociologist and administrator, was brought to the NSF to head this effort as Program Director for Social Sciences. He proceeded cautiously and developed a small but expanding program that won the respect of social scientists and the administrators of the NSF. In 1957, the program was expanded to permit support of basic social science irrespective of convergence with natural sciences. Henry Reicken took over the direction of the expanded program in 1958 and succeeded in further expanding the program. By the time he left the foundation (1966) to become President of the Social Science Research Council, he had become Associate Director for social sciences and the social sciences had gained a solid place in the structure of the foundation. Since then, other changes have further strengthened the position of the social sciences in the NSF but they need not be detailed here.[2] The successful struggle to bring these changes about in the NSF required the efforts of a number of energetic and devoted social scientists. My contribution was as a member of advisory committees that urged the officers of the foundation initially to extend support to the social sciences, then to expand this program greatly and give it a secure place in the basic structure of the foundation, and finally to fund the sociology section adequately.

Although this support has been threatened several times over the years, especially by maverick members of congress and more recently by the current administration, the NSF continues to be a major source of basic sociological research funding. It was a great satisfaction to me that, when President Reagan in 1980 cut the budget for sociology by 60%, and that of the other social sciences by nearly as much, we were able to rally support in Congress to reduce the cuts by about one half and later succeeded in restoring the social science budget to its earlier levels. The major credit for staving off total disaster goes to the Consortium of Social Science Associations and the Social Science Research Council for rallying social science leaders to testify before Congress and to enlist the aid of their representatives in the House and Senate in support of social science funding.

In a number of less direct ways, I participated in efforts to increase the acceptance and prestige of social science research through serving on committees of the Social Science Research Council; as a research consultant to several government agencies; as a trustee of nonprofit organizations, including the National Opinion Research Center and the Agricultural Development Council; as a member of the Executive Committee of the Division of Social Sciences of the National Research Council and its panels on the research needs of the social sciences; as Chairman of the Section on Social and Political Sciences in the National Academy of Sciences; and as Chairman of the National Commission on Research. In all of these endeavors, I tried to represent the best interests of sociology and the social sciences. I believe that

2. For additional information on the struggle to gain acceptance of the social sciences in the NSF, see Parsons (1946), Lundberg (1947), Alpert (1954, 1955, 1958), and Riley (1986).

the efforts of social scientists who served on these and other committees and commissions have helped to improve the national recognition of the social sciences, including sociology. But it is also my conviction that the struggle is not over and will require the constant efforts of younger colleagues to protect and improve the situation.

The Rebuilding of the Wisconsin
Sociology Department

During the time that I had been active in the wider affairs of the social sciences, the Wisconsin Sociology Department, although it had added several new faculty members, remained badly divided and directionless. Finally in 1957, the sociology faculty and the dean of the college asked me to join the department full-time as its Chair. The dean generously continued my half-time research appointment out of his budget and gave me a very light teaching load so that I could continue my research and still devote a great deal of attention to the affairs of the department.

The rebuilding of the department was made possible by a number of things. One of the most important factors was that most members gave me their solid support in this activity. The quarreling that had so marked the department lessened and, after the deaths of two of the combatants and the resignation of another, ceased. Another major factor was the growing popularity of our undergraduate offerings. This was part of a national trend but was especially marked at Wisconsin. The growth of our enrollments meant that we could add greatly to our staff. I insisted that our recruitment efforts should concentrate on bringing in bright young Ph.D.s from the major graduate departments. I went on recruiting tours seeking out young people who had demonstrated strong research interests. Because of the emerging scientific structure within the university, we were able to obtain research funds that permitted us to offer tenure-track appointments with part-time release from teaching. This enabled our recruits to develop their research programs to the point that their proposals would be likely competitors for outside funding. I advised the members of the department on sources of support and assisted with proposal writing. I knew a good deal about these matters from my own experience in seeking funding for my research and from the inside knowledge gained from serving on research grant committees in Washington.

In these ways, we increased the size of the department from 10 to 35 members in a five-year period. All but three of the new members came into the Department as assistant professors. Several were rapidly promoted to Associate Professors and one was so productive and so much in demand that he was made a full Professor in five years, just a month or so before reaching age 30. When I took over the leadership of the department, I was the only member who had an outside research grant. By the time I completed my term, more than two-thirds of the faculty had funded research, including some senior members who had never before applied for such support.

Another factor that contributed to our continuing growth was that we took full advantage of the opportunity to institute research training programs and facilities, with funding from the NIH and the NSF. These grants enabled us to expand our faculty and graduate student body by providing fully funded research training fellowships for graduate and postdoctoral students in six different training programs. The most prominent were the medical sociology, quantitative research methods, and demography and ecology training programs. During this time, we also inaugurated two research centers. Funds for our large research facilities were provided by the NSF and the university. Meanwhile, our undergraduate program continued to remain popular and to attract more than its share of outstanding students.

Thus, in the space of a few years, our department was transformed from a relatively small traditional teaching department into a large modern department, emphasizing scientific research as well as graduate and undergraduate teaching. Also, it was rapidly becoming one of the leading centers for quantitative research in social psychology, social stratification, and demography and human ecology. The transformation of the department was made possible, in large part, by the opening up of research and training funds for the support of the social sciences at the local and national levels.

In all honesty, I find it hard to be completely modest in assessing my contribution to the current high prestige of the department. But perhaps it would not be entirely wrong to say that I took full advantage of the opportunities that the developing institutional structure for the support of social sciences provided. Fortunately, I was able to enlist the support of my faculty colleagues and some top members of the university administration in this endeavor—in part because several social scientists were by this time in key administrative positions in the university. Also, I had established a general pattern that my very capable successors in the Chair followed, not without making their own innovations and improvements, however, in the department's teaching and research programs.

Our Research on Aspiration and Attainment

I now turn to my research on aspirations and attainment, which has occupied much of my attention for the past 25 years. From the beginning of my career, I have been interested in the extent and nature of social mobility in our society and, particularly, in why some individuals are socially mobile in the course of their lives and others are not. I have never doubted that social structural factors, particularly socioeconomic, ethnic, race, and community background, influence one's life chances; but neither have I doubted that such social psychological characteristics as intelligence, motivation, and aspirations also play an important part. I thought that differences in career achievements might well be explained by variations in aspirations, resulting from differences in individual and social background characteristics.

My colleagues and I had done preliminary research along these lines in the early 1950s, but never with adequate data to establish this position. The one article that came the closest demonstrated, for a large sample of high school youth, that parent's occupational status and student's measured ability both make substantial independent and joint contributions to educational and occupational aspirations (Sewell, Haller, and Straus, 1957). Our data were from records that did not contain information on achievements, so we could not extend our analysis to educational and occupational attainments.

This line of research was interrupted temporarily by an appointment to a Ford Foundation Visiting Professorship in India during 1956 to 1957. On my return from India, I took over the department leadership and had little time in the next few years to launch any further research along these lines. I did learn, however, that one of my colleagues in the School of Education, J. Kenneth Little, had conducted a questionnaire survey of all seniors in Wisconsin high schools in 1957 to determine their plans for education beyond high school. He had completed his use of the data and, knowing of my interest in educational aspirations, offered the questionnaires and coded IBM cards to me for further analysis. I looked over these materials and found that they contained information that I could exploit on social background; school experiences; relations with parents, teachers, peers; and educational and occupational aspirations. Meanwhile, I had accepted an invitation to be a Fellow at the Center for Advanced Study in Behavioral Sciences at Stanford, for the academic year 1959-1960, and decided to begin preliminary examination of the data while there.

With my wife as my research assistant, we ran numerous cross-tabulations and correlations to learn more about the data. I reported on preliminary results at the Center and at Stanford, the University of California, Berkeley, and the University of California, Los Angeles, obtaining valuable criticism and suggestions from colleagues at all of these places. After returning to Madison, I submitted a research proposal to the NIMH and received generous funding for a five-year period. The grant enabled us to draw a random sample of approximately 10,000 cases, recode information from the questionnaires, obtain information from public sources, begin our analysis of the data, and plan a follow-up survey to determine the achievements of the members of our sample. This project, "Social and Psychological Factors in Educational and Occupational Aspirations and Achievement," commonly known as the "Wisconsin Longitudinal Survey," was renewed periodically through 1980 by the NIMH and has had support since then from the NSF, the Spencer Foundation, and the University of Wisconsin.

During the early years of the project, we examined the effects of community, neighborhood, and school on educational and occupational aspirations. We found that each of these contexts had statistically significant but quite small effects, once socioeconomic background, measured intelligence, and gender of respondent were controlled (Sewell, 1964; Sewell and Armer, 1966a, 1966b; Sewell and Haller, 1965). Other analyses along these lines showed that parents, teachers, and peers all have significant influence on students' aspirations (Sewell and Shah, 1968a, 1968b).

In 1964, we completed a follow-up study (with an 87% response rate) that provided us with information on the educational and occupational attainments of our sample. We then began developing simple causal models of educational and occupational status attainments. Our work on models was greatly influenced by consultations with Otis Dudley Duncan and by his writings on linear causal models (1966, 1969). Our first published models demonstrated the direct and indirect effects of socioeconomic status and measured intelligence, as mediated by educational aspirations, on the attainment of higher education (Sewell and Shah, 1967). We developed other simple linear causal models involving socioeconomic status and measured ability, with single intervening variables, such as rank in high school class, teacher encouragement, and peer influence, in which aspirations and achievements were the dependent variables. All of this work, however, was only preparatory to the development of more complex models of educational and occupational attainment.

Building on the work of Blau and Duncan (1967), my colleagues Archibald O. Haller and Alejandro Portes and I (1969) developed a linear causal model to explain the relationship between socioeconomic origins and educational and occupational achievements (which the Blau-Duncan model had demonstrated) by adding social psychological variables as mediators between origins and later attainments. Our model attempted to explain the effects of socioeconomic background and measured intelligence, first on educational attainments, and then on early occupational achievements, as mediated by social psychological variables, including academic achievement in high school, the perceived influence of significant others, and educational and occupational aspirations. In this first paper on the model, we presented its theoretical rationale and tested it on a sample of farm males. We demonstrated that this model successfully elaborates the complex process by which social psychological variables mediate the influence of status origins on educational and occupational attainments.

The model was then further tested for subsamples representing a wide range of community size categories (Sewell, Haller, and Ohlendorf, 1970). The results were essentially the same, but minor adjustments were made to take into account some indirect paths that we had not fully anticipated. The revised model succeeded in explaining much of the variance in educational achievement and occupational attainment. The model reported in these papers has come to be known as the "Wisconsin Model."

Later my colleague Robert M. Hauser and I further elaborated the model by disaggregating the socioeconomic status index and the significant others' measure into their component parts (Sewell, 1971; Hauser, 1973; Sewell and Hauser, 1972). This enabled us to estimate the individual role of each of the component variables in educational and early occupational attainment. Later we used this model to explain the earnings of the men in our sample several years after their high school graduation (Sewell and Hauser, 1972, 1975). The disaggregated model has been used in most of our studies since that time.

In 1976, we completed a second follow-up study of our sample (with approximately a 90% response rate). The survey involved detailed interviews covering the composition of the respondent's family of origin and procreation, educational history, work experience, social participation, and other matters not available to us from other sources. A number of studies have been made using these data, but I will mention only our comparative analysis of the educational and occupational attainments of the women and men in our sample. Previous research had indicated that the process of status attainment was essentially the same for women and men (Sewell, 1971; Hout and Morgan, 1975; Treiman and Terrell, 1975; McClendon, 1976). With our new data on achievements at mid-life, we could determine for the first time how women's and men's later occupational achievements are affected by differences in educational attainments and by early occupational experience (Sewell, Hauser, and Wolf, 1980). The addition of these variables to our model revealed that at only one stage in the attainment process do women have an advantage over men: They obtain first jobs whose occupational status on average is considerably higher than men's. At mid-life, however, men's mean occupational status is several points higher than women's. In other words, women have lost ground over the course of their work lives while men have gained. Further analysis indicates that women are forced at mid-life to rely on formal educational qualifications for occupational placement because they are frequently reapplying to the labor market after interruptions, whereas men build on their earlier occupational experiences because of their more continuous work histories. Women also tend to enter female-dominated occupations that generally offer limited opportunities for advancement. On the basis of this analysis and recent studies by economists on women's earnings, it is clear that women suffer from structural and discriminatory practices that so far have proved to be difficult to correct in our society (Treiman and Hartmann, 1981).

Sibling Models

Our most recent research has involved the effects of family structure on the achievements of siblings. The new data required for this research comes from a 1977 survey of a sample of the siblings of our original respondents. The resemblance of siblings raised together is, of course, a fundamental indicator of the force with which the family functions to create and maintain systems of social differentiation and inequality. Sibling similarity captures the effects of social and economic (as well as genetic) background, of family structure, and of all other commonalities of social and psychological functioning of the family. We have developed theoretical and analytical designs for our research (Sewell and Hauser, 1977) and have published several papers on the results of our analysis (Hauser, Sewell, and Clarridge, 1982; Hauser and Mossel, 1985; Hauser and Sewell, 1985, 1986). I need mention only briefly two of these papers.

The first deals with the influence of birth order on educational attainment among more than 9000 of our original respondents and among their full sibships, which include more than 30,000 persons (Hauser and Sewell, 1985). Whether we look at selection into our original sample of respondents, their postsecondary educational achievements, or educational attainments within full-sibships, we find no systematic effects of birth order on schooling, when such relevant variables as age, gender, and number of siblings are controlled. This, of course, is contrary to the expectations of the well-known Zajonc and Markus confluence theory (Zajonc, 1983; Zajonc and Markus, 1975; Zajonc, Markus, and Markus, 1979) and to the recent sensational claims about sibling effects reported in the popular press.

The second study deals with family effects in models of education, occupational status, and earnings (Hauser and Sewell, 1986). Using fraternal pairs, we develop and test simple structural equation models of the effects of measured and unmeasured family background factors, mental ability, and schooling on occupational status and earnings. These models permit direct comparisons of within- and between-family regressions. We find no evidence that family background leads to overestimation of the effects of ability on schooling or of schooling on occupation; but, at the same time, we find that family background has notable independent effects on ability, schooling, and socioeconomic attainments.

The Influence of the Wisconsin Research

It is difficult for me to assess the influence of our Wisconsin research on the study of social stratification. The sheer number of publications is impressive: More than 70 articles and chapters in books and five monographs have been published reporting its results. Twenty Ph.D. dissertations have been based on project data. Several of our articles have become "Citation Classics" and many textbooks include discussions of our models. These models have been applied in various national, regional, state, and community studies. They have been used by others to interpret differences in the aspirations and achievements of blacks and whites, ethnic groups, and developed and developing nations. In most instances, these are not exact replications. In some studies, key variables are omitted because of lack of data. In other instances, new variables have been added to the models. (See Sewell and Hauser, 1980, for a detailed review of these studies.) We have been impressed, however, with the extent to which our models have been confirmed when similar measurements and variables are employed. (Recent evaluations of our work, both favorable and critical, are to be found in articles by Featherman, 1981, and Campbell, 1983.)

Before leaving this account of the Wisconsin research on aspiration and attainment, I must point out that a program of the magnitude of the Wisconsin Longitudinal Study would have been impossible had not the institutional structure of scientific research been expanded to include the funding of social science research. Neither would the analysis that was undertaken have been feasible without the recent development of mathematical statistical models for the analysis of survey data. The application of these models depended on the development of computer technology, which provided adequate storage capacity and computational power to permit the rapid solution of these statistical models. Moreover, such projects require a complex organizational structure, including a survey research facility to provide sampling, interviewing, and coding; computer programmers to put the data on tapes and disks and to adapt or create data analysis programs; and a project manager to tend to the day-to-day business and to manage and maintain the data files. But most of all, a project of this magnitude requires the collaboration of faculty and graduate student colleagues who have creative ideas and the methodological skills to share in the analysis of the data and in the writing of papers and reports.[3] This, of course, is in sharp contrast to the typical situation in the 1930s, when I began my career in sociology. At that

3. I wish to acknowledge fully that the work on this research program has been made possible by the theoretical and methodological contributions of my faculty and student collaborators. The two faculty colleagues who have contributed most are Archie O. Haller, especially during the earlier years of the project, and, more recently, Robert M. Hauser. These two have made theoretical, substantive, and methodological contributions to most of the research that has been produced and have shared in the analysis and writing of its most important publications. Other faculty colleagues who helped greatly in establishing the data base are Kenneth Lutterman, Ronald Pavalko, Janet Fisher, and Wendy C. Wolf. Each has coauthored several papers resulting from the project. Graduate students who served as research assistants and coauthored papers on the project include Michael Armer, Duane Alwin, William Bielby, Richard Campbell, Brian Clarridge, Thomas Daymont, Nancy Dunton, Peter Dickenson, Dorothy Ellegaard, Neil Fligstein, Ruth Gasson, David Grusky, Randy Hodson, Susan Janssen, Victor Jesudason, Michael Massagli, Peter Mossel, Norma Nager, George Ohlendorf, Allen Orenstein, Alejandro Portes, Rosanda Richards, Rachel Rosenfeld, Vimal Shah, Linda Sheehy, Hershel Shosteck, Kenneth Spenner, Matthew Snipp, Annemette Sorensen, Robin Stryker, Hazel Symonette, Shu-Ling Tsai, Eldon Wagner, Richard Williams, Alexandra Wright, and Charlotte Yang. All of us have been highly dependent on Taissa Hauser, our project manager, for her devoted and unstinting assistance. And, of course, I must acknowledge my great debt to my former undergraduate student, faculty colleague, frequent consultant, and longtime friend, Otis Dudley Duncan.

time, a lone scholar, with the assistance of a student or two, would undertake a research project with very limited funding, obtain information on a small nonprobability sample, employ simple counting or cross-tabular procedures in the analysis of the data, write up the results, and hope to get an article or monograph published in one of the then limited outlets for sociological research studies.

SUMMARY

I have witnessed a great transformation in the scale, methodology, social organization, scope, and funding of research, and in the training of graduate students, during the half century that I have been a sociologist. I have shown how my career has been influenced by these changes in the organization of the social sciences in general and of sociology in particular. Moreover, I have attempted to indicate how my efforts, in concert with others, may have contributed to these changes and to the way sociology is done at Wisconsin and in many of the leading graduate departments of sociology in America.

I am not yet prepared to evaluate the impact of these changes. Please ask me to do so in another ten or more years, say around my 90th birthday, if I am not still too involved in them to be objective! My guess is that the quantitative scientific revolution in sociology will continue to dominate American Sociology for many years to come, despite some vigorous competition from several quarters. I would predict also that in the future large national sample surveys and well-designed longitudinal studies will provide much of the data for sociological analysis, that data from these studies will be made readily and rapidly available in machine-readable form for all who wish to analyze them, and that complex statistical techniques will be developed to exploit the data more fully. All this will require large-scale funding by government agencies. I trust too that the foundations and government agencies will continue to support innovative and exploratory studies that do not require so much funding and infrastructure.

References

Alpert, Harry. 1954. "The National Science Foundation and Social Science Research." *American Sociological Review* 19(April):208-211.
———. 1955. "The Social Sciences and the National Science Foundation: 1945-1955." *American Sociological Review* 20(December):653-661.
———. 1957. "The Social Science Research Program of the National Science Foundation." *American Sociological Review* 22(October):582-585.
Blau, Peter M. and Otis Dudley Duncan. 1967. *The American Occupational Structure*. New York: John Wiley.
Campbell, Richard T. 1983. "Status Attainment Research: End of the Beginning or Beginning of the End." *Sociology of Education* 56(January):47-62.

Chapin, F. Stuart. 1933. "A Scale for Rating Living Room Equipment" (Circular No. 3). Minneapolis: Institute of Child Welfare.

Clausen, John A. 1950. "Social Science Research and the National Mental Health Program." *American Sociological Review* 15(June):402-408.

DuBois, Cora A. 1944. *The People of Alor: A Social-Psychological Study of an East Indian Island.* Minneapolis: University of Minnesota Press.

Duncan, Otis Dudley. 1966. "Path Analysis: Sociological Examples." *American Journal of Sociology* 72(July):1-16.

———. 1969. "Contingencies in Constructing Causal Models." Pp. 74-112 in *Sociological Methodology*, edited by E. F. Borgotta. San Francisco: Jossey-Bass.

Erikson, Erik H. 1939. "Observations on Sioux Education." *Journal of Psychology* 7:101-156.

———. 1950. *Childhood and Society.* New York: Norton.

Featherman, David A. 1981. "Stratification and Social Mobility." Pp. 79-100 in *The State of Sociology: Problems and Prospects*, edited by James E. Short, Jr. Beverly Hills, CA: Sage.

Fromm, Erich. 1941. *Escape from Freedom.* New York: Farrar & Rinehart.

Gorer, Geoffrey. 1943. "Themes in Japanese Culture." *Transactions of the New York Academy of Sciences* 5:106-124.

———. 1948. *The American People.* New York: Norton.

Hauser, Robert M. 1973. "Disaggregating a Social-Psychological Model of Educational Attainment." Pp. 255-284 in *Structural Equation Models in the Social Sciences*, edited by A. S. Goldberger and O. D. Duncan. New York: Seminar Press.

Hauser, Robert M. and Peter A. Mossel. 1985. "Fraternal Resemblance in Educational Attainment and Occupational Status." *American Journal of Sociology* 91(November):650-673.

Hauser, R. M. and William H. Sewell. 1985. "Birth Order and Educational Attainment in Full Sibships." *American Educational Research Journal* 22(Spring):1-23.

———. 1986. "Family Effects in Simple Models of Education, Occupational Status and Earnings: Findings from the Wisconsin and Kalamazoo Studies." *Journal of Labor Economics* 4(Part 2, April):S83-S115.

———. and Duane F. Alwin. 1976. "High School Effects on Achievement." Pp. 309-341 in *Schooling and Achievement in American Society*, edited by W. H. Sewell, R. M. Hauser, and D. A. Featherman. New York: Academic Press.

Hauser, Robert M., William H. Sewell, and Brian R. Clarridge. 1982. "The Influence of Family Structure on Socioeconomic Achievement: A Progress Report" (Working Paper 82-59). Madison: University of Wisconsin, Center for Demography and Human Ecology.

Hauser, Robert M., Shu-Ling Tsai, and William H. Sewell. 1983. "A Model of Stratification with Response Error in Social and Psychological Variables." *Sociology of Education* 56(January):20-46.

Henry, Jules. 1940. "Some Cultural Determinants of Hostility in Pilaga Indian Children." *American Journal of Orthopsychiatry* 11:111-119.

———. and Zunia Henry. 1944. "The Doll Play of Pilaga Indian Children" (Research Monograph No. 4). American Society of Orthopsychiatry.

Hout, Michael and William R. Morgan. 1975. "Race & Sex Variation in the Expected Attainments of High School Seniors." *American Journal of Sociology* 81(September):364-394.

Kardiner, Abram. 1939. *The Individual and His Society.* New York: Columbia University Press.

———. 1945. *The Psychological Frontiers of Society.* New York: Columbia University Press.

Linton, Ralph. 1945. *The Cultural Background of Personality.* New York: Appleton-Century.

Lundberg, George A. 1947. "The Senate Ponders Social Science." *The Scientific Monthly* 64(May):397-411.

McClendon, McKee J. 1976. "The Occupational Attainment Process of Males and Females." *American Sociological Review* 41(February):52-64.

Parsons, Talcott. 1946. "Science Legislation and the Role of the Social Sciences." *American Sociological Review* 11(December):653-666.

Riley, John W., Jr. 1986. "The Status of the Social Sciences, 1950: A Tale of Two Reports."
Pp. 113-120 in *The Nationalization of the Social Sciences,* edited by S. Z. Klausner and V. M.
Lidz. Philadelphia: University of Pennsylvania Press.

Sewell, William H. 1940a, April. *The Construction and Standardization of a Scale for the
Measurement of Socio-Economic Status of Oklahoma Farm Families* (Tech. Bull. No. 9).
Stillwater: Oklahoma Agricultural Experiment Station.

———. 1940b. "A Scale for the Measurement of Farm Family Socio-Economic Status."
Southwestern Social Science Quarterly 21(September):125-137.

———. 1949. "Field Techniques in Social Psychological Study in a Rural Community."
American Sociological Review 14(December):718-726.

———. 1952. "Infant Training and the Personality of the Child." *American Journal of Sociology*
58(September):150-159.

———. 1956. "Some Observations on Theory Testing." *Rural Sociology* 21(March):1-12.
(Reprinted in Bobbs-Merrill Reprint Series, #S506)

———. 1961. "Social Class and Childhood Personality." *Sociometry* 24(December):340-356.

———. 1963. "Some Recent Developments in Socialization Theory and Research." *The Annals
of the American Academy of Political and Social Science* 349(September):163-181.

———. 1964. "Community of Residence and College Plans." *American Sociological Review*
29(February):24-38.

———. 1971. "Inequality of Opportunity for Higher Education." *American Sociological Review*
36(October):793-809.

———. and J. Michael Armer. 1966. "Neighborhood Context and College Plans." *American
Sociological Review* 31(April):159-168.

Sewell, William H. and Archibald O. Haller. 1956. "Social Status and the Personality Adjustment
of the Child." *Sociometry* 19(June):114-125.

———. 1959. "Factors in the Relationships Between Social Status and the Personality
Adjustment of the Child." *American Sociological Review* 24(August):511-520.

———. 1965. "Educational and Occupational Perspectives of Farm and Rural Youth." Pp.
149-169 in *Rural Youth in Crisis: Facts, Myths, and Social Change,* edited by L. G. Burchinal.
Washington, DC: DHEW, Government Printing Office.

———. and George W. Ohlendorf. 1970. "The Educational and Early Occupational Status
Attainment Process: Replication and Revision." *American Sociological Review*
35(December):1014-1027.

Sewell, William H., Archibald O. Haller, and Alejandro Portes. 1969. "The Educational and
Early Occupational Attainment Process." *American Sociological Review* 34(February):82-92.

Sewell, William H., Archibald O. Haller, and M. A. Straus. 1957. "Social Status and Educational
and Occupational Aspirations." *American Sociological Review* 22(February):67-73.

Sewell, William H. and Robert M. Hauser. 1972. "Causes and Consequences of Higher
Education: Models of the Status Attainment Process." *American Journal of Agricultural
Economics* 54(December):851-861.

———. 1977. "On the Effects of Families and Family Structure on Achievements." Pp. 255-283 in
*Kinometrics: The Determinants of Educational Attainment, Mental Ability, and Occupa-
tional Success Within and Between Families,* edited by P. Taubman. Amsterdam: North
Holland.

———. 1980. "The Wisconsin Longitudinal Study of Social and Psychological Factors in
Aspirations and Achievements." Pp. 59-99 in *Research in Sociology of Education and
Socialization,* Vol. 1, edited by A. C. Kerckhoff. Greenwich, CT: JAI Press.

———. and Wendy C. Wolf. 1980. "Sex, Schooling, and Occupational Status." *American
Journal of Sociology* 86(November):551-583.

Sewell, William H., Robert M. Hauser et al. 1975. *Education, Occupation and Earnings:
Achievement in the Early Career.* New York: Academic Press.

Sewell, William H. and P. H. Mussen. 1952. "The Effects of Feeding, Weaning, and Scheduling Procedures on Childhood Adjustment and the Formation of Oral Symptoms." *Childhood Development* 23(September):185-191.

———. and C. W. Harris. 1955. *American Sociological Review* 20(April):137-148.

Sewell, William H. and Alan W. Orenstein. 1965. "Community of Residence and Occupational Choice." *American Journal of Sociology* 70(March):551-563.

Sewell, William H. and Vimal P. Shah. 1967. "Socioeconomic Status, Intelligence, and the Attainment of Higher Education." *Sociology of Education* 40(Winter):1-23.

———. 1968a. "Parents' Education and Children's Educational Aspirations and Achievements." *American Sociological Review* 33(April):191-209.

———. 1968b. "Social Class, Parental Encouragement, and Educational Aspirations." *American Journal of Sociology* 73(March):559-572.

Treiman, Donald J. and Heidi I. Hartmann, eds. 1981. *Women, Wages and Work: Equal Pay for Equal Value*. Washington: National Academy Press.

Treiman, Donald J. and Kermit Terrell. 1975. "Sex and the Process of Status Attainment: A Comparison of Men and Women." *American Sociological Review* 40(April):174-200.

U.S. Strategic Bombing Survey. 1947. *The Effects of U.S. Strategic Bombing on Japanese Civilian Morale* (Pacific War Series No. 14). Washington: Government Printing Office.

Zajonc, R. B. 1983. "Validating the Confluence Model." *Psychological Bulletin* 93:457-480.

———. and G. B. Markus. 1975. "Birth Order and Intellectual Development." *Psychological Review* 82:74-88.

Zajonc, R. B., H. Markus, and G. B. Markus. (1979). "The Birth Order Puzzle." *Journal of Personality and Social Psychology* 37:1325-1341.

10

An "Uppity Generation" and the Revitalization of Macroscopic Sociology

Reflections at Midcareer by a Woman from the 1960s

Theda Skocpol

"HOW DID SOMEONE from your background come to write such a book?" The questioner was Perry Anderson, and the query was directed at me, Theda Skocpol, as the two of us sat together on a wintry day in 1978, eating lunch at Grendel's Den, down Boylston street from Harvard Square. I had just finished the manuscript for *States and Social Revolutions: A Comparative Analysis of France, Russia, and China* (Skocpol, 1979). Anderson and I knew one another by reputation, but this was our first personal discussion. I had described the arguments and the historical scope of my new book to him, and he had then asked me about my background. Where had I come from; and what was my education? Anderson (1974a, 1974b) was himself the author of a recently published two-volume masterpiece, *Passages from Antiquity to Feudalism* and *Lineages of the Absolutist State*, a study that analyzed European civilization and European states over 2000 years of history.

The connections of Perry Anderson's comparative-historical work to his past were comprehensible, for Anderson had received an elite British education majoring in languages at Oxford, and was a nonprofessional leftist intellectual of independent means. But as I had explained to him, I was "nothing special" in American terms. I grew up in the Midwest, in Michigan, where both sets of grandparents had been farmers, my father a high school teacher, and my mother a homemaker and substitute teacher. Nor had I gone to an elite university. My undergraduate education, with a major in Sociology, was at a huge, state-supported "land-grant" institution, Michigan State University. Only after I married a physics major and completed my B.A. degree there, did we make our way to Harvard for graduate study. At Harvard, I ended up studying with Barrington Moore, Jr., along with Seymour Martin Lipset, Ezra Vogel, Daniel Bell, and George Homans. Their intellectual impact on me could certainly be seen in the book I had just completed during my third year as a Harvard junior faculty member. Yet, after all, where had I ever found the breadth of imagination and the sheer ambitious daring to embark on a Ph.D. thesis comparing three great social revolutions and six countries altogether, while knowing the languages of only two of them?

As I tried, a bit lamely, to explain to Perry Anderson that day, the answer lies partly in the impact on my thinking—and on the thinking of many others who were then becoming young adults and students of society—of the indelible domestic and international events of the 1960s. The 1960s created an "uppity generation," which has not only caused trouble for its elders in all of America's major institutions, but has also revitalized the macroscopic and critical sides of our discipline. The answer to Anderson's question about me also lies in something more traditionally American: in the special wonders that an open and competitive university system can work on an ambitious middle-class youngster who is willing to climb away from her community of origin in search of national professional success.

Let me talk about each of these matters in turn. Afterward, I will turn to another set of formative experiences for myself and others: those having to do with the sharp transformations in the roles of women that have come in the United States during the last two decades. These transformations too have had momentous intellectual consequences for our discipline, consequences that in my opinion are going to play out for many years to come.

THE 1960s AND THE
SOCIOLOGICAL IMAGINATION

Two tensions have run through the sociological enterprise since its origins, and especially since it became academically institutionalized between 1890 and 1930 in the United States. First, is sociology about long-term social change and entire configurations of social relations; or is it about more narrowly defined "social" problems or "social" areas of life not already claimed by other social scientists such as economists and political scientists? Second, is sociology an "objective and cumulative" science (however that is defined in a given epoch); or is sociology a critical enterprise, devoted to promoting the reform of existing social arrangements? In truth, sociology is—and must always be—all of these things, despite the practical difficulties of holding them together in shared professional arrangements.

In different historical periods, the balance among the tendencies shifts, as one or another emphasis is revitalized through sociologists' experiences in, and links to, the larger society—and especially through the experiences of younger cohorts who are just entering the discipline in a given period. For those of us who believe that American sociologists can think big and critically, that they can attempt to grasp the interrelations of institutions and understand the conflicts and contradictions that cause them to change over time, in short, for those of us who are "macroscopic sociologists," there have been three periods in modern U.S. history that have been especially revitalizing. The first was the turn of the twentieth century, when the problems of industrial labor and urban living inspired new conceptions of social interrelatedness and drew many social analysts into progressive reform movements. The second period of revitalization stretched from the New Deal through World War II, when successive (albeit contrasting) national crises, and collective efforts to manage them, inspired attempts at grand macrosociological theorizing and involved many sociologists with domestic and foreign policymaking. Finally, the third period of revitalization, which brought experiences and orientations in many ways at odds with those inspired by the second period, was "the 1960s." This decade (stretching into the early 1970s) witnessed the civil rights and black power movements, demands for "student power" on the campuses, the launching of women's movements, and widespread opposition among American middle-class youth to U.S. involvement in the Vietnam War.

The ferment of the 1960s commenced just ahead of the time that the demographic bulge of the postwar "baby boom" arrived at young adulthood. Thus the sense of scarce opportunities that would hit later, as large, crowded cohorts came onto the postcollege labor markets, was not there at first. The ferment of the 1960s also came at a time of national economic prosperity, and I can remember well the sense of optimism and freedom that gave to young people. No matter how much we protested, we felt that future opportunities for careers remained open, when—and if—we got around to them.

Politically, of course, varied experiences in this decade delivered different messages to subgroups of young Americans. For quite a few working-class men outside the colleges, the decade may have had little special effect, until the draft recruiters came and they (unlike their college brethren) went off to Vietnam, often not to return. But for young people in the colleges and universities, this was an exhilarating and wrenching time of intense political engagement, and perhaps cultural alienation. Some "dropped out" of career-oriented American middle-class life as a result, but usually just temporarily. Many young people participated and protested without ever dropping out or going to jail.

What most of the generation came to share, I think, was an acute sense that existing relations of power in state, economy, and society could be very unjust, and that authorities in all institutional spheres were not necessarily honest or automatically worthy of trust. At the same time, we gained a sense that protests and rebellions could make a difference: After mass demonstrations and the deaths of three young civil rights workers, the federal government finally enforced desegregation in the South; campus authorities did often back down in the face of students sit-ins; and, in the bitter end, the United States withdrew from Vietnam.

For the discipline of sociology (along with other social sciences), the 1960s were a source of internal trouble, as well as of intellectual reorientation and renewal. Until the middle-1970s, at least, the troubling effects were more obvious, especially from the point of view of the elders of the discipline. For one thing, the protests of the 1960s aroused a lot of sympathy and participation from sociologists, which often put sociology departments on collision courses with university administrators.

More important, many 1960s-generation student protesters chose to go to graduate school in sociology, seeing the discipline as a way to continue and intellectualize critical stances toward society. This meant that, by the middle 1970s, very bright and articulate 1960s-generation Ph.D.s were on the market for assistant professor jobs; and five to eight years later, they were expecting tenure in sociology departments around the country. But the passage upward was often not smooth, for these were members of an "uppity generation" in two senses. First, they were self-consciously and loudly critical of the theories and sometimes also the methods that had guided the careers of their elders. Many of the elders had experienced America as a victor over Depression and Nazism, and had defined worldviews grounded in cold war oppositions between "freedom" and "tyranny." The young people of the 1960s generation, however, were skeptical both of American goodness and of U.S. efficacy in the world.

Second, not only were these youngsters intellectually at odds with many of their elders, they were also people who wouldn't take "no" for an answer if they felt an injustice had been done in the tenure process. Time after time, therefore, 1960s-generation sociologists were denied promotions by tenured colleagues who did not understand or like their new "marxist" or "radical" or "feminist" teaching and research. And time after time, aggrieved 1960s-generation sociologists filed complaints or lawsuits to get these tenure denials reversed. Sometimes they succeeded after several years of bitter disputes, usually leaving university administrators more convinced than ever that sociology was an "unscientific" and hopelessly divided discipline.

I have put the foregoing in the past tense, because in most colleges and universities this phase ended by the early 1980s, as the 1960s-generation sociologists who were going to get tenure—in one way or another—got it and began to settle into their departmental and university establishments. Meanwhile, the reinvigorating effects of their scholarly productivity have been incorporated into the discipline's journals and reading lists, especially on the macroscopic and critical sides of the discipline. What are those effects? Overall, I see three very important ones.

First, 1960s-generation macrosociologists have rejected the preoccupation of social scientists in the 1950s with consensual and systemic models of social order, in favor of enduring concerns about understanding sources of domination by some classes or elites or groups over others. Furthermore, 1960s-generation people are fascinated by conflict, including the possibilities for protests against domination to lead to better social arrangements. It is not incidental that 1960s-generation sociologists, along with a few older ones whose work resonated well with the experiences of the 1960s, have led the way in reorienting much of sociological theorizing and research from the study of prestige and mobility to the study of class relations, from the study of political attitudes to the study of the state, and from the study of irrational deviance to the study of resourceful collective action.

Second, 1960s-generation macrosociologists have discarded the progressive-developmentalist and U.S.-centered view of the world characteristic of "modernization theory." They have replaced this, not with any one new view, but with debates about "the capitalist world system," with research on the diverse class and state structures of various Third World areas, and with a sense of the varied political and cultural trajectories of nations caught up in world economic and geopolitical transitions that transcend the control of any one country, including the United States. The sense in which all of these new views are part of the post-Vietnam era should be obvious.

Third, and perhaps least obvious, it seems to me that 1960s-generation sociologists of all sorts, not just macroscopically oriented ones, have—finally—brought a new tolerance for diversity into the departmental and professional settings of our discipline. Partly this has happened because we ourselves had to be "tolerated" as we grew up; as we have become tenured and reached middle age, we have become less determined to criticize the shortcomings of our elders! In addition, 1960s-generation sociologists (and so far those who have followed us into the discipline) are more comfortable with theoretical, methodological, and political differences of opinion than were sociologists who experienced career success in the 1950s.

We 1960s-generation people do not yearn for one grand sociological theory such as Parsonsian structure-functionalism; nor do we imagine that sociology can be a pure, cumulative, technically grounded science. Some of us are Marxists and leftists, and all of us know that such folks are valuable to the discipline. All of us have been socialized at a time when the proper research methodologies of sociology broadened from interviews and statistics to include various historical and interpretive methods. And most of us enjoy close intellectual ties to age-peers in one or another different discipline, thus causing us to be less defensive about sociology's boundaries than sociologists were in the 1950s.

Sociology as a discipline, in sum, has survived the raucous advent of a generation of ex-student-protesters. As a result, sociology has much more vivid and interesting things to say about the United States and the world. Frequently, to be sure, these things are critical of established authorities and ways of life, which means that the discipline remains less than favored in a period of conservative national politics. Still it really doesn't matter that the critical and macroscopic parts of sociology have not played well in Washington, D.C. For these are the discipline's long-term resources, the grounds from which it generates new research ideas for the future, ideas that can sometimes capture the imagination of broader audiences. And if I am right that the discipline is also becoming more internally tolerant as a result of the incorporation of the 1960s generation, then it will be able to benefit from these long-term benefits, while still having plenty of room for more problem-oriented and technically sophisticated colleagues whose work might gain more favor in Washington.

AN UPWARDLY MOBILE MIDWESTERNER:
FROM MICHIGAN STATE TO HARVARD

So far I have spoken of the 1960s generation of American sociologists in collective terms. But what about my personal trajectory, my unique variation on the themes of this generation? After all, generations do not write books; and Perry Anderson could well have wondered, not how *someone* from the U.S. 1960s generation could write *States and Social Revolutions*, but how a person from a nonelite midwestern background, from "Moo U" rather than the Ivy League, could do it, or would ever want to.

Major books in macroscopic sociology have been produced over the last ten years by 1960s-generation people who come from eastern, upper-middle-class backgrounds, especially Jewish upper-middle-class backgrounds, and who have received undergraduate degrees from Ivy League universities. Interestingly, these have mostly been books about American society and its history, and not comparative works like *States and Social Revolutions*. Probably a book like my first one, about other people's countries and events in the past, takes less self-confidence than a "big" and critical book about one's own nation.

In any event, I am certain that if I had accepted one of the offers of admission that I—as a midwestern high school valedictorian and Merit Scholar—received from the Ivy League colleges, I would never have ended up doing macroscopic sociology of any kind. Upward social mobility for a young person not already from a cosmopolitan professional or upper-class background needs to come in measured steps if it is to produce growing self-confidence rather than a sense of being limited and not first rate. In the United States, fortunately, the higher education system is competitive and open enough to allow a step-by-step climb like mine.

Michigan State University was a wonderful place for a bright Midwesterner to be an undergraduate in the late 1960s. The university is huge, and therefore reasonably cosmopolitan. Moreover, at that time, with the auto industry and the state's finances booming, MSU was "on the make" in everything from football to academic excellence. In the latter field, as in the former, MSU had a national recruitment campaign and used special scholarships to attract bright students from all over the country. Once students arrived at MSU, they found that an elite Honors College within the overall mass university catered to those defined as "the academic elite." Even as a Michigan native at a public state university, therefore, I could attend special, small classes with very smart—and often very radical—peers from all parts of the United States. I could have the feeling of being fully part of the political and cultural ferment of the decade, yet still get on with my academic studies in a way essential to someone not from a privileged background. As protesters and organizers, many of my friends took much greater risks than I did. As always, I was hitting the books.

The MSU Sociology Department had marvelous teachers—especially James McKee and John and Ruth Useem—who gave undergraduates a sense that macroscopic and critical sociology could be at once exciting and solidly based in empirical knowledge about America and the rest of the world. In general, MSU sociology had many engaging and critically minded professors, but they were not so "trendy" as to be spending their time on European theories rather than on the study of actual social patterns, and I benefited from their groundedness. (I did not hear about Louis Althusser until I got to Harvard, which was fortunate!) What is more, flexible MSU rules about majors for honors students allowed me to range freely in the social sciences and literature, and not remain confined to undergraduate lecture courses. I took many courses in anthropology, political science, and French literature. I took one graduate seminar that introduced me to the work of Barrington Moore, Jr., and gave me the idea that I could go to Harvard and study with him. And I took an intensive history course that surveyed all of the American past at a very high level of mastery. These experiences planted the seeds that have since grown into the major projects I have pursued as a mature sociologist.

Equally important, at MSU everything was manageable for me, even as it was plenty challenging. I gained a sense of being "special" and "on top" of a large university world. If I had gone as a Midwesterner to the Ivy League, I could not have gained that feeling and the self-confidence it breeds. Nor, for that matter, would I probably have been able to win the fellowships from the Danforth Foundation and the National Science Foundation that gave me the indispensable material means to do continuous graduate study.

Next, it was important to my development into a macroscopic comparative-historical sociologist that I went from MSU to Harvard, and studied there in the early 1970s, rather than earlier or later. The hegemony of Parsonsian structure-functionalism had faded by the time I arrived at Harvard, leaving a legacy of respect for macroscopic sociology without the confining embrace of an abstract paradigm. Of greater practical importance, I got to Harvard just after the biggest radical protests, so I was not tempted to do things that would get me suspended (as others were, just a year or two ahead of me). And Barrington Moore's seminars were there for me to join.

Moreover, the Harvard Sociology Department was in an excellent period back then. Graduate classes included 15 to 25 students per year, hardworking, ambitious, and very intelligent students from all over the world. This was a period when broad-minded sociology was highly esteemed in the larger society, and also inside Harvard, to the degree that any sociology has ever been esteemed there. We Harvard graduate students of the 1970s got attention from distinguished teachers, and even more attention from one another. The ones considered the best among us were encouraged to do ambitious dissertations, well beyond what any professionally sensible graduate training program would encourage in its Ph.D. students.

Thus, when I wrote a 100-page paper comparing the French, Russian, and Chinese Revolutions, and used the comparison to criticize and reorient sociological theory in this area, Daniel Bell declared that I had the beginnings of a thesis there. Given that it was nonprofessional Harvard, self-styled as the center of the intellectual world, I believed him, and so was foolhardy enough to undertake a dissertation on a huge topic I really cared about, rather than doing a limited exercise. My studies with Ezra Vogel on China and with Barrington Moore on Europe had convinced me that I understood new things about revolutions in modern world history. What is more, a comparative-historical study was a "dispassionate" and scholarly way for me to get at themes about power, the state, and social change that were on my mind in this era of protest over U.S. involvement in the Vietnamese revolution.

In sum, along with the climate of the 1960s, a scholarly but not very professional Harvard graduate education, coming on top of an MSU honors undergraduate education, gave me the chutzpah to undertake the virtually impossible. Many painful months later (after I had been teaching for a year as a prospective assistant professor at Harvard) my ambitious Ph.D. dissertation was approved. I had the basis for what would become, after a couple of years of further work and revisions, a major book in comparative-historical sociology, the kind of book that usually is written only by a grand old man at the end of a long career that started with more circumscribed research—or else by an Oxford-educated British leftist not worried about a professional career at all!

NEW POSSIBILITIES FOR WOMEN, NEW PROBLEMS FOR EVERYONE— AND ANOTHER SOURCE OF REVITALIZATION FOR SOCIOLOGY

I have presented matters to this point as if being a woman made little difference in my life, as if the identity as a 1960s-generation Midwesterner who went to Harvard was more important. This reflects the way I thought about things most of the time as an undergraduate and graduate student. In turn, my experiences through my student years facilitated my sense of self as a high-achieving student with all possibilities before her, regardless of what might have typically happened to other young females.

I am the older daughter in a two-daughter family. In school, I was always "the brain" rather than a popular beauty, and I drowned my sorrows about this in books. Then, when I got to college, I found I could have books and good friends at the same time, and I flourished. I married very early, as an undergraduate, but this step felt like a liberation from parental supervision rather than an acceptance of new constraints. Bill Skocpol and I had fallen in love while working together as student volunteers on a civil rights education project in Mississippi, and our relationship was always premised on the idea that we would proceed together to graduate training and careers as university teachers. I have little doubt that this excellent marriage to an egalitarian man of the 1960s, a marriage now over two decades in duration, has always been a major factor in my career achievements as well as my long-term personal happiness.

For about a year after getting married in 1967 as a junior, I did experience the shock of certain teachers suddenly redefining me as someone without an independent future. I had been planning to graduate one year early along with Bill, but I had to back off, because it took months to convince certain professors that as a married woman I should still be seriously recommended for fellowships and for the best graduate departments. Bill and I talked openly with our teachers about the incipient discrimination I was facing, and upon reflection everyone changed their outlooks. I took very valuable courses that extra year, and I was recommended for—and won—the national fellowships I needed to get on with it. Moreover, Bill and I were able to proceed to graduate school at exactly the same time, and afterward we would always face major career hurdles and transitions at about the same time. In contrast to the more typical situation where the woman follows after a more advanced male career, this situation has reinforced our egalitarian attitudes toward one another and given each of us equal leverage in the decisions about our life and work.

Once I arrived at Harvard for graduate study, my gender identity simply receded. Because my class entered during the Vietnam draft, when men could not get deferrals for graduate study, the class, a large one, was half women. A clique of women emerged as the leadership cadre in my graduate cohort. The women's movement was getting off the ground in those years, and I attended a consciousness-raising group. But we women and men in the Harvard graduate program seemed already to have achieved an egalitarian situation. The senior faculty, of course, were another matter, yet at first it only seemed necessary to "raise their consciousness" through a combination of mild protests and suggestions of "qualified" women for them to hire. At that time, in the early 1970s, the federal government was demanding that Harvard and other universities draw up affirmative action guidelines, and many professors and administrators were genuinely eager to recruit women at the assistant professor level.

After a couple of frustrating years in which, somehow, women got pushed aside in favor of male protégés of senior faculty, the Harvard Sociology Department was finally ready to take the plunge—just as I was completing my Ph.D. and getting some national notice for my work. In the space of two years, three women assistant professors were suddenly hired, to make up half of a junior faculty that had previously had no women except off-line lecturers. I was one of the women hired. Ironically, I probably felt like the "safest" candidate to most of my professors, for I was their own product, a known quantity. Anyway, the two and then three of us women were happy to be together, and we had excellent collegial relations with our junior male counterparts. Again, just as it had seemed while I was a graduate student, the issue of "femaleness" became irrelevant. Harvard Sociology had decided to incorporate women, we all felt, and before too long senior women would be hired or promoted strictly according to their merits. It was all going to happen naturally, without any great fuss, as long as we kept making good suggestions of "qualified women." Across the nation, such women were emerging in large numbers at all levels of the discipline of sociology, so surely Harvard would soon find suitable senior women.

Well, it didn't turn out that way, as anyone who hasn't been asleep in recent years surely knows! During 1980 to 1981, after two increasingly tense years as the only remaining woman on the Harvard Sociology faculty, I became one of the uppitiest of all uppity generation sociologists. After I had, in my own view and the view of many others around the country, "earned" tenure at Harvard, I was denied it with no explanation that I found credible, other than what I felt were reactions against me as an ambitious woman. I filed a protest, the first internal grievance ever pursued at Harvard about tenure and about gender discrimination. No doubt, the same overweening self-confidence, partly Harvard-bred, that helped me to conceive and write *States and Social Revolutions* encouraged me to protest (albeit after much anguish and with well-founded fears about the consequences). Certainly, too, the general esteem in which protest against perceived injustice is held by my generation gave me the courage to sustain what turned out to be a many-year game of "chicken" with the leaders of the most arrogant university in the Western world.

I did not expect to "win" my original 1980-1981 grievance, but ultimately I did, achieving the right to have my case decided on its scholarly merits by Harvard's President Derek Bok. Then I had to keep asking over many years for a "final" decision from President Bok. Yet these were years during which I flourished happily and productively as a tenured faculty member at the University of Chicago, where I learned the skills of leading a research group and building a collegial center, things I could not easily have learned at Harvard. The only drawback to remaining forever at Chicago, America's greatest scholarly university, was that my husband and I had to live and work in two places. Finally, in late 1984, I was offered the Harvard tenured professorship that I am convinced would have been mine in 1981 if I had been "Theodore" rather than "Theda." Because I wanted to improve my chances to stop commuting and live year-round with my husband, I accepted the Harvard offer and returned there in the fall of 1986. I was not welcomed and am not yet allowed to function normally as a senior member of the faculty at Harvard. I greatly miss the collegiality of the University of Chicago. But my husband and I are able to live and work together in Boston, and I must simply endure the hostilities until they abate.

This, however, is all I am going to say about the events between Harvard and myself. If you want to know the rest, you must read the wonderfully juicy memoirs I will write in about 25 years! For now, let me conclude with some more general reflections about changing women's roles and the reverberations in sociological scholarship.

Although many women of the 1960s generation—as well as many older women whose lives were transformed midstream by the women's movement—became self-conscious feminists much earlier than I did, I suspect that my trajectory reverberates with general experiences in one important respect. In the heady days of the late 1960s and early 1970s, many of us imagined that changes in women's roles at workplaces and within families might come all at once. No doubt there would be much travail for a bit, but then we could all settle down to a new normality. Many of us younger women expected that, of course, we and our successors would henceforth be able to "have it all": meritocratic careers (with no problems about getting the promotions we earned); enduring love-relationships; and children. For many middle-class career women, however—including the significant proportions of us now in the ranks as professional sociologists—the last decade has been a prolonged lesson in how difficult it is—impossible, really—to "have it all." (Or if one does succeed, as the character in the Lily Tomlin play exclaims: "If I'd known this is what it would be like to have it all, I might have been willing to settle for less"!—Wagner, 1985, p. 184.) The last decade has also been a time of multiple challenges and frustrations for the men—changing and unchanged alike—who have been dealing with us changing women. (Arlie Russell Hochschild gave a talk at the University of Chicago titled "Changing Women and Unchanged Men.")

By now, almost everyone is confused and worried about where these gender-role changes are going to come out, both in their own lives, and for American society as a whole. Women are in all levels of the work force to stay. But ambitious women are still not accepted at the top and, no matter what their achievements, they still have to endure the worst personal insults and struggle without end against virtually insuperable obstacles to their having real power. Many American families, meanwhile, do not feel as if they are working correctly, either as loving partnerships or as ways to sustain children. Some of the frustrations over all of this are taken out in bitter disputes between men and women, especially over domestic relations, and over issues of sexual harassment or women's career advancement. Yet many of the frustrations are also being taken out by women on each other. The sad fact is that, within given work places, professions, and communities, as well as within the society as a whole, subgroups of women who have chosen—or been pushed by circumstances into—contrasting relationships to men, children, and work morally condemn one another in ways ranging from gossip to political movements over abortion.

As was the case with the student-centered ferment of the 1960s, the upheavals subsequently highlighted by the women's movement and propelled by underlying longer-term changes in gender relations are proving to be a source of intellectual revitalization for the discipline of sociology. The various points I made in the previous paragraph came not only from my experiences and those of others I know personally. They also come from the outpouring of marvelous sociological studies recently published on women's situations and changing gender relations in American society. They come from what I have learned through the scholarship of leading sociologists such as Alice Rossi, Kristin Luker, Kathleen Gerson, Carole Joffe, Rosabeth Kanter, Barbara Laslett, Arlie Hochschild, Ruth Sidel, Lenore Weitzman, Jane Mansbridge, Beth Hess, and Myra Feree, and quite a few others. When things get tough in society, we sociologists get going—one might say! Lately, sociologists (mostly women) who study gender issues have especially gotten going. They are producing excellent scholarship on matters that will not be subsumed by the newly fashionable economistic "rational choice" theories favored by many male academics. For this sociological scholarship uses methods ranging from statistics, to history, to intensive interviews, to participant observation, to tell us about the intractable dilemmas and trade-offs that men and women face today in American society. These are matters of personal concern to all of us, and matters of almost obsessive concern to the society as a whole. For many years to come, therefore, sociology will gain enormously from those who can write vividly, macroscopically, and with some critical edge about changing gender relations and their reverberations in families, workplaces, and the nation's politics.

Yet what, finally, does all of this have to do with Theda Skocpol? It is all well and good for her to read books by women fellow sociologists about matters of gender, but we all know that she has never done such research herself. She has written about states, wars, and revolutions, all decidedly "male" phenomena, and she has not even highlighted the gender dimensions of the phenomena she has studied.

Fair enough. The central theme of my sociological scholarship has always been "the state." I have done comparative-historical studies of various kinds of large-scale social change—especially revolutions and the rise of modern welfare states—in order to explore ways in which states as organizations and as institutional arrangements independently affect political conflicts and their outcomes (see, e.g., Skocpol, 1979, 1984; Evans, Rueschemeyer, and Skocpol, 1985). These have been my variations on the central themes of 1960s-generation scholarship, my way of dealing with issues of domination and conflict. And I have never wanted to write about "women's issues" unless they seemed directly relevant to my primary research concerns.

In recent years, however, I have been coming to see that women's movements and gender relations are, in fact, central to the formation of modern welfare states and, in particular, critical to the early stages of modern social policies in the twentieth-century United States. Perhaps not surprising, my time at the University of Chicago has coincided with research on the temporal and geographic variations within the United States, even as I have retained a cross-national purview (see Amenta et al., 1987). This intensive look at America's past has finally led me to gender issues. While many "women's studies" scholars in sociology, political science, and social history are beginning self-conscious attempts to write about gender relations in relation to societywide political and economic processes, I have been discovering from another direction the many ways in which "bringing the state back in" also means bringing gender identities and relationships to a central place. The new insights I have gained in the process have given me more intellectual excitement than anything since discovering the core ideas of my first book.

For example, fundamental things about the entire history of public social provision in the United States fell together for me for the first time when I realized what a difference it had made that women alone—rather than women plus working-class men as in most other nations—were excluded from the first 100 years of American mass electoral democracy. In response, American women shaped many public policies as they mobilized outside of regular political channels. From the 1880s to the 1920s, European bureaucrats, politicians, and workers were originating "paternalist" welfare states. But the origins of modern American social provision are much more distinctively "maternalist," both because American women were uniquely mobilized, and because American men had no bureaucratic state through which to shape and therefore control early welfare measures. Since the Progressive era, women's efforts and gender relations have continued to shape basic aspects of U.S. social policies, right down to the current debates about the "feminization of poverty," about "the divorce revolution," and about the "right to life" versus the "right to choose" an abortion.

My next major book is a macroscopic reflection on American history over the last 100 years, tracing the development of U.S. social policies from Civil War pensions, through the Progressive Era and the New Deal, through to the present-day debates over the future of social security and welfare. I am still a sociologist from the 1960s who likes to think very big and critically, and my recent years in the Midwest, as well as my roots there, ensured that I would in due course turn that proclivity to the understanding of our own nation. Yet the evolution of this current project also reflects the extent to which I have become, as an adult woman, increasingly feminist in my thinking—and not only at the personal level. For the analysis of gender relations figures centrally in this project, along with analyses of state formation and the politics of race and class.

C. Wright Mills once pointed out that it is the job of good sociology to reveal the public issues inherent in troubles personally felt. Along with many others over the last ten years, I have personally felt the gender dimensions of life with special intensity. I hope that as a macroscopic historical student of politics, a child of the American 1960s, I can join the many others in our discipline who are already drawing on the travails of changing gender relations to enrich the sociological imagination. We should be able to do it for many years to come.

References

Amenta, Edwin, Elisabeth Clemens, Jefren Olsen, Sunita Parikh, and Theda Skocpol. 1987. "The Political Origins of Unemployment Insurance in Five American States." *Studies in American Political Development* 2:137-182.

Anderson, Perry. 1974a. *Passages from Antiquity to Feudalism*. London: New Left Books.
———. 1974b. *Lineages of the Absolutist State*. London: New Left Books.
Evans, Peter, Dietrich Rueschemeyer, and Theda Skocpol, eds. 1985. *Bringing the State Back In*. Cambridge: Cambridge University Press.
Skocpol, Theda. 1979. *States and Social Revolutions: A Comparative Analysis of France, Russia, and China*. Cambridge: Cambridge University Press.
———. 1984. "Why Not Equal Protection? Explaining the Politics of Public Social Spending in Britain, 1900-1911, and the United States, 1880s-1920." *American Sociological Review* 49:726-750.
Wagner, Jane. 1985. *In Search for Signs of Intelligent Life in the Universe*. New York: Harper & Row.

Epilogue

11

Commentary on
Sociological Lives

Charles Vert Willie

ANY COMMENTARY ON this set of glimpses into eight sociological lives should, at the least, contain a few observations on the nature of auto-biographies and the influence of those powerful enough to write them. Because these topics are covered in the Introduction to this book, with one exception, I shall not comment on either of them. Rather, I propose to identify some of the sociological themes that crosscut the eight fascinating essays. First, I shall call attention to the variety of routes taken by these influentials in becoming sociologists. Then I shall, in effect, ask some questions: about their views on ethics and moralities, on stability and change, on the problems of conceptualization and level of abstraction, and finally on their images of the scope of sociology.

The one exception that runs through these various questions and that may infringe—but ever so slightly—on the introductory essays by Robert Merton and Matilda Riley, concerns the idea of power. And here, in the spirit of this volume, I shall draw on some of my own ideas and experiences with that pervasive and relevant concept.

ON BECOMING A SOCIOLOGIST

Judging from the testimony of these eight scholars, they became sociologists by a variety of routes. The discipline of sociology was not the one they were inclined to enter as first choice.

Physics was Tad Blalock's first major. He switched to mathematics. Then in graduate school he changed from mathematics to sociology "almost sight unseen," he said, because he did not want to spend his life being "quite so pure" in pursuit of an understanding of pure mathematics. Moreover, he considered such pursuits "something of an escape from reality."

Bernice Neugarten received an undergraduate degree in English and French literatures and a master's in educational psychology. Because she was too young to find a job as a high school teacher, she accepted the offer of an assistantship from her professor to enter the Human Development (then called Child Development) doctoral program at the University of Chicago. Thus Neugarten claims her entry into sociology was accidental. She was neither pushed from another field nor pulled toward this one.

Alice Rossi wanted to be a writer and poet. She was an English major but changed to sociology during her undergraduate career after experiencing an enthusiastic and challenging sociology teacher who was sufficiently secure to introduce some of his courses with poems. When her poetry-reading professor moved on to Freud, Veblen, and Weber, Rossi was so excited that she changed her major to sociology before the semester ended.

Lewis Coser was initially interested in literature. He studied comparative literature and how the literature of different nations was associated with their varying social structures. He switched to sociology because of the narrow perspective of his professor who thought that such an inquiry was a study in sociology and not comparative literature. Coser was more interested in the study than in its classification and switched to sociology so that he could fulfill his intellectual interest without horrifying a professor.

Rosabeth Moss Kanter, a very private person, does not tell us when she decided to become a sociologist, but she does tell us why. Kanter was interested in the frontiers of social organization, "in the possibility of creating frameworks for social life that would satisfy utopian longings." (She joined a kibbutz in Israel.)

William Wilson got caught up in the civil rights revolution that was in full swing when he was in graduate school. By the time that he accepted his first full-time academic job, in 1965, Wilson had decided that race and ethnic relations would be his field of specialization. There are utopian longings in Wilson's orientation too; he wanted to challenge "liberal orthodoxy," advance a "social democratic public policy agenda," and get the public's attention for the purpose of improving life-chances of the "truly disadvantaged."

Theda Skocpol did have an undergraduate major in sociology but her interests were hardly traditional. She continued in graduate school, where she could study macroscopic and critical sociology. She studied sociology to gain an understanding of conflict and protest.

William Sewell finished courses required of premedical majors yet he came into sociology as an undergraduate. Long before completing his work for the baccalaureate degree, his interest in becoming a physician had waned.

Immediately after graduating from college, Sewell enrolled in graduate school to study how science could be brought to bear on social phenomenon. Early on, he was committed to the development of quantitative sociology.

In thinking about this variety of sociological lives, I now try to identify some of the crosscutting themes that they variously share. They are all distinguished sociologists, and in my reflective account they will largely speak for themselves, although I know full well that they may often disagree with my categorizations.

SOCIAL ORGANIZATION ISSUES:
MORALITY AND ETHICS

Blalock, Kanter, Skocpol, and Coser may be classified as ethical moralists who want a better world and hope sociology can help them achieve this goal. Blalock was pushed from the disciplines of his first choice because physicists either refused to take responsibility for the destructive outcomes of science or they more or less avoided the reality of social problems. Kanter was pulled to sociology as an instrument "to reshape [reality] to include the best of human aspiration," and Skocpol was attracted to the discipline "as a way to continue and intellectualize critical stances toward society" that could "lead to better social arrangements." Whether pushed from other disciplines or pulled to sociology, these outstanding scholars experienced "the call" for moral and ethical reasons.

While Coser should also be classified as an ethical moralist, he claims that his "moral partisanship" is walled off from his "pure sociological analysis." Nevertheless, he acknowledges that his writings have been inspired and motivated by his life experiences—such as those in the concentration camp, in revolutionary Europe, and in the turmoil of war. Moreover, he sees sociological theories as "tools for the elucidation of empirical problems." He is uncomfortable with sociological theorizing that is biased in a "conservative direction."

Rossi, who has used her sociology to understand age and gender variables, adopted this focus, in part, as a creative outlet because she was provoked. She was cheated out of a study in which she was passionately invested. After the experience of discrimination by one of her research employers, Rossi shifted her intellectual and political action concerns. The pain from that experience, she said, was the stimulus for venturing into the sociological study of gender and eventually her writings on gender equality. Thus Rossi was pulled toward an area of specialization in sociology that promised insight into ways of overcoming the social problem of discrimination.

Kanter also mentions discrimination as motivating a sense of urgency in the direction that her work took. She tells us, "It was very difficult for me to accept the legitimacy of the organizational and interpersonal barriers placed in the path of advancement for women." Indeed it was a source of great personal irritation for her to hear the failure of women to do as well as men in the public realm blamed on the psychology of the victim rather than the victimizers. Due largely to the inappropriateness of these conventional explanations, Kanter translated part of her interest in social organization "to an investigation of the barriers that inhibit women."

It is significant that Rossi and Kanter view their sociological studies of age and gender variables and of organizational designs as ways of overcoming discrimination, as well as making contributions to the discipline.

In like manner, the sociological study of race relations, one of Blalock's fields of specialization, also is concerned with the social problem of discrimination. He traces this interest, in part, to post-World War II experiences in the Far East and his gradual awareness that science ought to be concerned about ethnocentrism, as revealed by the prejudices of American sailors who delighted in nightly fights with Chinese whom they insultingly called "Gooks" despite the fact that they had been our allies during the war. Eventually Blalock developed a sense of guilt about the absence of contact with blacks other than domestic servants in Hartford where he grew up. Similarly Coser was concerned about the contemptuous way servants were treated in his family of orientation in Germany.

William Wilson emphasizes that an understanding of discrimination was the goal that drew him to the sociology of racial and ethnic relations. But he was concerned not so much with discrimination against him as he was with the "widening gap between the haves and the have-nots among blacks." Wilson wanted to understand the "deteriorating conditions of the black underclass."

Guilt, outrage, concern, and understanding about the social problem of discrimination were among the reactions that pulled or pushed these sociologists into their areas of specialization in the discipline.

Skocpol reports that she has personally experienced gender discrimination from one of her university employers. While she believes improving gender relations "to be a source of intellectual revitalization for the discipline of sociology," her sociological research has been not about matters of gender but about "state, wars, and revolutions." Wilson also wanted to understand the role of "the state . . . in the emerging controversy over affirmative action." He found the changing social structure of blacks in America a subject of "intellectual curiosity" and decided to make it his field of concentration.

Neugarten reported no gender discrimination in her work but she has been concerned about age discrimination. She has contested age discrimination actions as a citizen in the university and in the community. Her sociological research has largely focused on issues of age discrimination.

Sewell found discrimination against social science in the various universities where he was employed. As one of the "young Turks," he joined with others to force a change. His efforts on behalf of financial support for social science, including sociology, extended beyond the university to the federal government. Sewell's research interests, however, have not focused on the sociology of support for social science. His efforts on behalf of social science have been implemented largely in his role as policymaker in the university and federal government and in voluntary national associations concerned with research.

Skocpol, Rossi, and Kanter demonstrate that sociologists may make dissimilar professional responses to similar circumstances of gender discrimination.

Why have I classified some sociologists as ethical moralists (Willie, 1981, pp. 147-148)? Ethical action, it seems to me, involves making a proper estimation of others' needs and then acting on the basis of such information to fulfill those needs in ways that are fair to all group or association participants. Moral behavior, in contrast, has to do with what is right or wrong in terms of the standards or values of groups or associations with which one identifies and to which one pledges allegiance. Morality and ethics are linked in that it would be unfair to require ethical behavior to fulfill the self-interests of others that are immoral, that violate one's own interests or the interests of the groups with which one identifies. Likewise, it would be unfair to require moral behavior— the fulfillment of one's own interests—that is unethical because it violates the interests of others. The puzzlement over such a social question is this: How may individuals and groups fulfill their own interests without violating the interests of others? Societal failures to solve this puzzlement, particularly with reference to age, gender, race, and the state, have intrigued and challenged sociologists over the years, as testimonies of these scholars have revealed.

If the life experiences in social structures of this panel of sociologists are representative of others, then it is beyond happenstance that the national association that is a companion to the American Sociological Association is called the Society for the Study of Social Problems. Concern with social problems has been an abiding and stimulating force in the careers of many sociologists.

ON STABILITY AND CHANGE

These sociologists have discussed their professional lives and changing social structures using a number of different perspectives. Kanter embraces Peter Drucker's characterization of this period as the *age of discontinuity*. Such a period, she believes, has been a boon to a sociology that searches for unintended consequences. Coser, who has written extensively about *social conflict*, classifies himself as a "heretic in the functionalist school." He cannot fully accept sociological theory biased in favor of equilibrium and harmonious adjustment.

Rossi speaks of her own experience as manifesting *age-status discordance* resulting in "off time" in family and career developments. Neugarten's career has been affected by *discontinuity*, by "off-time" and "out-time" events. She was ahead of her age cohort as a teenager in college, received her Ph.D. degree "on time," but spent eight years "out," raising two children, and therefore was tenured a bit later than usual. Both Rossi and Neugarten talk about the positive as well as the negative aspect of "out time" or "off time." Sewell is pleased to have participated in *transforming* a relatively small traditional teaching department of sociology into a large research enterprise, in the *struggle to improve* the prestige of the social sciences, including sociology, and in the *struggle to change* the institutional structure of research at the national level.

Skocpol states that sociology must be concerned with *"reform* of existing social arrangements" and with "long-term *social change"* (emphasis added), and she credits the sociologists of the 1960s generation with fostering big thoughts and critical thoughts on such matters. William Wilson, a sociologist of the 1960s, also is interested in the *"changing social structure* for blacks in America" and the *"changing social environments* in [the city's] variegated ethnic neighborhoods." With almost a fixation on discontinuity, discordance, conflict, transformation, reform, and how to do things differently, sociologists, one may conclude, are almost obsessed with social change. Neugarten and Sewell, who were not attracted to sociology as an instrument of reform, are professionally interested in social change; but they also focus on continuities.

Professionally, some of the panel members describe themselves as marginal people betwixt and between. Both Blalock and Rossi felt that they were marginal: Blalock because of where he came from and his increasing "tolerance for ambiguity" in the intense disputes about theory and research, and qualitative and quantitative research methods; and Rossi because of where she is going, her fresh perspective, and her less inhibited feelings about striking out and exploring new areas of knowledge. Coser describes his situation as one of "dual allegiances to divergent sociological traditions."

While Kanter does not self-classify her professional role, she affirms that we should never accept reality but should continually try to reshape it. Her orientation probably is shared by others and may explain why "so many sociologists appear more comfortable," according to Kanter, "with the role of critic or gadfly." Neugarten, who is not so much concerned with social reform, has become increasingly interested in social policy and believes that there is a role for social scientists. Whether or not one is a gadfly, she believes that "common sense is not so common" and that "it is important to document one version of common sense over another."

Skocpol, of the 1960s generation of scholars, said her cohort learned that "protest and rebellion could make a difference," and gave itself the task of doing just that—of reorienting and renewing sociology from the study of prestige and mobility to the study of class relations, from the study of political attitudes to the study of the state, from the study of individual deviance to the study of collective action. Wilson, who calls himself a "democratic socialist," regrets that, as his thinking about the field of race relations in America began to change, in his earlier writing he had "paid so little attention to the role of class."

The "1960s generation" of scholars, as we have seen, was marginal; however, they are not unlike the other cohorts of scholars represented on this panel. Most sociologists, it would seem, think of themselves as marginal and in pursuit of change. The orientations of these sociologists bring into sharp focus one of the contemporary problems of the discipline—how to reconcile the concern for social change with a deeper understanding of social stability.

As is well known, it is appropriate to conceptualize social organization as both *homeostatic* and *homeokinetic*. Physiologist Walter Canon discussed the tendency of systems to maintain a steady state, an equilibrium that corrects for imbalance. But microbiologist Rene Dubos described living systems also as having a steady rate of change, overcoming the tendency toward inertia. Homeokinesis is a concept not so much in opposition to homeostasis as it is complementary to it. Social systems have the tendency both to stabilize and to change. Stability without change may be harmful as is change without stability (Willie, 1975, pp. 45-46). The two complement each other. Neugarten acknowledges this principle in her studies that embrace an understanding of both social change and social control.

It seems to me that the moral and ethical issues that confront sociologists are how to stabilize and retain in social organization that which helps, and how to change and rid social organization of that which harms. Formulating the issues this way, sociology is committed to neither change nor stability. It is committed to understanding change and stability for the purpose of helping and not harming people, both of which, of course, are situational.

Blalock introduces his discussion with this idea: "Our behaviors and thoughts are a joint function of situation factors and our own interpretive processes." He is so convinced of the validity of this statement that he calls it a social science truism. I believe that he is correct. And because of this belief, I think it inappropriate for a situationist to call for more coordinated research that "moves beyond small-scale, exploratory research in many fields," one of Blalock's recommendations. He is on target in stating the need for "more ambitious and carefully coordinated longitudinal research . . . to enable us to get a better grasp of temporal sequences and lag periods." This is precisely what William Sewell and his colleagues have done in the Wisconsin Longitudinal Survey. Blalock, however, misses the mark in urging a winding down of "exploratory research in many fields" in sociology.

By favoring coordination and consolidation, Wilson lines up with Blalock and is also against diversity. He urges that specific studies of race relations should, when possible, be linked to a "comprehensive theoretical framework." Such a practice, he believes, will move "beyond race-specific policies" by "emphasizing programs to which the more advantaged groups of all races can positively relate." Wilson's call for coordination is not unlike that of Blalock's. Both overlook a principle emphasized by Matilda White Riley, that study of a specific variable often can clarify our general knowledge, "raise new research questions, demand new methodological approaches, and even enhance the integrative power of our discipline" (Riley, 1987, p. 1). Several decades ago, Georg Simmel, in an essay titled "The Problem of Sociology," reminded us that society emerges out of specific kinds of interactions, that human knowledge originates in practical needs, that every science grows by virtue of a decomposition of the totality into specific qualities and functions, and finally that "one would condemn science to sterility if before assuming new tasks one made a completely formulated methodology the condition for taking the first step" (Simmel, 1908).

I prefer Skocpol's assessment that there is "a new tolerance for diversity" within the discipline that embraces "theoretical, methodological, and political differences of opinion." She states that sociology must endure the tensions that have run through the enterprise since its origins "despite the practical difficulties of holding them together in shared professional arrangements." The tension between large-scale coordinated research and small-scale exploratory research, for example, should remain and not be resolved in favor of either. As we so often have been reminded by Peter Rossi of the traditional wisdom—in the house of sociology there are many mansions. Sewell, who believes that the quantitative scientific revolution in sociology will continue to dominate American sociology for many years to come also hopes that there will always be funding for innovative studies on a smaller scale and that there will be a place in the discipline for scholars who pursue such studies.

In the social system, quantity gives rise to quality, especially quantity that is diversified. Metaphorically, one should let a hundred flowers bloom, another way of saying that many different research projects are of value. As stated by social ethicist Harvey Cox (1969, p. 57), "innovation . . . requires a *variety* of experiments going on." Ezra Vogel reports that the "Japanese do not hesitate to overlap and duplicate their efforts to gather relevant information." When an issue becomes salient, he said, Japan assigns competing research projects to several institutes. According to Vogel, the Japanese believe that this increases the chance of reaching a wise decision (Vogel, 1979, p. 52). The quantity of information gathered is the means by which that society reaches its quality decisions. Rather than limit sociological research, which continues as a young discipline (so young that it is not even the first choice of some of its practitioners), I say let hundreds of flowers bloom, let thousands of flowers bloom, for their petals will mark the many different routes to valid sociological knowledge.

Rossi's review of research on gender, age, and family indicates the benefits to a discipline when it facilitates many different studies of an issue. Specifically, Rossi argues that family sociological research that had a "married adult bias" could not explain why postparent couples were so happy. Their happiness contradicted the "empty nest" hypothesis that explained why postparent married couples might be sad. Rossi said it required "a new generation of family researchers" with an "antinatalist ambiance" to discover the rejuvenation of sexual intimacy in postparent couples and other benefits of family life that emerge after the stress of everyday parenting had ended. A new generation of researchers would not have been free to make this discovery if they had been effectively coordinated by the older generation. Such coordination risks carry over the bias of the past into the present and future.

Sewell and his colleagues have found value in disaggregating their composite socioeconomic status index to estimate the individual role of each of the components. Wilson criticized his earlier research for not disaggregating the race variable and for "treat[ing] blacks as a monolithic socioeconomic group." Sociological research in general will probably benefit from the presence of disaggregated small-scale, exploratory research, as well as from the ambitious and carefully coordinated large-scale studies mentioned by Blalock, and from studies that identify population-specific needs and how they may be fulfilled, as well as from macro-structural studies that link problems associated with particular groups to "broader issues of societal organization" and "comprehensive theoretical formulations" as advocated by Wilson.

CONCEPTUALIZATION:
THE PERSISTING PROBLEM

Most of the scholars represented in this volume agree that conceptualization is a major and persisting problem in sociology. Blalock states that conceptual models in a science are largely unappreciated by sociologists. They understand that theoretical arguments necessarily rest on assumptions, he said, but ignore the importance of making explicitly stated assumptions. Moreover, according to Blalock, sociologists need models that can handle "large numbers of complexities"; structural-equation modeling may be of assistance in this regard. Many of the other earlier attempts at modeling Blalock reacted to negatively as "too simplistic."

Drawing on the work of Peter Blau and Otis Dudley Duncan (1967), Sewell and his associates developed "a linear causal model" that has been helpful in explaining the relationship between socioeconomic origin and several social and psychological variables. He states that some of the analyses made by the

Wisconsin Longitudinal Study would have been impossible without the development of mathematical statistical models for the analysis of survey data.

Kanter calls our age one of discontinuity, but she cannot muster an explanatory model for it and its institutions other than a reliance on Hegelian dialectics. The components of her dialectical model for societies and individuals are hope, the period of utopian possibilities; cynicism, the period of opposition and estrangement when the ability of institutions to actually deliver on what they promised is tested and often found wanting; and finally tentative integration or the merger of hope and cynicism, a process that involves the acceptance of institutions as they are, including their imperfections. While Kanter believes the dialectical model is of some value, she recognizes its limitations: that it may be too simplistic to explain successive iterations or simultaneous occurrences, and circular development as opposed to stage development; and that it does not take into account how power is implemented and the harmful potential of repressive or totalitarian behavior in utopian experiments. Though not using the language of the dialectic model, Skocpol discusses conceptual models of the sociologists of the 1960s generation and how these differ from other conceptualizations of social relations. She said the 1960s generation rejected consensual and systemic models of social order in favor of models that facilitate an understanding of the sources of class and group domination. She further argued that models for understanding conflict are particularly fascinating to sociologists of the 1960s generation, who tend to pursue both a macroscopic and a critical analysis.

Rossi is blunt. She states that sociology is in a "conceptual muddle," particularly with reference to research on age and gender. Apparently, the conceptual models offered by Kanter and Skocpol are not sufficient to deal with the issues with which Rossi is concerned. The muddle exists, she believes, because we persist in using, for example, sex as a biological variable without comprehending its other dimensions. She found Robert Merton's "levels analysis" scheme to be of value. According to Rossi, this analytical scheme places sociological variables in a broader context that embraces cultural-historical, psychological, and biological levels.[1] Outstanding scholarship embraces all levels. She concludes that "age and gender are major variables in almost all sociological specialities, hence our paradigms cannot be adequate without building into them cultural meaning, psychological traits, and physiological attributes and processes."

1. Talcott Parsons also developed a levels-of-analysis scheme (Parsons, 1949, pp. 8-12, 25-28, 46-51, 251-274). Caroline Hodges Persell has found such a scheme of great value in understanding, for example, the relationship between education and inequality (Persell, 1977, p. 5). Obviously such a scheme contributes to a fuller understanding of gender.

Our concepts identify and describe the sociological facts that we measure and link together in theoretical schemes. Conrad Taueber, when he accepted the American Sociological Association award in 1986 for a distinguished career in sociological practice, said that if our concepts are faulty, our sophisticated methods of measurement will be of very limited benefit. Thus it is important for sociologists to make concept clarification a continuous task. Neugarten believes that, in her field of study, "new conceptual approaches" rather than "theoretical advances" are the most dramatic prospects for the future.

RAISING THE
LEVEL OF ABSTRACTION

Rossi's insistence on placing sociological variables in a broader context ties in with Blalock's counsel to "raise the level of abstraction." He believes that we should make more substantial efforts to do this in our empirical research. Blalock believes this will come to pass when we formulate research problems in such a way that they have relevance at least to theories of the middle range discussed by Merton (Merton, 1949). By raising the level of abstraction, we are better able to see similarities in the different and differences in the similar. Skocpol has worked to this end in her comparative studies that use a macroscopic perspective.

Kanter, who has tried to raise the level of abstraction in her work, said that she had difficulty getting the argument accepted by "certain establishment scholars" that many of the values of the youth movement of the 1960s have been adopted in the workplace by older adults in the 1970s and 1980s. Specifically, she mentions the value of participation that new corporations like Apple Computer have emphasized.

Many older adults have had difficulty realizing and accepting the fact that they are similar in some ways to younger people, that they have patterned some of their own behavior to the models introduced by the young whose pioneering behavior they previously had rejected. Similarly, other dominant people of power both in the discipline and in the society at large attempt to deny or render invisible new ideas, concepts, and patterns of interaction that have emerged from women, racial minorities, and other subdominant people of power. Customs and conventions initiated by subdominants may be borrowed and integrated into the mainstream, but their origins are forgotten or ignored. Subdominants are seldom credited as social innovators in the discipline of sociology. More comparative studies of disaggregated population groups might prevent such denials and oversights in the future.

By not attending to the social implications of our research, Neugarten asserts that "we students of society have sometimes missed out on some of the big social issues." One issue, of course, was the prediction and proper understanding of the civil rights movement, which Everett Hughes emphasized in his Presidential address to the American Sociological Association. Similarly, Neugarten insists on a "demographic imperative" created by the dramatic increase in life expectancy.

An abstract level with which I have been working has to do with power in social relationships. In all social situations, some people have more and others have less power. Those with more power I label dominants and those with less power I label subdominants. Because a social system cannot exist without dominants and subdominants, wise dominants are generous and tend to give more to subdominants than they are required to give as a way of encouraging subdominants to continue participating in the social system. Similarly, wise subdominants tend to be magnanimous and take less than they are entitled to receive as a way of encouraging dominants to continue participating in the social system. Participation by dominants and subdominants has check and balance functions. Because of these functions, there is no intrinsic value in being either dominant or subdominant. Both categories are essential in effectively functioning societies.

Generosity or magnanimity is a function of the status position of dominance or subdominance and not a characteristic or property of the individual. When women function as dominants, they are obligated to be generous; and when men function as subdominants, they may be magnanimous. Dominant and subdominant roles complement each other, regardless of the characteristics of the individuals who fill them. Thus generosity and magnanimity are not ascribed characteristics, for example, of any gender category.

By raising the level of abstraction to that of dominance and subdominance, we overcome the error of attributing the disadvantaged circumstances of blacks in the United States to their minority status, knowing that they too are disadvantaged in South Africa, where they are the majority. By raising the level of abstraction to that of dominance and subdominance, we overcome the error of attributing the advantaged circumstances of males in the United States to their stronger muscular structure compared to women, knowing that adolescents and young adults are disadvantaged despite their stronger muscular structure than most middle-aged men. By raising the level of abstraction to that of dominance and subdominance, we recognize similarities among blacks, women, and younger people in this society, despite their differences. Racial minorities referred to by Blalock, women mentioned by Rossi and Neugarten, younger people discussed by Kanter and Skocpol, and the underclass analyzed by Wilson are different in particular ways but all have in common in this society a socially imposed subdominant status in the power structure.

Finally, by raising the level of abstraction, we understand how whites, men, and middle-aged adults may act like blacks or other racial minorities, women, and younger people when they function as subdominants. By raising the level of abstraction, we overcome the error of particularity, go beyond the principle of difference to that of complementarity, recognizing (as stated earlier) similarities in different population groups and differences in similar population groups.

MULTIDISCIPLINARY APPROACH

The concept of complementarity leads to a final observation of a theme present in all essays of this panel. Blalock asserted that scholars who have had the greatest impact on his thinking have been those intrigued with general philosophical questions that crosscut disciplines. Rossi spoke of "the ambience of a small liberal arts college" and her faculty position there that was conducive to indulging her interests in a wider array of disciplines than just sociology and finding "kindred spirits" in these other fields. Sewell's work on the strategic bombing survey during World War II was his first experience in interdisciplinary research. He liked it and has continued throughout his career to work in other interdisciplinary groups such as those sponsored by the Social Science Research Council. Skocpol enjoys "close intellectual ties to age-peers in one or another different discipline" and states that this experience has caused her to be "less defensive about sociology's boundaries." Neugarten came into sociology by way of an interdisciplinary route, the Committee on Human Development at the University of Chicago. Wilson's aspiration for the future of sociology is that it become more interdisciplinary. Beyond having such an aspiration for the field, Coser personally has incorporated multiple perspectives in his work: "I supplement my purely sociological concerns with writings of a critical and moral-political nature." On the basis of these responses, one may conclude that the leading sociologists in the United States believe their field is and should continue to be inclusive.

The presentations of these sociologists have more than fulfilled the goals that Matilda White Riley had for the 1986 Annual Meeting of the American Sociological Association—"the emphasis on multiple independent levels of the society or group, and the emphasis on the multidimensionality of sociological concerns as they touch on related aspects of other disciplines" (Riley, 1987, p. 1).

References

Blau, Peter M. and Otis Dudley Duncan. 1967. *The American Occupational Structure*. New York: John Wiley.

Canon, Walter B. 1939. *The Wisdom of the Body*. New York: Norton.

Cox, Harvey. 1969. "Feasibility and Fantasy: Sources of Transcendence." In *Transcendence*, edited by Herbert Richardson and Donald Cutler. Boston: Beacon.

Dubos, Rene. 1972. *A God Within*. New York: Scribner.

Merton, Robert K. 1949. *Social Structure and Social Theory*. New York: Free Press.

Parsons, Talcott. 1949. *Essays in Sociological Theory, Pure and Applied*. New York: Free Press.

Persell, Caroline Hodges. 1977. *Education and Inequality*. New York: Free Press.

Riley, Matilda White. 1987. "On the Significance of Age in Sociology." *American Sociological Review* 52(February):1-14.

Sewell, William H. 1971. "Inequality of Opportunity for Higher Education." *American Sociological Review* 36(October):793-809.

Sewell, William H. and Robert M. Hauser. 1972. "Causes and Consequences of Higher Education: Models of the Status Attainment Process." *American Journal of Agricultural Economics* 54(December):850-861.

Simmel, Georg. 1908. *Georg Simmel 1858-1918*. Columbus: Ohio State University Press. (1959)

Vogel, Ezra F. 1979. *Japan as Number 1*. New York: Harper.

Willie, Charles V. 1975. *Oreo*. Wakefield, MA: Parameter Press.

Willie, Charles V. 1981. *The Ivory and Ebony Towers*. Lexington, MA: Lexington Books.

Index

Aberle, David, 124
Abortion, public attitudes toward, 47
Abstraction, raising the level of, 173-175
Academic career, shape of, gender and cohort differences in, 49-52
Academic controversy and intellectual growth, 79-90
Academic field, aging as, 93-94
Academic research, federal funding of, 50
Activity theory and old age, 102
Adams, Donald, 124
Adolescence: acting-out behavior, 59; disturbances, 58; limit testing, 58, 59; sexual behavior, 61; studies by Neugarten, 96
Adult development, gender differences in, 47
Adulthood, personality change in, 96
Age, 166
—advocacy organizations, 102-103
—of discontinuity, 167; societal and sociological inquiry in, 71-78; three phases of, 73-74
—future research on, 57
—Rossi on, 43
—sociology of, 36, 101; communication problems, 37; conceptual confusion, 38; current obstacles for, 37; emerging interests, 38-39; misdirected sociological influence and, 38; terminological confusion, 38
—Sorokin on, 36
—stratification, 38
—study of, sociology not ready for, 37
Age-status discordance, 167-168; social marginality with, 49
Aggressive responses: and androgenic hormones, 62
Aging, 36; as academic field, 93-94; Federal Council on, 97; interplay with structural changes, 11; maturational effects of, 56; no single pattern of, 102; processes, 36; society and, 91-106; successful, no single pattern for, 102; White House Conference on, 1981, 97-98
Alpert, Harry, 131
Althusser, Louis, 151
American history, Skocpol on, 158
Anderson, Perry, 145

Anomie and social structure, 54
Arensberg, Conrad, 124
Aron, Raymond, 66
Aspiration, Sewell's research on, 134-137
Asynchrony, 28
Atomic bomb and physicists, 116
Attainment, Sewell's research on, 134-137
Autobiographers: memory of, 18; observation of, errors in, 18
Autobiography: art and craft of, 17; sociological, 17-21

Baby boom, 147; generation, 73
Bain, Reed, 121
Bales, Freed, 31
Ballachey, Egerton, 124
Barton, Allen, 53
Becker, George, 70
Bell, Daniel, 72, 146, 152
Bendix, Reinhard, 18, 68
Benedict, Ruth, 54
Biographical illusions, 80
Biology, in gender differences, 61
Black population, deepening economic schism in, 82
Black protest movement, 80-82
Black sociologists, concern over *The Declining Significance of Race*, 79
Blalock, Hubert M., Jr., 30, 31-32, 34, 81
—becoming a sociologist, 109-110
—biography on, short, 7
—at Brown University, 109-110
—on careful conceptualization efforts, 114-115
—drafted, 107
—as ethical moralist, 165
—finding history boring, 107
—gaps, ambiguities, and disputes, 110-113
—learning: about ethnocentrism, 108; about reward system, 113-114; about war, 108
—marginality experience by, 110
—on multidisciplinary approach, 175
—on social phenomena not studies in depth, 114
—*Social Statistics*, 113
—*Sociological Theory and Research*, 32
—socialization to sociology by culture shock, 107-117

NOTES

NOTES

NOTES

NOTES

NOTES

NOTES

NOTES

The Headway Readers

President and Publisher
M. Blouke Carus

Executive Vice President
Paul Carus

Education Director
Carl Bereiter

General Manager
André W. Carus

Editorial Director
Dale E. Howard

**Coordinator of Editorial
Services**
Juanita A. Raman

Production Manager
LeRoy Ceresa

Art Director
Todd Sanders

Project Leader
Marilyn F. Cunningham

Permissions Editor
Diane M. Sikora

The Place Called Morning

The Headway Program
Level F

Editor
Marianne Carus

Reading and Language Arts Curriculum Development Center
Catherine E. Anderson, Director

Open Court   La Salle, Illinois

ACKNOWLEDGMENTS:

FOR PERMISSION to reprint copyrighted material, grateful acknowledgment is made to the following publishers and persons:

Crown Publishers, Inc., for "The Umbrella" from *A Treasury of Jewish Folklore* edited by Nathan Ausubel, copyright 1948 by Crown Publishers, Inc.

The Dial Press for an adaptation of *Mandy's Grandmother* by Liesel Moak Skorpen, copyrighted © 1975 by Liesel Moak Skorpen, as it appeared in *Cricket,* September 1975.

Doubleday Publishing Company for "A Voyage to the Moon" adapted from *A Voyage to the Moon* by Savinien Cyrano de Bergerac.

E. P. Dutton & Co., Inc., and A. B. P. International for Chapter II from *Winnie-The-Pooh* by A. A. Milne. Illustrated by E. H. Shepard, Copyright 1926, by E. P. Dutton & Co., Inc. Renewal 1954, by A. A. Milne. Reprinted by permission of the publishers.

Follett Publishing Company, a division of Follett Corporation, for "The Great Minu" abridged from *The Great Minu* as retold by Beth P. Wilson, copyright © 1974 by Beth P. Wilson.

Funk & Wagnalls Company for "Love Like Salt," reprinted from *The Soup Stone: The Magic of Familiar Things* by Maria Leach.

Grosset & Dunlap, Inc., for "The Lady with the Lamp" from *The Story of Florence Nightingale* by Margaret Leighton. Copyright 1952, copyright renewed © 1980 by Margaret Leighton.

Harper & Row, Publishers, for "Alexander and His Horse" from *History Stories of Our Lands* from the volume *Tales From Far and Near,* edited by Arthur Guy Terry; and for "Narcissa" from *Bronzeville Boys and Girls* by Gwendolyn Brooks. Copyright 1956 by Gwendolyn Brooks Blakely.

Harper & Row, Publishers, Inc., for "Boa Constrictor," from *Where the Sidewalk Ends* by Shel Silverstein, copyright © 1974 by Shel Silverstein.

Holt, Rinehart and Winston, Inc., for "Stopping by Woods on a Snowy Evening," from *You Come Too* by Robert Frost. Copyright 1923, by Holt, Rinehart and Winston, Inc. Copyright renewed 1951 by Robert Frost.

Scholastic Inc. for *The Dead Tree* by Alvin Tresselt, text copyright © 1972 by Alvin Tresselt.

Time-Life Picture Agency © Time Inc. for Margaret Bourke-White photographs on pages 177, 179, 180, and 181.

All possible care has been taken to trace ownership and obtain permission for each selection included. If any errors or omissions have occurred, they will be corrected in subsequent editions, provided they are brought to the publisher's attention.

Contents

Part One: Stories and Poems Everyone Likes

Part Two: Famous People

Part Three: Science and Nature

Part Four: For Readers Brave and Bold

Part Five: On Your Own

ILLUSTRATORS:
Enrico Arno (5, 13, 26), Melanie Arwin (100, 148-150), Joseph Cellini (94, 103, 109, 110, 162, 166), David Cunningham (133, 135), JoAnn Daley (117), Pat Doyle (35), Mike Eagle (81, 89-91), Paul Foley (120), Imero Gobatto (3, 32, 39, 41, 42, 154, 156, 159, 169), Lee Hill (6-9), Trina Schart Hyman (15, 17, 19, 21, 22, 48, 50, 54), Bill Jacobson (68, 113), Robin Jacques (45), Randy Jones (65, 136), Diane Magnuson (14), Dick Martin (84), Victor Mays (98, 124), Charles McBarron (77), Barbara McClintock (79), Vernon McKissack (186, 189, 191-195, 197), Barbara Pritzen (cover), E. H. Shepard (58, 61, 63, 64), Krystyna Stasiak (29, 31, 151), George Suyeoka (72), Lorna Tomei (119), Wally Tripp (70).

PHOTOGRAPHY:
Bettman Archives, Inc. (87), Margaret Bourke-White (177, 179, 180, 181, 183), Culver Pictures (130).

DESIGN:
John Grandits, James Buddenbaum.

Part One

Stories and Poems
Everyone Likes

The Lion in His Den

Aesop

In the forest many years ago there lived an old lion. This lion was so old that he could no longer run and catch little animals for his food. He knew that the only way to get enough to eat was to make the other animals come to him.

So he crawled into his den and made believe that he was sick. He groaned and groaned. The little animals would hear the groans. They felt sorry for the old lion, and they would go in the den to see if they could help him. Then the lion would snap them up for his food. In this way many animals lost their lives.

One day a fox was passing by the lion's den and he heard the lion groan. The fox did not go into the den, but he stood in the entrance and said, "What's the matter, my friend?"

"Oh, I am very sick," replied the lion. "I will not live very long now. Come into my den so that I can say good-bye to you."

When the fox heard these words, he replied, "Please pardon me, friend lion, but I do not think I will come in. I see many paw prints pointing into your den, but I don't see any pointing out."

QUESTIONS

1. What trick did the old lion use to get his food?
2. Did he catch many animals by this trick?
3. Why didn't he catch the fox with his trick?
4. What is the point of this fable?

THE DEER

Old Fable

One time a deer came up to the edge of a river to get a drink. He saw himself in the water, and he was very pleased to see how large and broad his antlers were. But then he saw his legs reflected in the water, and he said to himself, "How thin and ugly my legs are!"

Suddenly a lion jumped out of the bushes and ran after the deer. The deer started to run across the open field. He was nearly out of sight of the lion when his antlers became tangled in a tree branch. The lion almost caught him. But the deer got his antlers untangled just in time. After he had run a safe distance from the lion, he said to himself, "How stupid I am! I thought that my legs were thin and ugly, and yet they have saved me. I was glad that my antlers were big and broad, but because of them I almost lost my life!"

Across the ocean and far away, a poor African farmer prepared to journey to the big city of Accra, in Ghana. He walked around his small farm, taking note of the yams and corn growing in the garden. Then he fed his chickens and goats, latched his thatched-roof hut, and started down the narrow, dusty road.

All morning and all afternoon the farmer trudged down the road, stopping only at midday for a bite to eat and a short rest. At last he reached the farms on the outskirts of the city. There he noticed a great herd of cows. Who could own such a great herd, he wondered. Seeing a man with them, he asked, "To whom do these cows belong?" The man did not know the

THE GREAT MINU

Retold by
Beth P. Wilson

language of the farmer, who had traveled so
far, so he shrugged his shoulders and said,
"Minu," meaning "I do not understand."
The traveler thought Minu must be a person

and exclaimed, "Mr. Minu must be very rich!"

Entering the city, the traveler saw some large new buildings in the town square. He wondered who might own these buildings. But the man he asked could not understand his question, so he also answered, "Minu."

"Good heavens!" cried the traveler. "What a

rich fellow Mr. Minu must be to own all those cows and these large new buildings, too!"

Soon he came to a grand hotel surrounded by beautiful grounds and mahogany trees. A group of fashionably dressed African ladies came down the front steps of the hotel. The traveler stepped up to them and asked who might be the owner of such a grand hotel. The ladies smiled and said softly, "Minu." "How wealthy Mr. Minu is!" exclaimed the astonished traveler.

He wandered from one neighborhood to another and finally came to the harbor where he saw men loading bananas, cocoa beans, and mahogany onto a fine big ship. With the blue sky above, the foamy green ocean below, and the sailors rushing about on board ship, it was an impressive sight. The traveler inquired of a bystander, "To whom does this fine big ship belong?" "Minu," replied the puzzled man who couldn't understand a word of the question. The traveler gasped. "To the great Minu also? He is the richest man I ever heard of!"

Just as the traveler was setting out for home, he saw men carrying a coffin down the main street of Accra. A long procession of people, all dressed in black, followed the men. People on the sidelines shook their heads slowly. Sad faces looked up now and then. When the traveler asked one of the mourners the name of the dead person, he received the usual reply, "Minu."

"Mr. Minu is dead?" wailed the traveler. "Poor Mr. Minu! So he had to leave all his wealth—his great herd of cows, his large new buildings and grand hotel, and his fine big ship—and die just like a poor person. Well, well, in the future I'll be content with my little hut, on my little farm, in my little village."

The long, dusty road back didn't seem as long as it had before. When the farmer arrived home, he unlatched the door of his hut and looked around inside. Then he climbed into his own snug bed and dreamed of the good foo-foo he would eat the next day.

QUESTIONS

1. Who is Mr. Minu?
2. What did the farmer learn from his trip to Accra?
3. Find the city of Accra, and the country of Ghana, on a map of Africa.
4. If somebody asks you what "foo-foo" is, what is your answer?

My Shadow

Robert Louis Stevenson

I have a little shadow that goes in and out
  with me,
And what can be the use of him is more than
  I can see.
He is very, very like me from the heels up to
  the head;
And I see him jump before me, when I jump
  into my bed.

The funniest thing about him is the way he
  likes to grow—
Not at all like proper children, which is always
  very slow;
For he sometimes shoots up taller like an
  India-rubber ball,
And he sometimes gets so little that there's
  none of him at all.

One morning, very early, before the sun was up,
I rose and found the shining dew on every
  buttercup;
But my lazy little shadow, like an arrant sleepy-
  head,
Had stayed at home behind me and was fast
  asleep in bed.

The Boy Who Cried Wolf

Aesop

Once there was a shepherd boy who took care of his sheep on a lonely hillside in the country. He had no one to talk to, and he was very lonely. One day the boy thought of a way to find some excitement. He ran down the hill and shouted, "A wolf! A wolf!"

The farmers who were working in the nearby fields heard the shouts. They thought that a wolf was eating up the boy's sheep, so they stopped their work and ran to help him.

But when they got to the hillside, the boy laughed and said, "I was only playing a joke." The farmers did not think that the boy's joke was very funny, and they were angry with him.

A few days later the boy did the same thing again. "A wolf! A wolf!" he cried. Again the farmers dropped their tools and ran to help him. But when they saw that the boy had fooled them a second time, they were very angry.

Then on the very next day a wolf did come.

"Wolf! Wolf!" cried the boy. But this time the farmers did not believe him. They went on with their work, and the wolf ate up many of the boy's sheep. The boy was very sad, but he had learned a hard lesson: If you are a liar, no one will believe you, even when you are telling the truth.

QUESTIONS

1. Why did the boy cry "Wolf" the first time?
2. Why didn't the farmers think the boy's joke was a good one?
3. Why didn't the farmers come the last time the boy cried "Wolf"?
4. What lesson did the boy learn?

MANDY'S GRANDMOTHER

Liesel Moak Skorpen

Mandy's grandmother was coming for a visit. Mandy's mother was cleaning the house. Even the closets and the drawers.

"Will my grandmother peek in our drawers?" Mandy asked.

"Of course she won't," her mother said. "I'm just in a mood for cleaning drawers. You wouldn't understand."

WORDS TO WATCH

entertain	fumbling	scurvy
precious	formula	casting on

"I don't," said Mandy.

"How will I manage?" said Mandy's mother later. "What with the baby teething and all?"

Mandy was helping her mother make the guest room bed. "That's a bad baby," she said. "All he does is cry."

"It isn't his fault," replied her mother. "You cried too when you were cutting teeth."

"I doubt it," Mandy said.

Mandy's mother smoothed the spread. She was in a hurry. She was always in a hurry now. "You'll have to help me entertain your grandmother," she said.

"I don't know how to entertain," said Mandy.

Mandy had a picture book with a grandmother in the story. That grandmother took the little girl for walks and to the zoo. She had plenty of time to hold the girl on her lap. Mandy looked at all the pictures carefully, especially the ones with the girl on the grandmother's lap. Sometimes she liked to sit on somebody's lap. Sometimes she didn't, but sometimes she really did.

On the day that her grandmother was coming, Mandy had to pick up her room, take a bath, and change her clothes. "Do I have to take down my fort?" Mandy asked.

"Oh, I suppose not," said Mandy's mother, hurrying.

Mandy put on clean jeans and her favorite sweater and her floppy old, sloppy old hat.

"Couldn't you put on a dress?" asked her mother, holding the crying baby.

"My grandmother will like my hat," said Mandy.

Mandy's grandmother came in a furry coat and a funny

hat with flowers. She had two interesting boxes in her arms. Mandy's mother brought the baby down. He was crying again. "Isn't he precious?" her grandmother said. "And who is this little fellow?" she said to Mandy.

"Why, that's our Mandy," said Mandy's mother quickly.

"Oh, dear," said Mandy's grandmother, fumbling with her packages and trying to smile.

In the baby's box were a soft toy horse, some silly-looking suits, and a fat yellow puff that Mandy liked and wanted for herself. "I can hardly wait to see Mandy in hers," Mandy's grandmother said.

"Maybe it's cowboy clothes," Mandy thought, tearing the ribbons off her box. The dress was yellow. So was the hat. The purse had a little lace hanky inside. "Thank you," said Mandy softly but politely. She tried to smile, but it came out crooked.

The next day it rained. Mandy looked out of the kitchen window. "Yuck," she said. Mandy had the same breakfast every day: a peanut butter and banana sandwich, and tea with honey but mostly milk. "That's not a healthy breakfast," Mandy's grandmother said. "I'll fix you some oatmeal and some eggs."

"Yuck," said Mandy. "I hate eggs."

Mandy's mother was making formula. The baby was crying in his chair. Formula stuff was spread all over the kitchen. "Do me a favor, honey," said her mother. "Go in and talk to Grandmother a while." Mandy went in the living room.

"Show me your dolls," said Grandmother brightly. "How your mother used to love her dolls."

"I don't have dolls," said Mandy. "I don't like them. I have a frog, though," she said hopefully. "His name is Wart." She lifted her hat, and there was Wart sleeping on her

head. Mandy's grandmother screamed, her mother came
running, and Mandy was sent outside.

"What I know about grandmothers," Mandy said to Wart,
"is that they're very boring." Mandy was mad at everyone,
even Wart. Wart hopped on the pirate ship she had built for
them. "Not today, you scurvy toad," said Mandy.

Mandy's grandmother took a walk by herself down to the
mailboxes and back. She walked in the wet garden, frowning
at the weeds. She sat on the porch writing letters.

The next day Mandy's grandmother didn't come down.

"Take her up this cup of tea," Mandy's mother said.

"She doesn't like me," Mandy said.

"Of course she does," said her mother sternly. "She loves you."

Mandy knocked.

"Come in," said Mandy's grandmother softly. She was sitting by the window. Her eyes were closed.

Mandy set the tea on the table. She was thinking about the picture book, because she was feeling like sitting on somebody's lap. "I brought some tea," she said.

"Thank you, dear," Mandy's grandmother said, "but I'm not feeling very well."

Mandy saw that her grandmother had been crying. It made her stomach feel queer to think about grown-ups crying. "Tea's very good for you," she said. "It warms you up."

Mandy's grandmother closed her eyes again. She didn't take the tea.

"I think you must be very sad," said Mandy.

"I am a little sad," Mandy's grandmother said. "I was thinking about when your mother was little like you. I used to like to hold her on my lap."

"I like laps, too," said Mandy quickly. "I like laps a lot."

Mandy's grandmother held out her arms, and there was Mandy on her lap. Mandy's arms were around her neck, and Mandy's face was pressed against her shoulder.

"Are you crying?" Mandy's grandmother asked.

"No," said Mandy, crying.

They had their breakfast together by the window. Mandy had a sandwich. Mandy's grandmother had scrambled eggs and toast. They both had tea with honey and mostly milk.

After breakfast Mandy showed her grandmother the barn.
She showed her the chickens and the goats and introduced
her to Strawberry Pony.

"Does he bite?" her grandmother asked.

"Not if he likes you," Mandy said.

Mandy's grandmother fed him carrot sticks, and Strawberry licked her hand.

"Would you like to ride him?" Mandy asked. "Sometimes
he bucks a little bit."

Mandy's grandmother thought that she wouldn't. "Hip
Hip Harray!" she shouted as Mandy and Strawberry came
galloping down the lane.

21

Mandy showed her the pirate ship. Her grandmother took a good look at Wart, but she didn't want to hold him.

"Friends don't have to share everything," she said.

Mandy thought that over and decided she was right. She showed her grandmother the secret blackberry bush. "Promise you'll never tell," she said. Her grandmother crossed her heart. They packed a lunch and ate it on the picnic rock halfway up the hill.

The next day was wet again. They talked a lot. Mandy's grandmother told her stories of when her mother was a little girl. About how she made cookies once with salt instead of

sugar, and how she used to write poems for Grandfather's birthday, and how she fell in her uncle's pond with her Easter bonnet on.

They made popcorn by the fire. Mandy's grandmother taught her how to knit. Mandy taught her grandmother how to whistle. They had hamburgers and blackberry buckle for supper. In the evening they sat by the fire and whistled and knit.

It was time for Mandy's grandmother to go.

"Will you start casting on for me?" said Mandy. They were sitting in the airport.

"How many stitches?" her grandmother asked.

"I think about a thousand," Mandy said.

"What are we making?" her grandmother asked.

"A blanket for Strawberry," Mandy said.

Mandy's grandmother didn't laugh. She sat in her furry coat and flowered hat, waiting for the airplane to come, smiling and casting on stitches: one, two, three, four.

"I love you, Mandy," her grandmother said.

"I love you, too," said Mandy, because she did.

QUESTIONS

1. Why was Mandy's mother always in a hurry just before Mandy's grandmother visited them?
2. What did Mandy's grandmother bring for Mandy and the baby?
3. Did Mandy like her new dress and hat?
4. Name some of Mandy's favorite things.
5. Tell how Mandy and her grandmother became friends.

The Boy Who Flew Too Close to the Sun

Greek Myth

Many years ago on an island called Crete there lived a wicked king named Minos. Minos had a wife, and his wife was the mother of a strange monster called the *Minotaur*. The Minotaur was half man and half bull.

Minos did not want anybody to know that his wife was the mother of a monster, so he thought of a way to keep it a secret.

He asked a clever man named Daedalus to build a labyrinth. A labyrinth is a place with so many passageways that it is very hard to find one's way out. Daedalus lived in the country of Greece, and he had a little son named Icarus. Together Daedalus and Icarus sailed to Crete to build a labyrinth to keep the Minotaur in. Daedalus built such a good labyrinth that when the Minotaur was placed inside it, he could not find a way out no matter how hard he tried.

King Minos was happy again, and he thanked Daedalus for helping him. But when Daedalus wanted to sail with his son back to Greece, Minos would not let him go. He wanted Daedalus to stay and invent many new things that would help

---

WORDS TO WATCH

Crete	Daedalus	Greece
Minos	labyrinth	Icarus
Minotaur	passageway	prison

24

him. Minos had Daedalus and Icarus put in prison so that they would have to stay in Crete.

Daedalus and Icarus wanted very much to go home, but they did not know how to escape from prison. Then Daedalus thought of a way to get back home. He said to his little son, "Minos has blocked all my ways of escape by land and by water. But he does not rule the air. We will escape by air. I will make some wings for us, and we will fly back home."

So Daedalus set to work to make wings. He took some feathers and placed them so that the largest feathers were at one end and the smallest feathers at the other. Then he stuck the feathers together with wax so that they looked just like the wings of a large bird. He tied one pair of these wings to his son's arms, and he tied the other pair to his own arms.

Before they tried out their wings, Daedalus said to his son, "Icarus, you must not fly too high nor too low. If you fly too low, you may fall into the sea and drown. If you fly too high, the sun will melt the wax that holds your wings together. The best thing to do is to follow me."

Then they began flapping their wings. At once they rose into the air. Soon they were high above their prison, and they started flying toward home. Icarus was having a good time flying through the air. He forgot all about what his father had told him. Instead of following his father, he flew higher and higher in the sky. He wanted to see how high his wings could carry him. Soon the heat of the sun began to melt the wax. Feathers began to fall off, and his wings began to come apart. Down and down he fell. Icarus kept flapping, but he was flapping only his bare arms. He fell into the sea.

Icarus cried out to his father, but the waves closed over him and his cries were heard no more. Daedalus saw some feathers from his little son's wings floating on the water. He flew down and took up the boy's body and flew with it to the shore. There he buried it. Daedalus was heartbroken that he had lost his son and wished that he had never thought of inventing wings.

QUESTIONS

1. Why did Daedalus and his son go to Crete?
2. Why did Minos put Daedalus and Icarus in prison?
3. How did Daedalus make the wings?
4. What did Daedalus tell Icarus not to do?
5. What happened when Icarus did not obey his father?
6. Do you feel more sorry for Daedalus or for Icarus? Why?
7. Write or tell about what you would do if you could fly.
8. Find out more about Crete.

Compound Words

I. Read and Spell

ladybug	outdoors	pancake
sidewalk	airplane	highway
something	penknife	newspaper
skyscraper	grandmother	railroad
tablespoon	strawberry	horseshoe
daylight	afternoon	cannot
bulldog	fireworks	crossroad
turtledove	sunflower	springtime
pigskin	notebook	sheepdog

II. Read and Answer
1. What words are in each of the compound words in Part I?
2. Make three compound words using these words:
   bill   foot   ship   board   ball
3. Think of some more compound words.

III. Write
Write five sentences, each one using a word in Part I.

Love Like Salt

Maria Leach

One day an old king returned from a journey and asked his three daughters if they were glad to see him.

"Your return is like the return of the sun," said the eldest.

"To see you again is like light to my eyes," said the second.

"To have you back is as good as salt," said the youngest.

"WHAT!" said the king to his youngest daughter. "That doesn't sound as though you love me very much."

"I love you as meat loves salt," said the little girl.

This made the king angry, and he scolded her. She was impudent, he said. But she would not change her words.

WORDS TO WATCH		
value	banish	guest
journey	tended	sipped
forgiven	shepherd	knelt
impudent	page	saltcellar

29

So he drove her away. The old king told everybody in his kingdom that he was banishing his youngest daughter because she was impudent and did not love him as much as she should.

The young princess ran out of the house in the night, but she did not know where to go. Suddenly she remembered a little house on the side of a hill where lived a kind old man who tended her father's sheep. He took her in gladly and gave her a bowl of warm milk and bread for her supper and let her lie down to sleep on a soft white sheepskin before the fire. She stayed with the old shepherd a long time after that and helped tend the sheep on the hills.

One day she heard that the king was giving a big feast at the castle. And she decided that she would go and help serve at the table. So she dressed herself in the clothes of a young page and went to the kitchen.

The cook was an old friend of hers who had loved the little princess ever since she was a tiny girl.

"Don't put any salt in anything," she begged the cook. And because the cook thought the old king had it coming to him, he didn't.

When the feast was served, the soup was without salt. The guests sipped at it politely and said nothing. But the king was angry and decided he would have to speak to the cook. When the meat was served, it was tasteless; every dish was without flavor.

So the king did send for the cook. But instead of the cook, a young page came and knelt before the king. "It was my order," said the page. "I thought you did not care for salt."

"And who are you?" said the king.

"I am the child who loves the king like salt," said the girl.

With that the king gave a shout and threw his arms around her. Now he knew the value of salt, and the little princess was forgiven. The servants brought in the saltcellars; the food was salted. The feast went on, and everybody was happy.

QUESTIONS

1. Why did the king think that his youngest daughter did not love him?
2. Where did the princess go after the king turned her out of her home?
3. What did the princess tell the cook to do? Why?
4. What finally made the king know that his daughter really did love him?
5. Do you think that the youngest daughter loved her father more than her sisters did?

The Owl and the Pussy Cat

Edward Lear

The Owl and the Pussycat went to sea
  In a beautiful pea-green boat.
They took some honey, and plenty of money
  Wrapped up in a five-pound note.
The Owl looked up to the stars above,
  And sang to a small guitar,
"Oh lovely Pussy, O Pussy, my love,
  What a beautiful Pussy you are,
    You are,
    You are!
  What a beautiful Pussy you are!"

Pussy said to the Owl, "You elegant fowl,
    How charmingly sweet you sing!
Oh! let us be married; too long we have tarried:
    But what shall we do for a ring?"
They sailed away, for a year and a day,
    To the land where the bong-tree grows,
And there in a wood a Piggy-wig stood,
    With a ring at the end of his nose,
        His nose,
        His nose,
    With a ring at the end of his nose.

"Dear Pig, are you willing to sell for one shilling
    Your ring?" Said the Piggy, "I will."
So they took it away, and were married next day
    By the turkey who lives on the hill.
They dined on mince and slices of quince,
    Which they ate with a runcible spoon;
And hand in hand, on the edge of the sand,
    They danced by the light of the moon,
        The moon,
        The moon,
    They danced by the light of the moon.

David and Goliath

The Bible

Many, many years ago in the land of Israel lived a boy named David. David was very brave and loved God with all his heart.

In those days the people of Israel were at war with the Philistines, who had invaded their country to plunder and steal. The Israelites could not chase the Philistines out of their country, nor could they win a single victory over them. They did not even dare to attack them because they were afraid of Goliath, who was a terrible giant—a man as tall as a tree. His body was covered with armor, and he wore a brass helmet. Every day Goliath walked over to the Israelites and mocked them.

"Come on now," he shouted, "why don't you send over one of your great heroes to fight with me? Are you afraid, you cowards? I am stronger than all of you put together!" And he roared with laughter and cursed the Israelites and also cursed God. Nobody dared to chase him away because everyone trembled with fear just to look at him.

WORDS TO WATCH

Israel	Israelite	mock
Philistine	coward	champion
Goliath	sling	victory
insult	plunder	brass
cursed	fled	swayed

34

David's brothers were soldiers in the Israelite army. One day David went to visit them. Just when he arrived, Goliath was shouting his insults again. David heard him mock the soldiers and curse God, and he became very angry. "Why do you let this giant frighten you?" he asked the soldiers. "Have you forgotten that God is on our side? If no one will fight against Goliath, I will fight him myself."

The soldiers of the Israelites tried to stop him. "Goliath is big and powerful," they said, "and you are only a young boy. You do not even know how to fight."

But these warnings did not stop David. He trusted in God. He remembered when he had guarded his father's sheep. Sometimes a bear or a lion would come out of the woods to steal a lamb. But David had killed each lion and bear, and he knew that God had helped him. He thought to himself, "I will kill Goliath just as I did the bear and the lion, for God will protect me."

When the time came for the fight, Goliath came dressed in his armor and brass helmet, and he carried a spear. At his side he wore a huge sword.

But David did not wear any armor, and instead of a spear and a sword, he had only a sling and five smooth stones.

When Goliath saw David coming without sword or armor, he laughed and shouted, "Whom do we have here? Look at the little boy who cannot even carry a sword! Do you think I am a dog so you can chase me away with your stick? Come on, I'll show you! I'll kill you so that the wild beasts can eat you!" Everybody who heard him speak started trembling with fear, all except David.

David replied, "You come to me with a sword and a spear, but I come to you because you mocked God, and God will give me the victory over you."

Then David put a stone in his sling, took aim, and before Goliath could throw his spear, the stone had hit the giant squarely on the forehead. For a moment Goliath swayed back and forth, and then he fell to the ground.

When the Philistines saw that their champion had been killed by a young boy, they fled in terror. David won a great victory for the people of Israel that day, and years later he became their king.

QUESTIONS

1. Why were the soldiers of Israel afraid to fight Goliath?
2. Why wasn't David afraid to fight Goliath?
3. What did David do when he was guarding his father's sheep to show that he was brave?
4. What did David and Goliath use to fight each other?
5. Why did the Philistines run away?
6. How did the Israelites reward David for his bravery?

Games Children Like

I. Read and Spell

Cards	Chess	Hide-and-Seek
Hopscotch	Tag	Tic-Tac-Toe
Checkers	Gossip	Riddles
Musical Chairs	Hangman	Categories
You Are Getting Hot	Spelling Bee	Tiddlywinks
Dreidel	Jump Rope	Charades
Earth, Fire, Water, and Air	Red Light/ Green Light	Snake Marbles
Piñata	Stickball	Simon Says
Red Rover	Four-Square	Jacks
Capture the Flag	Captain, May I?	

II. Find Out and Answer

1. How are these games played?
2. Which of these games have you played?
3. Which game do you like to play best?
4. Name some other kinds of games you like.

III. Write

1. Write a story about the game you like most.
2. Explain the rules of one of the games of Part I that you like to play.

Pinocchio

Carlo Collodi

Gepetto lived in a small room with no light except that which came through the doorway. The furniture in his room was very simple: an old chair, a bad bed, and a broken-down table. At the end of the room was a fireplace with a lighted fire, but the fire was painted. Beside the fire was a pot boiling merrily, but the pot was painted on too, and so was the steam that rose from the pot.

Gepetto lived all alone, and sometimes he was very lonely. One day he decided to carve a puppet out of wood so that he

WORDS TO WATCH		
Gepetto	earnestly	clog
fashion	smothered	bawl
puppet	numb	ungrateful
Pinocchio	cobblestone	Carlo Collodi

39

could have someone to talk to. He got out his tools and set to work to fashion a puppet.

"What name shall I give him?" he said to himself. "I think I will call him Pinocchio. It is a name that will bring him luck. I once knew a whole family by that name. There were Pinocchio the father, Pinocchia the mother, and Pinocchi the children, and all of them did well. The richest of them was a beggar."

After Gepetto found a name for his puppet, he set earnestly to work to make it. First he made the hair, then the forehead, and then the eyes.

The very moment he finished the eyes, he was amazed to see that they moved and that they were staring at him.

"Wicked wooden eyes, why do you stare at me?" he asked.

There was no answer.

Then he began to carve the nose, but no sooner was the nose finished than it began to grow. It grew and grew and grew until it seemed that it would never end. Poor Gepetto kept cutting it off; but the more he cut it off, the more the impudent nose grew.

As soon as the mouth was finished, it began to laugh at Gepetto and make fun of him.

"Stop laughing!" said Gepetto, who was becoming angry. But he might as well have been talking to a wall.

"Stop laughing, I say!" Gepetto roared.

The mouth stopped laughing, but then it stuck out its tongue as far as it would go. Gepetto pretended not to see and went on with his work. After the mouth, he made the chin, then the neck, then the shoulders, the stomach, the arms, and then the hands.

Just as he finished the hands, he felt his wig being snatched from his head. He looked up, and what did he see? He saw his yellow wig in the puppet's hand.

"Pinocchio, give me back my wig!" cried the old man. "Give it back at once."

But instead of giving it back, Pinocchio put it on his own head and almost smothered himself. When Gepetto saw how rude Pinocchio was, he became sadder than he had ever been in his life. He turned to Pinocchio and said to him: "You naughty rascal! You are not even finished yet, and already you have begun to make fun of your poor father. That is bad, my boy, *very bad*." And he wiped away a tear.

Everything was made now, except the legs and feet. The moment that Gepetto finished the feet, he felt a kick on the end of his nose.

"I deserve it!" he said to himself. "I should have thought of it sooner! Now it is too late!"

Gepetto then picked up the puppet and set him on the floor to teach him to walk. Pinocchio's legs were stiff and numb at

first, and he could not move. But Gepetto led him by the hand and showed him how to put one leg in front of the other.

Soon Pinocchio was able to walk by himself and to run around the room. Suddenly he darted through the door, out into the street, and was gone.

Poor Gepetto rushed out after him, but he could not catch him because Pinocchio was running like a scared rabbit. His wooden feet clattered on the cobblestones like the sound of twenty pairs of peasants' clogs.

"Stop him! Stop him!" shouted Gepetto, but the people who saw the puppet running down the street like a race horse were too astonished to do anything. Then they laughed until they could laugh no more.

At last a policeman appeared. He heard the clatter, and thinking that a young horse had got loose, he planted himself in the middle of the street with legs apart. He was determined to stop the runaway and prevent worse things from happening.

When Pinocchio saw the policeman blocking the street ahead of him, he tried to take the policeman by surprise and run underneath his legs. But he failed.

The policeman caught him easily by his long nose and handed him over to Gepetto. Gepetto wanted to punish the puppet by slapping his ears, but to his surprise he discovered that Pinocchio had no ears. In his hurry to make him, Gepetto had forgotten to give him ears.

He then took him by the back of the neck and led him towards his house, all the while saying in a threatening voice, "I will take care of you, young man, when we get home. You can be sure of that."

When Pinocchio heard these words, he threw himself on the ground and would not take another step. Meanwhile a crowd of idle people began to gather around them, talking about Pinocchio. Several of them said, "Poor puppet. No wonder he runs away from home. Who knows how hard that bad old Gepetto beats him!" And others added, "Gepetto seems like a good man, but he doesn't like children. If we leave that puppet in his hands, he may tear him to pieces!"

When the policeman heard all this talk, he turned Pinocchio loose and led Gepetto away to prison. The poor old man could not make the policeman believe what had really happened. All he could do was bawl like a calf.

As he was being led away to prison he cried out, "Ungrateful boy! And to think how hard I worked to make him a good puppet. But it serves me right! I should have thought of it sooner!"

What happens afterward, you will not believe. Do you want to learn how Pinocchio almost gets killed, how he is rescued by a good fairy, how his nose grows longer when he lies, how he turns into a donkey, how he gets swallowed by a terrible whale, and how he turns into a real boy at last? If you do, you can read the whole story in the book called *The Adventures of Pinocchio* by Carlo Collodi.

QUESTIONS

1. What happened when Gepetto made Pinocchio's eyes? What happened when he made his nose? His mouth? His hands? His feet?
2. When Gepetto was leading Pinocchio home, what did the people say?
3. Do you think the policeman made a mistake in setting Pinocchio free and putting Gepetto in jail? Why?

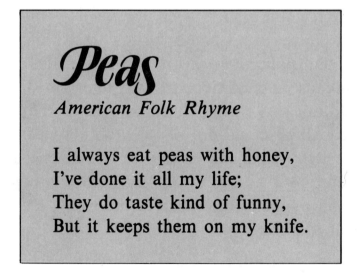

Peas

American Folk Rhyme

I always eat peas with honey,
I've done it all my life;
They do taste kind of funny,
But it keeps them on my knife.

Narcissa

Gwendolyn Brooks

Some of the girls are playing jacks.
Some are playing ball.
But small Narcissa is not playing
Anything at all.

Small Narcissa sits upon
A brick in her back yard
And looks at tiger-lilies,
And shakes her pigtails hard.

First she is an ancient queen
In pomp and purple veil.
Soon she is a singing wind.
And, next, a nightingale.

How fine to be Narcissa,
A-changing like all that!
While sitting still, as still, as still
As anyone ever sat!

Animal Names

I. Read and Spell

Animal	Male	Female	Baby
bear	he-bear	she-bear	cub
cow	bull	cow	calf
deer	buck	doe	fawn
elephant	bull	cow	calf
fox	dog	vixen	cub
whale	bull	cow	calf
lion	lion	lioness	cub
goose	gander	goose	gosling

II. Read and Answer

1. What are the babies of these animals called?

    cat dog horse pig swan sheep

2. What is the male of these animals called?

    cat duck pig sheep chicken horse

3. What is the female of these animals called?

    chicken tiger sheep horse pig

III. Write

1. Write a story about your favorite animal.
2. Write the funniest story you can remember about your pet or the pet of someone you know.

Snow White and the Seven Dwarfs

Brothers Grimm

Once upon a time a queen sat sewing in front of a window with an ebony frame. It was the middle of the winter, and flakes of snow were falling from the sky like feathers. While the queen was sewing and watching the snow, she pricked her finger with her needle, and three drops of blood fell onto the snow. The crimson color on the white snow looked so beautiful that the queen said to herself, "Oh, if only I had a child with skin as white as snow, with lips as red as blood, and with hair as black as the wood of this ebony frame!"

Some time later she gave birth to a little daughter with skin as white as snow, with lips as red as blood, and with hair as black as ebony. She named the child Snow White. But soon afterward the queen died.

After a year had gone by, the king took another wife. She was beautiful, but proud and haughty and jealous of anyone who seemed to be more beautiful. She had a magic mirror, and whenever she looked at herself in it, she said,

"Mirror, mirror, on the wall,
Who's the fairest one of all?"

WORDS TO WATCH		
envy	startled	falsehood
ebony	endure	rage
crimson	dwarf	mined
mourned	haughty	peasant

Then the mirror replied,

"Lady queen, so grand and tall,
You are the fairest of them all."

And she was satisfied, for she knew the mirror always told the truth.

As time passed, the little child named Snow White grew taller and more beautiful every day, until at last she was more beautiful than the queen herself. So once when the queen asked her mirror,

"Mirror, mirror, on the wall,
Who's the fairest one of all?"

it answered,

"Lady queen, you are tall and grand,
But Snow White is fairest in the land."

Then the queen was startled and turned green with envy. From that hour, she burned with secret envy whenever she saw Snow White.

Finally, she called a huntsman and said, "Take the child into the forest, for I will no longer endure her in my sight. Kill her, and bring back her heart as proof."

The huntsman obeyed and led the child away. But when he had drawn his hunting knife, Snow White began to cry.

The huntsman took pity on her because she looked so lovely and said, "Run away then, poor child!"

As he returned to the castle, the huntsman came upon a bear, which he killed. He then removed its heart and brought it back to the queen, who laughed wickedly when she saw it, believing it to be Snow White's.

The poor child was now all alone in the great dark forest, and she felt frightened as she looked around. She didn't know what to do, so she began to run. She ran over sharp stones and through thorn bushes. Wild animals passed close to her but did her no harm.

She ran as long as her feet could carry her, and when evening came, she saw a little house and went into it to rest.

Everything in the house was very small. There stood a little table, covered with a white tablecloth, on which were seven little plates. There were also seven little spoons, knives, forks, and seven little cups. Up against the walls stood seven little beds with sheets as white as snow.

Snow White was hungry and thirsty, so she ate a little of the vegetables and bread on each plate and drank a little from every cup, because she did not want to eat all of anyone's meal.

Then she grew sleepy, so she lay down in one of the beds, but she could not make herself comfortable, for each bed was either too long or too short. Luckily the seventh bed was just right—so she stayed there, said her prayers, and fell asleep.

When it had grown quite dark, the masters of the house, seven dwarfs who mined for iron among the mountains, came home. They lighted their seven candles, and as soon as there was a light in the kitchen, they saw that someone had been there.

The first said, "Who has been sitting on my chair?"

The second said, "Who has eaten off my plate?"

The third said, "Who has taken part of my bread?"

The fourth said, "Who has touched my vegetables?"

The fifth said, "Who has used my fork?"

The sixth said, "Who has cut with my knife?"

The seventh said, "Who has drunk out of my little cup?"

Then the first dwarf looked around and saw that there was a slight hollow in his bed, so he asked, "Who has been lying in my little bed?"

The others came running, and each called out, "Someone has been lying in my bed too."

But the seventh, when he looked in his bed, saw Snow White there, sound asleep. He called the others, who flocked around with cries of surprise. They fetched their seven candles and cast the light on Snow White. "What a lovely child!" they cried.

The seven dwarfs were so pleased that they would not wake her but let her sleep on in the little bed. The seventh dwarf slept with the others in turn, an hour with each, and so they spent the night.

When morning came, Snow White woke up and was frightened when she saw the seven dwarfs. But they were very friendly to her.

"What is your name?" they asked.

"Snow White," she answered.

"How did you find your way to our house?" the dwarfs asked.

Snow White told them how her stepmother had tried to kill her, how the huntsman had spared her life, and how she had run all day till at last she had found their little house.

Then the dwarfs said, "If you will keep house for us, you may stay here with us."

"Gladly," said Snow White. And so it was agreed.

When the good dwarfs left for the mine in the morning, they warned Snow White. "Beware of your wicked stepmother," they said. "She may soon find out that you are here. Don't let anyone into the house."

The queen, back at the castle, had no doubt that she was again the first and fairest woman in the world. She walked up to her mirror and asked,

"Mirror, mirror, on the wall,
Who's the fairest one of all?"

The mirror replied,

"Lady queen, so grand and tall,
Here, you are fairest of them all;
But over the hills, with the seven dwarfs old,
Lives Snow White, fairer a hundredfold."

The queen trembled with rage, for she knew that the mirror never told a falsehood. So Snow White was still alive!

"Snow White shall die," she cried, "if it costs my own life!"

Then she went to a secret and lonely room where no one ever disturbed her. For hours she stayed in there, making a poisoned apple. Ripe and rosy, it was indeed a beautiful sight to see, but it brought instant death to anyone who ate it.

When the apple was ready, the queen painted her face, disguised herself as a peasant woman, and traveled over the seven hills to where the seven dwarfs lived.

At the sound of the knock, Snow White put her head out of the window and said, "I cannot open the door to anybody. The seven dwarfs have forbidden me to do so."

"Very well," replied the peasant woman. "I only want to get rid of my apples. Here, I will give you one of them!"

"I dare not take it," said Snow White.

"Are you afraid of being poisoned?" said the old woman. "Look here, I will cut the apple in two, and you shall eat the rosy side, and I, the white."

Now the fruit was so cleverly made that only the rosy side

was poisoned. Snow White longed for the pretty apple, and when she saw the peasant woman eating it, she stretched out her hand and took the poisoned half. She had scarcely tasted it when she fell lifeless to the ground.

The queen laughed loudly and watched her for a moment; then she dashed away.

When she got home, she asked the mirror,

"Mirror, mirror, on the wall,
Who's the fairest of us all?"

The mirror at last replied,

"Lady queen, so grand and tall,
You are the fairest of them all."

When the dwarfs came home in the evening, they found Snow White lying on the ground without any sign of life. They lifted her up and washed her with water and wine, but nothing helped. They tried to waken her, but she did not breathe. She was dead.

They laid Snow White on a bed, sat around her, and wept for three days and three nights. Then they wanted to bury her, but since she looked so beautiful, they decided to place her in a glass case. They carried the case up to the mountain above, and one of them always stayed by it and guarded it. But there was little need to guard it, for even the birds and wild animals came and mourned for Snow White.

For many years Snow White lay unchanged in her glass case, looking as though she were asleep. Her skin was still white as snow, her lips red as blood, and her hair black as ebony.

At last the son of a king chanced to wander into the forest and come to the dwarfs' house for a night's shelter. He saw the case with the beautiful Snow White in it. Then he said to the dwarfs, "Let me have it. I will give you whatever you like for it."

But the dwarfs answered, "We would not part with it for all the gold in the world."

He said again, "Yet give it to me, for I cannot live without seeing Snow White, and though she is dead, I will prize and honor her as my beloved forevermore."

Then the good dwarfs took pity on him and gave him the glass case. The prince lifted it up, but as he did so, a tiny piece of the poisoned apple fell from Snow White's lips. Immediately she opened her eyes and sat up, alive once more. "Where am I?" she asked.

The prince answered joyfully, "With me," and he told her what had happened.

"I love you more dearly than anything else in the world," he said. "Come with me to my father's castle and be my wife." Snow White was well pleased when she heard these words. She went with the prince, and they were married amid much rejoicing.

The wicked stepmother was invited to the feast. She dressed herself in her richest clothes and stood in front of the mirror saying,

"Mirror, mirror, on the wall,
Who's the fairest one of all?"

The mirror answered,

"Lady queen, so grand and tall,
Here, you are fairest of them all;
But the young queen over the mountains old,
Is fairer than you a thousandfold."

The evil-hearted woman could scarcely believe her ears. But curiosity would not allow her to rest. She went to the wedding to see who that young queen could be, who was the most beautiful in all the world. When she came and found that it was Snow White alive again, she tore her hair and stamped away, never to be heard from again, and the handsome prince and Snow White lived happily ever after.

QUESTIONS

1. What did the huntsman do when the queen told him to take Snow White into the forest and kill her?
2. How did the queen learn that Snow White was still alive?
3. How did the queen make the poisoned apple?
4. How did Snow White come to life again after she ate the poisoned apple?
5. What happened to Snow White in the end?
6. What happened to the queen in the end?

Musical Instruments

I. Read and Spell

drum	viola	clarinet
piano	trombone	tuba
flute	accordion	saxophone
trumpet	organ	English horn
cello	piccolo	oboe
harp	guitar	bassoon
kettledrum	French horn	bass viol
bugle	violin	snare drum

II. Read and Answer

1. Which of these instruments are played with a bow?
2. Which of these instruments are played by blowing into them?
3. Which of these instruments are played by striking them?
4. Which of these instruments have keys?
5. Which of these instruments is the smallest?
6. Which is the largest?
7. Name some other musical instruments.
8. If you play an instrument, tell the class which one you play. If not, which one would you like to play?

III. Write

1. Write five sentences, each using a word in Part I.
2. Write a little story telling about the musical instrument you like best.

winnie-the-pooh

A. A. Milne

Edward Bear, known to his friends as Winnie-the-Pooh, or Pooh for short, was walking through the forest one day, humming proudly to himself. He had made up a little hum that very morning, as he was doing his Stoutness Exercises in front of the glass: *Tra-la-la, tra-la-la,* as he stretched up as high as he could go, and then *Tra-la-la, tra-la—oh, help!—la,* as he tried to reach his toes. After breakfast he had said it over and over to himself until he had learned it all by heart, and now he was humming it right through, properly. It went like this:

> *Tra-la-la, tra-la-la,*
> *Tra-la-la, tra-la-la,*
> *Rum-tum-tiddle-um-tum.*

> *Tiddle-iddle, tiddle-iddle,*
> *Tiddle-iddle, tiddle-iddle,*
> *Rum-tum-tum-tiddle-um.*

Well, he was humming this hum to himself and walking along gaily, wondering what everybody else was doing and

---

WORDS TO WATCH

stoutness	mug	convenient
properly	greedy	sigh
scuffling	larder	slenderer
Winnie-the-Pooh	towel-horse	relation

57

what it felt like, being somebody else, when suddenly he came to a sandy bank, and in the bank was a large hole.

"Aha!" said Pooh. (*Rum-tum-tiddle-um-tum.*) "If I know anything about anything, that hole means Rabbit," he said, "and Rabbit means Company," he said, "and Company means Food and Listening-to-Me-Humming and such like. *Rum-tum-tum-tiddle-um.*"

So he bent down, put his head into the hole, and called out:
"Is anybody at home?"

There was a sudden scuffling noise from inside the hole, and then silence.

"What I said was, 'Is anybody at home?'" called out Pooh very loudly.

"No!" said a voice; and then added, "You needn't shout so loud. I heard you quite well the first time."

"Bother!" said Pooh. "Isn't there anybody here at all?"

"Nobody."

Winnie-the-Pooh took his head out of the hole and thought for a little, and he thought to himself, "There must be somebody there, because somebody must have said 'Nobody.'" So he put his head back in the hole and said:

"Hallo, Rabbit, isn't that you?"

"No," said Rabbit, in a different sort of voice this time.

"But isn't that Rabbit's voice?"

"I don't think so," said Rabbit. "It isn't meant to be."

"Oh!" said Pooh.

He took his head out of the hole and had another think, and then he put it back, and said:

"Well, could you very kindly tell me where Rabbit is?"

"He has gone to see his friend Pooh Bear, who is a great friend of his."

"But this is Me!" said Bear, very much surprised.

"What sort of Me?"

"Pooh Bear."

"Are you sure?" said Rabbit, still more surprised.

"Quite, quite sure," said Pooh.

"Oh, well, then, come in."

So Pooh pushed and pushed and pushed his way through the hole, and at last he got in.

"You were quite right," said Rabbit, looking at him all over. "It is you. Glad to see you."

"Who did you think it was?"

"Well, I wasn't sure. You know how it is in the Forest. One can't have *anybody* coming into one's house. One has to be careful. What about a mouthful of something?"

Pooh always liked a little something at eleven o'clock in the morning, and he was very glad to see Rabbit getting out the plates and mugs; and when Rabbit said, "Honey or condensed milk with your bread?" he was so excited that he said, "Both," and then, so as not to seem greedy, he added, "But don't bother about the bread, please." And for a long time after that he said nothing . . . until at last, humming to himself in a rather sticky voice, he got up, shook Rabbit lovingly by the paw, and said that he must be going on.

"Must you?" said Rabbit politely.

"Well," said Pooh, "I could stay a little longer if it—if you—" and he tried very hard to look in the direction of the larder.

"As a matter of fact," said Rabbit, "I was going out myself directly."

"Oh, well, then, I'll be going on. Good-bye."

"Well, good-bye, if you're sure you won't have any more."

"Is there any more?" asked Pooh quickly.

Rabbit took the covers off the dishes and said, "No, there wasn't."

"I thought not," said Pooh, nodding to himself. "Well, good-bye. I must be going on."

So he started to climb out of the hole. He pulled with his front paws, and pushed with his back paws, and in a little while his nose was out in the open again . . . and then his ears . . . and then his front paws . . . and then his shoulders . . . and then—

"Oh, help!" said Pooh. "I'd better go back."

"Oh, bother!" said Pooh. "I shall have to go on."

"I can't do that either!" said Pooh. "Oh, help and bother!"

Now by this time Rabbit wanted to go for a walk too, and finding the front door full, he went out by the back door, and came round to Pooh, and looked at him.

"Hallo, are you stuck?" he asked.

"N-no," said Pooh carelessly. "Just resting and thinking and humming to myself."

"Here, give us a paw."

Pooh Bear stretched out a paw, and Rabbit pulled and pulled and pulled. . . .

"Ow!" cried Pooh. "You're hurting!"

"The fact is," said Rabbit, "you're stuck."

"It all comes," said Pooh crossly, "of not having front doors big enough."

"It all comes," said Rabbit sternly, "of eating too much. I thought at the time," said Rabbit, "only I didn't like to say anything," said Rabbit, "that one of us was eating too much," said Rabbit, "and I knew it wasn't *me*," he said. "Well, well, I shall go and fetch Christopher Robin."

Christopher Robin lived at the other end of the Forest, and when he came back with Rabbit and saw the front half of Pooh, he said, "Silly old Bear," in such a loving voice that everybody felt quite hopeful again.

"I was just beginning to think," said Bear, sniffing slightly, "that Rabbit might never be able to use his front door again. And I should *hate* that," he said.

"So should I," said Rabbit.

"Use his front door again?" said Christopher Robin. "Of course he'll use his front door again."

"Good," said Rabbit.

"If we can't pull you out, Pooh, we might push you back."

Rabbit scratched his whiskers thoughtfully and pointed out that when once Pooh was pushed back, he was back, and of course nobody was more glad to see Pooh than he was, still there it was, some lived in trees and some lived underground, and—

"You mean I'd *never* get out?" said Pooh.

"I mean," said Rabbit, "that having got *so* far, it seems a pity to waste it."

Christopher Robin nodded.

"Then there's only one thing to be done," he said. "We shall have to wait for you to get thin again."

"How long does getting thin take?" asked Pooh anxiously.

"About a week, I should think."

"But I can't stay here for a *week*."

"You can *stay* here all right, silly old Bear. It's getting you out which is so difficult."

"We'll read to you," said Rabbit cheerfully. "And I hope it won't snow," he added. "And I say, old fellow, you're taking up a good deal of room in my house—do you mind if I use your back legs as a towel-horse? Because, I mean, there they are—doing nothing—and it would be very convenient just to hang the towels on them."

"A week!" said Pooh gloomily. "What about meals?"

"I'm afraid no meals," said Christopher Robin, "because of getting thin quicker. But we *will* read to you."

Bear began to sigh and then found he couldn't because he was so tightly stuck, and a tear rolled down his eye, as he said:

"Then would you read a Sustaining Book, such as would help and comfort a Wedged Bear in Great Tightness?"

So for a week Christopher Robin read that sort of book at the north end of Pooh, and Rabbit hung his washing on the south end—and in between Bear felt himself getting slenderer and slenderer. And at the end of the week Christopher Robin said, *"Now!"*

So he took hold of Pooh's front paws, and Rabbit took hold of Christopher Robin, and all Rabbit's friends and relations took hold of Rabbit, and they all pulled together. . . .

And for a long time Pooh only said "Ow!" . . .

And "Oh!" . . .

And then, all of a sudden, he said "Pop!" just as if a cork were coming out of a bottle.

And Christopher Robin and Rabbit and all Rabbit's friends and relations went head-over-heels backwards . . . and on the top of them came Winnie-the-Pooh—free!

So, with a nod of thanks to his friends, he went on with his walk through the forest, humming proudly to himself. But Christopher Robin looked after him lovingly, and said to himself, "Silly old Bear!"

Boa Constrictor

Shel Silverstein

Oh I'm being eaten by a boa constrictor,
A boa constrictor, a boa constrictor,
I'm being eaten by a boa constrictor,
And I don't like it . . . one bit!
Well what do you know . . . it's nibbling my toe,
Oh gee . . . it's up to my knee,
Oh my . . . it's up to my thigh,
Oh fiddle . . . it's up to my middle,
Oh heck . . . it's up to my neck,
Oh dread . . . it's . . . MMFFF.

Some Famous Books

I. Read and Remember

Title	Author
Fables	Aesop
The Adventures of Pinocchio	Carlo Collodi
Peter Pan in Kensington Gardens	J. B. Barrie
Alice's Adventures in Wonderland	Lewis Carroll
Just So Stories	Rudyard Kipling
Fairy Tales	Hans Christian Andersen
Heidi	Johanna Spyri
Robin Hood and Little John	Anonymous
A Child's Garden of Verses	Robert Louis Stevenson
Fairy Tales	The Brothers Grimm
Winnie-the-Pooh	A. A. Milne

II. Find Out and Answer

1. Which of these books have you read?
2. Find out about these books and read one of them.
3. Tell the class about some parts or stories that you remember from one of these books.
4. Find out the titles and authors of other good books.

III. Write

1. Write a report about a book you read and liked.
2. Read one of these books and write a report about it.

Part Two

Famous People

Alexander and His Horse

Greek Legend

A long, long time ago there lived a king named Philip. One day King Philip received a beautiful horse as a present. The king took his new horse out on a wide plain to ride him. He took some of his men with him and also his son Alexander.

But they soon found out that the horse was very wild. It kicked and reared so that no man could mount upon its back. The king was furious that so wild an animal should have been sent to him, and he gave orders for it to be taken back at once.

But Prince Alexander was sorry when he heard this.

WORDS TO WATCH		
Philip	mount	trot
Alexander	gallop	Bucephalus
reared	plain	restless

"It is a pity to lose such a fine horse because no man is brave enough to mount it," said he.

The king thought his son spoke without thinking.

"Your words are bold," he said, "but are you bold enough to mount the horse yourself?"

The young prince went up to the restless animal. He took the bridle and turned its head toward the sun. He did so because he had seen that the horse was afraid of its own black shadow, which kept moving upon the ground before its eyes.

With its face to the sun, the horse could no longer see the shadow, which now fell on the ground behind it. It soon became quiet. Then the prince stroked it and patted it gently, and by and by he sprang quickly upon its back.

The horse at once set off at a gallop over the plain with the boy bravely holding on. The king and his men were in great fear, for they thought the prince would be thrown to the ground and killed. But they need not have been afraid.

Soon the horse grew tired of its gallop and began to trot. Then Alexander turned and gently rode it back. The men shouted, and the king took his son in his arms and shed tears of joy.

The horse was given to the young prince. It loved its master and would kneel down for him to mount, but it would not let any other person get upon its back.

At last, after many years, Alexander's horse was hurt in a fight. But it carried its master to a safe place. Then it lay down and died.

Alexander built a city at that place. He named the city Bucephalus because Bucephalus was the name of his horse.

1. Who was Alexander the Great?
2. Why did Alexander's father not want to keep the horse?
3. Tell how Alexander tamed the horse.
4. How did Alexander show that he was brave?

THE OWL

Anonymous

There was an old owl who lived in an oak;
The more he heard, the less he spoke.
The less he spoke, the more he heard.
Why aren't we like that wise old bird?

Cleopatra

Helen Webber

The kingdom of ancient Egypt lay in northeast Africa and Asia Minor. Its capital city, Alexandria, was a great center of learning. Egypt was called the *gift of the Nile* because each summer that great river flooded its banks and left black soil on the land. The Egyptian farmers planted their crops in this rich soil. Beyond the Nile River valley stretched the desert.

Now the queen of ancient Egypt two thousand years ago was Cleopatra. Cleopatra was the last of the Ptolemies, a family that had ruled Egypt for 300 years. She was intelligent, ambitious, and crafty. She was also so beautiful that she became a legend in her own time.

Cleopatra was just eighteen when she became queen. It was a time when Egypt feared the growing power of Rome. In her public life, Cleopatra wanted to keep power for herself and to keep Egypt strong and free. In her private life, she wanted luxury and love. She tried to make these two parts of her life work together. And, for a while at least, she succeeded. Two great Roman conquerors, Julius Caesar and Mark Antony, made alliances with her and helped to further her plans.

Julius Caesar had conquered much of Europe and then had chased his enemy into Egypt. When he came to the city of Alexandria he met Cleopatra and at once fell in love with her. He took her side in a civil war she was fighting and helped her gain more power in Egypt. They were united, and Cleopatra went back to Rome with Caesar. When Caesar died two years later, she returned to Egypt with their son, Caesarion.

Mark Antony had hoped to inherit all of Caesar's power as Roman emperor, but he had to settle for a part of it. Antony's share of the Roman Empire was in the East, and so he too came to Alexandria. When Cleopatra heard that he was coming, she decided to try to win his heart as she had won Caesar's. She hoped in this way to keep her power in Egypt and perhaps to rule in Rome as well.

She dressed herself as the goddess of love and her maids as nymphs and mermaids. Then she floated down the Nile to meet Antony in a boat so richly ornamented that the people lined the banks of the river for miles just to see her pass.

"The barge she sat in, like a burnished throne,
Burned on the water. . . .
Purple the sails, and so perfumed that
The winds were lovesick with them. The oars were silver,
Which to the tune of flutes kept stroke. . . ."

Antony liked luxury as much as Cleopatra did. And he was as charmed by her beauty and cleverness as Caesar had been. So Antony, too, fell in love with her.

After some years had passed, Antony's followers in Rome grew angry with him for staying in Egypt so long and for marrying Cleopatra. Another powerful Roman leader, Octavian, made war on Antony and Cleopatra. Octavian's fleet defeated the fleets of Antony and Cleopatra at the great naval battle of Actium. Then the couple fled to Alexandria, followed by Octavian. And here their ambitions and their love came to a bitter end.

Antony was led to believe that Cleopatra had taken her own life, so he threw himself on his sword. When he heard that she was really alive, he had himself carried into her presence. Then he spoke to her: "I am dying, Egypt, dying. . . ." She took him in her arms and there he died. Then Cleopatra took a poisonous snake on her arm and let it bite her. She was buried beside Antony. Her death marked the start of Roman rule in Egypt.

Twenty centuries have passed since the time of Cleopatra, but poets and painters through the ages have been fascinated by her story and have told or pictured it in a great many ways. For as the greatest of our poets, Shakespeare, said of Cleopatra: "Age cannot wither her, nor custom stale her infinite variety."

QUESTIONS

1. Why was Egypt called the "gift of the Nile"?
2. What did Cleopatra want in her public life? In her private life?
3. How did Cleopatra prepare to meet Antony?
4. How did Cleopatra and Antony die?
5. On a map, find Rome, Egypt, the Nile River, and Alexandria.
6. Find out more about the Roman Empire, Julius Caesar, Mark Antony, and Octavian.

William Tell

Swiss Legend

Switzerland is a beautiful little country in Europe. A long time ago it was conquered by the Austrians, and a wicked, cruel Austrian named Gessler ruled over the Swiss people. Although Gessler had many soldiers, he could not make the proud Swiss bow down when he passed by.

Boiling with rage, he thought of a way to make them feel his power. In the market place of the village of Altdorf, he set up a high pole and placed his Austrian hat on top of it. He ordered every Swiss man, woman, and child to bow to the hat whenever they passed by it.

One day William Tell came down from his home in the mountains to visit friends in Altdorf. He was tall and strong, known as the finest archer in the country, who could shoot bears and wolves with his crossbow. With him was his only son, a boy ten years old.

They crossed the market place and passed by the pole, but they did not bow. At once several soldiers surrounded Tell and took him before Gessler.

"Why did you not bow to the hat?" asked Gessler.

WORDS TO WATCH

market place	Europe	Altdorf
Austria	measured	tyrant
Switzerland	power	dungeon
crossbow	pale	rudder
paces	country	spared

"I am a Swiss," replied Tell. "I do not have to bow to an Austrian hat."

"Bow or die," shouted Gessler.

"I would sooner die than bow to it," replied Tell proudly.

Then Gessler, who could hardly control his mounting anger, thought of something else.

"They tell me you shoot very well," he said with a wicked smile. "I will not punish you. Instead, we will see if you are as good as people say you are. Let your son stand a hundred paces from you. Put an apple on his head, and shoot an arrow through the apple. If you fail, you shall be put to death; if you succeed, your life will be spared."

"I'd rather die than aim an arrow at my own son," cried Tell. "You cannot ask a father to do such a horrible thing."

"Do as I order," shouted Gessler furiously, "or I'll put both you and your son to death!"

All the people who heard these words turned pale with fear, and other fathers held their sons close to them. But the little boy whispered to his father, "I am not afraid, Father. I will hold very still, and I will not even breathe or blink an eye."

Gessler's soldiers measured off the hundred paces, led the boy to the marked spot, and placed an apple on his head.

William Tell slowly took out two arrows, slipped one under his belt, and fitted the other to his crossbow. His son held his head high and stood motionless while he watched his father bend the crossbow and take aim. The crowd did not dare to breathe. Zing! The arrow sped from the crossbow, straight to the apple, and split it in two pieces. Not a hair of the boy's head was touched. The crowd cheered; everyone was overjoyed.

"A master shot," cried Gessler, "but tell me, did you not put a second arrow under your belt?"

"The second arrow was for you, if my son had been hurt," replied Tell.

"I gave my word to spare your life," shouted the Austrian furiously, "but I will teach you a lesson. Bind him," he ordered, "and take him across the lake to my castle. Throw him in the dungeon, where he will see neither sun nor moon as long as he lives. Then I shall be safe from his arrows!"

The soldiers bound William Tell with ropes and threw him into the bottom of a boat. When they were in the middle of the lake, a terrible storm arose, and the soldiers set Tell free so that he could help them with the boat. He took the rudder and steered the boat toward the rocks. As soon as they were close enough, he suddenly sprang ashore, kicking the boat back into the wild waves of the lake.

Tell escaped into the mountains, which no one else knew as well as he. He hid near the path which Gessler had to take to his castle, and he waited. His second arrow was ready, fitted to the crossbow. When Gessler passed by late that afternoon, the arrow did not miss, and the wicked tyrant fell dead.

Two Cats

Anonymous

There once were two cats of Kilkenny,
Each thought there was one cat too many;
So they fought and they fit,
And they scratched and they bit,
Till, excepting their nails
And the tips of their tails,
Instead of two cats, there weren't any.

Boadicea

Judith Barnard

More than 1,900 years ago, in 62 A.D., a huge army fought its way across Britain. The army was from Rome. It was part of an even greater army that was conquering countries all over Europe and even in Africa and Asia.

At that time, Britain had small, crowded towns instead of cities. Groups of people lived in tribes, each with its own name, each with its cluster of huts separated from other tribes by rough ground or marshes. Until the Roman soldiers came, there were few roads. The Romans built roads for their armies to move quickly as they defeated one tribe after another. When Roman soldiers marched along the roads, the earth shook, and the tramp-tramp-tramp of heavy feet could be heard for miles.

Roman troops became known for their cruelty to the people they had conquered. They took money and animals and food, often leaving nothing for the families they robbed. When crops were ready for harvest, the soldiers moved in and took what they wished from the fields; they left behind stripped plants or the poor crops they didn't want.

The soldiers made free with the people's homes, walking into huts where people ate or slept, taking women and children. There were no laws to protect the people; the only law was Roman force of arms. The people were always afraid, always angry—and always helpless.

But the people of the Iceni tribe thought they might not be

so helpless after all. They were one of the largest tribes; and they were a proud and hard-working people. Often they refused when Roman soldiers demanded food or higher taxes. For a while, their refusals brought only harsher treatment from the Romans. So the Iceni went to their queen to tell her they wanted to rebel.

The queen was Boadicea. The king had died the year before. After his death, the Romans became bolder in their demands, as if they felt a widowed queen could do nothing to stop them.

But Boadicea knew that a king or queen sometimes *follows* the people, as well as leading them. When her people talked of rebellion she could not ask them to be patient. And besides, she too was angry. She stood and held out her hands. "We will make our own weapons," she said. "Others we will steal from the Romans while they sleep. And we will drive out every Roman soldier. The land will be ours again!"

Thousands of Iceni men and women armed themselves with battering rams, catapults, stones, javelins, swords, and daggers. People from other tribes joined them. Howling great war cries that echoed in the cool dawn shadows, they attacked the Roman camp near London.

By nightfall, as the sun disappeared, twisted bodies covered the ground. Bushes were red with the blood of Roman and Iceni soldiers. The air was heavy and hushed; no birds sang, no dogs barked. Boadicea led her survivors back to camp. "We won this battle," she thought, "but we will lose in the end. Too many of our fighters were killed. The Romans have smaller armies but they have better weapons and they have training; we have none. But what else can we do?"

There was nothing else they could do. They fought on, and at first they won several important battles. The Iceni drove the Romans out of London, out of Colchester, out of Verulamium (later called St. Albans). A feeling of freedom and victory was everywhere. People slept at night without trembling at every sound, without wondering when Romans would steal women or children, or take all the food and animals for themselves.

But as Boadicea had foreseen, the victories did not last. Suetonius Paulinus, a Roman general, alarmed by the Iceni march that was driving Roman soldiers into retreat, led his army against Boadicea's army. The Romans crushed the Iceni; they crushed the tribal army beneath their feet. It seemed they would crush the last living things in Britain.

Finally the Roman soldiers reached Boadicea's camp and killed the Iceni guarding her. The Romans captured the queen and made plans to take her to Rome.

But Boadicea had no intention of going to Rome. Her armies were defeated, her land lay in ruins. Roman troops occupied every town. There was no escape, there would be no freedom, no more victories. But she belonged in Britain, not in Rome.

That night, alone in her prison hut, Boadicea took from a hiding place a poison she had been saving for the defeat she had foreseen. She held it up and then, without taking a moment to think, quickly swallowed it all.

In the morning, when the soldiers came to take her to the ship, she lay on the floor, very cold, very still. There was nothing the soldiers could do. Boadicea was dead; she would never be a slave of Rome.

QUESTIONS

1. Was Boadicea wise to keep fighting after she knew the Iceni could not win?
2. Why was the Roman army better than the Iceni army?
3. Find out more about the Romans in Britain. Who was Julius Caesar? What is Hadrian's Wall?

Happy Thought

Robert Louis Stevenson

The world is so full of a number of things,
I'm sure we should all be as happy as kings.

Occupations

I. Read and Spell

teacher	lawyer	plumber
doctor	police officer	physicist
nurse	chemist	carpenter
engineer	scientist	fire fighter
librarian	politician	banker
office worker	mechanic	photographer
professor	journalist	salesclerk
executive	veterinarian	farmer
astronaut	factory worker	interpreter
writer	merchant	soldier
architect	artist	pilot
sailor	musician	actor

II. Read and Answer

1. Tell what people do in each of these occupations.
2. What kind of education do you need for each of these occupations?
3. Name some other occupations.
4. What do you think you might like to be?
5. How would you prepare yourself for your work?
6. Can a woman be a police officer, a physicist, or a carpenter?

III. Write

1. Write five sentences, each using a word in Part I.
2. Write a story about what you want to be when you are grown up.

Mary Queen of Scots

Mary Stuart was born in Scotland over 400 years ago, in the days when Scotland and England were still separate kingdoms. She was crowned Queen of Scotland upon the death of her father, the king, when she was only one week old.

At the age of five, the child-queen was sent to the court of France to be educated. There she met the crown prince of France, who was to be her future husband. The two children grew up together as friends. They were married when Mary had become a tall and lovely girl of 15. The French people loved her for her sweetness and beauty. Many French poets wrote verses in praise of her.

By the time Mary was 16 her young husband had become king, and she had become the queen of France as well as of Scotland. But before a year had passed she was a widow. Mary had led a happy and protected young life. What lay ahead of her now was sorrow and tragedy.

She decided to return to the Scotland she had almost forgotten. There she missed the mild weather of France. She missed the music and dancing and other pleasant customs of the French court. Most painful of all, she found that her Catholic faith was out of favor in Scotland, which was becoming Protestant during her years in France.

Queen Mary tried to allow freedom of religion to all her people. But the people had not yet learned to respect each other's beliefs. The leader of the Protestants frowned on Mary, her church, and her customs. He complained that wicked Mary had "danced past midnight out of glee." The

Catholics, for their part, wanted Mary to restore their power and drive the Protestants out. Nothing she did really satisfied either side.

The troubles in Scotland turned into violent rebellion. Mary was captured by some of the Protestant nobles. She was imprisoned in a dark, grim castle on an island in the middle of a lake.

In disguise, Mary escaped from the island. She quickly raised a small army. But her army was defeated, and she had to flee. She might have fled to France, where she had friends and property. Instead, she sailed to England in a fishing boat and asked protection from her cousin, Queen Elizabeth I. This was Mary's worst mistake. Once in England she was drawn into Queen Elizabeth's spider web.

Elizabeth feared that Mary was plotting to make herself queen of England. So she had Mary put in prison. Mary suffered 19 long years in prison, broken in health. It was there that her religion became a great comfort to her. She gained peace of spirit at the cost of much pain.

At last, Elizabeth charged that Mary had plotted against her life. Mary was tried, found guilty, and beheaded. The courage and dignity with which she faced death has since become a legend.

The motto of Mary Queen of Scots was: "In my end is my beginning." Although Mary herself died an outcast, Scotland and England were united under the rule of her son, King James I. Every ruler of Britain since that time has been descended from her. So the end of Mary Stuart was the beginning of a long line of Stuart kings and queens.

A Good Thanksgiving

Marian Douglas

Said old Gentleman Ray, "On Thanksgiving day,
If you want a good time, then give something away."

So he sent a fat turkey to Shoemaker Price,
And the shoemaker said, "What a big bird! How nice.

"With such a good dinner before me, I ought
To give Widow Lee the small chicken I bought."

"This fine chicken, oh, see!" said the pleased Widow Lee,
"And the kindness that sent it, how precious to me.

"I would like to make someone as happy as I—
I'll give Washerwoman Biddy my big pumpkin pie."

"And oh sure!" Biddy said, " 'tis the queen of all pies!
And to look at its yellow face gladdens my eyes.

"Now it's my turn, I think; and a sweet ginger cake
For the motherless Finigan children I'll bake."

Said the Finigan children—Rose, Denny, and Hugh—
"It smells sweet of spice, and we'll carry a slice
To poor little lame Jake, who has nothing that's nice."

"Oh I thank you, and thank you," said the little lame Jake.
"What a beautiful, beautiful, beautiful cake!

"And such a big slice! I will save all the crumbs,
And give them to each little sparrow that comes."

And the sparrows they twittered, as if they would say,
Like old Gentleman Ray, "On Thanksgiving day,
If you want a good time, then give something away."

Holidays

I. Read and Remember

New Year's Day

Lincoln's Birthday

Valentine's Day

Passover

Easter Sunday

Memorial Day

Flag Day

Washington's Birthday

Martin Luther King's Birthday

Hanukkah

Independence Day

Labor Day

Rosh Hashanah

Christmas Day

Halloween

Columbus Day

Thanksgiving Day

Chinese New Year

St. Patrick's Day

II. Read and Answer

1. Why are these holidays celebrated?
2. When are these holidays celebrated?
3. How are these holidays celebrated?

III. Read and Write

Write a story about your favorite holiday.

Father Hidalgo

Helen Webber

In Mexico, our neighboring country to the south, September 16 is Independence Day. Each year on the eve of that day, the people of Mexico City gather in front of the president's palace. The president rings the liberty bell and gives the famous call, "Long live independence! Long live Mexico!" The people answer, shouting "*Viva* Mexico! Long live Mexico!" Then, perhaps, parents will tell their children why the liberty bell was brought to the palace from the church in Dolores, and how the priest of that church, Father Hidalgo, became the father of his country.

Father Hidalgo was the son of a Spanish family, and the Spanish had ruled Mexico for three hundred years. But he had been born in Mexico, and his heart was with the Mexican people. Although he was an educated man who had taught in a college, he chose to be a priest in the little village of Dolores. There the people were poor and hungry. Father Hidalgo was a strong and lively man, and one who loved a joke. But he was no longer young when he began the great work of his life.

He had many good ideas for helping his flock to learn trades that he hoped would lift them out of their poverty. He taught them how to grow grapes for making wine and how to grow mulberry trees and stock them with silkworms for making silk. But when the Spanish rulers heard of the priest's work, they sent men to destroy the crops. Mexicans were not

to be allowed to make wine and silk. Instead, they had to buy these things from Spain, at high prices that none but the rich could pay.

Then Father Hidalgo started a blacksmith's shop. He also taught brickmaking and pottery and other crafts to the people of Dolores. But progress was slow, and they still did not have enough to eat. He began to believe that Mexico must free herself from Spain. Other men and women shared his belief. Talk of freedom was everywhere. Together with his friends, the priest started to plan an uprising, but the Spanish found out about these plans. It was dangerous now to delay.

Father Hidalgo decided to act at once. His first thought was to ask the Virgin of Guadalupe, a saint much loved by poor Mexicans, to bless his attempt to free Mexico. Ringing his church bell—the same bell that became Mexico's liberty bell—he called the people from their homes to meet at the church. There he prayed to the Virgin and then spoke to the people he loved. He ended his speech with the call to in-

94

dependence that would be shouted throughout Mexico every September for years to come. "*Viva* Mexico!"

Then the priest, followed by a dozen men of Dolores, set out to raise an army. They walked from town to town, and soon the ragged band numbered eighty thousand men. They were armed mostly with sticks, stones, knives, and axes. Under the banner of the Virgin of Guadalupe, they fought the Spanish army. It is said that some of the Mexicans knew so little about fighting that they tried to stop the Spanish cannons by holding straw hats over the mouths of the cannons. But their desire for freedom made them fight on.

At first the Mexicans won battle after battle. Later, however, they could not stand up against the well-trained and well-armed Spanish soldiers. After a year of fighting, Father Hidalgo was captured and put to death. But the fight for freedom did not die with him. After ten more years, the Mexicans finally won their independence.

Although he did not live to see Mexico free from Spanish rule, perhaps Father Hidalgo guessed that Mexicans would one day govern themselves and would remember him as the father of their independence. Not only have the Mexicans remembered Father Hidalgo, they have also brought his church bell from Dolores to their capital city and made it their liberty bell.

QUESTIONS

1. Describe the Independence Day celebrations in Mexico.
2. How was Father Hidalgo's uprising against the Spanish like the American Revolution?
3. Find out something about the American liberty bell, which is now in Philadelphia.

The Lady with the Lamp

Margaret Leighton

Already as a little girl, Florence Nightingale took care of her sick dolls and pets. When she was a bit older, she visited and nursed the sick and poor people in her village. She loved her parents and her sister dearly, but she did not care about beautiful clothes, elegant parties, travel, and all the other things that her family enjoyed. More than anything she wanted to become a nurse! At that time, though, there were no nurses as we now know them. Hospitals in England and all over the world were the most horrible places one can imagine. Sick people would not think of going there if they could find anyone to nurse them at home. Hospitals were dirty and overrun by lice and fleas. The women who worked in them were uneducated and looked down upon. That's why Florence's parents did not allow her to work in a hospital. But Florence was strong-willed and determined. She secretly read and studied all she could find about hospitals and nursing. After many unhappy years, Florence got her way. She managed one hospital in London so successfully that she was called to serve when war broke out between England and Russia. She took 38 nurses to the Crimea to organize hospitals and nursing for the wounded soldiers. The following story begins the day after their arrival in the Crimea.

Florence Nightingale and her nurses slept very little that night. They were all cold and hungry. Fleas bit them, the wooden benches were hard, and rats ran about the room all night.

Florence rose in the early dawn and looked out at the bright sky.

Already she had made her plans. "We will set up the portable stoves which we brought from Marseilles in here," she told her nurses. "We will make hot, nourishing drinks and have them ready for the wounded when they are brought here from the ships."

The stretchers, loaded with sick and wounded soldiers, soon began to pour into the hospital. Miss Nightingale and her nurses were working in the wards, cleaning, dressing wounds, and caring for the sick.

The commander of the army sent word that five hundred more wounded men were being sent down from the fighting front to the Scutari hospitals.

"But there's no space left even on the floor!" exclaimed the officer in charge of the hospitals, when he heard this news.

"A whole wing of the Barrack Hospital is not in use," Florence said quietly. "I'm told it was destroyed by fire. Why not repair it?"

The officer shook his head. "That fire happened before we took this place over," he exclaimed. "I have no right to have repairs made there. I'd have to get permission from the War Office in London."

"I shall have it done myself, then," said Florence Nightingale. She hired workmen, bought lumber and supplies, and drew up plans. By the time the ships arrived bringing the wounded, the new wing was ready for them.

But still the disasters grew. The British Army had failed to supply its troops with warm clothing or proper food. Winter came. The men suffered cruelly in the icy trenches from

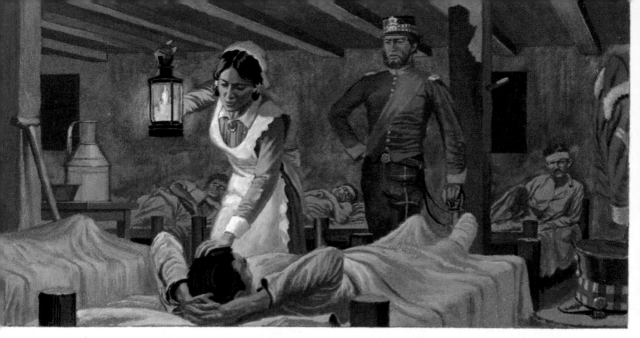

hunger and cold. The cholera increased. More than half the
Army lay wounded and sick. The Nightingale nurses worked
from before dawn to after dark with quiet heroism.

But night did not bring an end to Florence Nightingale's
labors.

One night a young transport sailor named William lay
restless and wakeful in his cot. It was almost midnight. The
great echoing wards of the Barrack Hospital were dark. The
only sound was the slow step of the sentry pacing the stone
floor.

William's throat burned with thirst. The pain of his
shattered leg seemed more than he could bear. Worst of all
was the fear growing in his heart.

"Tomorrow we'll operate," the surgeon had said.

"What does that mean?" William wondered. "Will they
cut my leg off? I think I'd rather die, here and now!"

Suddenly he noticed shadows sliding along the ceiling. A
light was moving, far down the ward. A whispered murmur
passed from man to man. "It's *her!* It's Nurse Nightingale,"
they said.

She came as quietly as a shadow. When she reached William's cot she set the lantern down and bent over him. Her cool hand touched his forehead. "You're hot and thirsty, William. Here's a drink for you."

Her arm steadied him while he gulped the water. "There, is that better?" she asked. In the lantern light her face was pale, but as kind and gentle as his own mother's.

"Nurse Nightingale," William said hoarsely, "are they going to cut off my leg tomorrow?"

Florence Nightingale's face was grave. "I don't know, William," she said. "But I promise you that I shall be there with you all the time. If they can save your leg, they will, you may be sure of that. And will you promise me something?"

"What do you mean, ma'am?" he asked doubtfully.

"Promise me that you will bear whatever they decide like the brave British sailor that you are," she asked.

He could not refuse *her*. "Yes, I'll promise," he said.

She smiled. "Now try to sleep." She touched his eyelids and he closed them. But when she moved on, he raised his head and watched the light of her lantern flickering down the long room. She spoke to a soldier here, and smiled at another there. William saw a brawny fellow turn his head and kiss her shadow as it lay for a moment on his pillow.

"She seems to know, somehow, whenever a fellow is a bit low, and she comes to cheer him up," the man next to William said. "She's an angel, and no mistake."

William turned over on his side. He could still feel the touch of her fingers on his eyelids. And what Florence Nightingale did for him that night she did for hundreds, yes, thousands of other men during that terrible and tragic winter.

The Coming of Morning

Emily Dickinson

Will there really be a morning?
  Is there such a thing as day?
Could I see it from the mountains
  If I were as tall as they?

Has it feet like water lilies?
  Has it feathers like a bird?
Is it brought from famous countries
  Of which I have never heard?

Oh, some scholar! Oh, some sailor!
  Oh, some wise man from the skies!
Please do tell a little pilgrim
  Where the place called morning lies!

Martin Luther King

Every American child learns in school that black people were first brought to this country as slaves. It took a bloody civil war to set them free. But perhaps not everyone knows that a hundred years after the Civil War, black Americans still did not have the right to live and work and play and go to school where they liked. The story of how they worked to gain these rights—which we call *civil rights*—is partly the story of a young minister named Martin Luther King. He became a hero to black people, as well as to a great many other people who care about freedom and peace. The events that were to make Martin Luther King a fighter for civil rights began in Montgomery, Alabama, on a winter day in 1955.

That day a black woman named Rosa Parks was riding a bus home. She was tired after a long day's work. In 1955, the law in Montgomery was that black people had to sit in the back of the bus. They also had to give up their seats if white passengers were standing. When the bus that Rosa Parks was riding became crowded, the driver ordered her to give her seat to a white man. With quiet courage, she refused. Then the police came and arrested her.

WORDS TO WATCH

civil	nonviolence	content
boycott	injustice	refuse
weary	racial	Montgomery

Black people were very angry to hear how Mrs. Parks had been treated. They knew that the law was wrong. They were tired of being treated unjustly because of their race. They decided to *boycott* the buses—to refuse to ride in them at all. If all the black people of Montgomery refused to ride in the buses, the bus company would make a lot less money.

Martin Luther King led this boycott, talking to his followers to give them strength and hope whenever they grew weary. For a whole year, thousands of blacks refused to ride the buses. Instead, they went to their jobs any way they could—some even riding mules, and many walking for miles. News of the Montgomery bus boycott spread all over America. Many people everywhere agreed with the blacks of Montgomery and did what they could to help change the laws. And, of course, the bus company made less money. At last the fighters for civil rights won, and the unjust bus laws were changed. Martin Luther King was proud that his people had won their victory without using any violence.

His belief in *nonviolence*—in the power of using peaceful means to attack injustice—was the idea that ruled his life. No matter how often he was the target of hate and violence, he never allowed himself or his followers to use violence in return. The fighters for civil rights went from victory to victory over racial injustice, both in the South and in the North. Martin Luther King went with them, walking at the front of his peaceful army wherever there was danger to face and a wrong to make right. He was even willing to go to jail many times for breaking those laws that he knew to be unjust. By the time his short life was over, there were people all over the country—indeed, all over the world—who believed in his ideas and wanted to carry on his work.

In 1963, the fighters for civil rights had a March on Washington to mark the hundredth anniversary of the freeing of the slaves. They wanted to remind the government that much work was still to be done. On that summer day, a quarter of a million people, black and white, stood before the Lincoln Memorial and heard Martin Luther King say:

I have a dream today. I have a dream that my four little children will one day live in a nation where they will not be judged by the color of their skin but by the content of their character. . . . When we let freedom ring, when we let it ring from every village and every town, from every state and every city, we will be able to speed up the day when all of God's children, black men and white men, . . . will be able to join hands and sing in the words of that old Negro song, "Free at last! Free at last! Thank God Almighty, we are free at last!"

Some Famous People of the World

I. Read and Spell

Plato	Dante	Mozart
Aristotle	Shakespeare	St. Frances Cabrini
Cleopatra	Leonardo da Vinci	Goethe
Julius Caesar	Bach	Darwin
Archimedes	Newton	Jane Austen
Napoleon	Marie Curie	Chief Joseph
Confucius	José Martí	Helen Keller
Chopin	Pablo Casals	Gregor Mendel
Mahatma Gandhi	Golda Meir	Max Planck
Geronimo	Lao-tze	Nefertiti
Joan of Arc	Lady Murasaki	Garibaldi
Toussaint L'Ouverture		Yuri Gagarin
Joseph Jenkins Roberts		Michelangelo

II. Find Out and Answer

1. Find out why ten of these people are famous.
2. Think of some other famous people.
3. Find out the names of some people who are famous as:
   - a. poets
   - b. scientists
   - c. world leaders
   - d. painters
   - e. composers
4. What makes people famous?
5. Can a person be great without being famous?

III. Write

1. Write a story about a famous person you like.
2. Write a story about what you would most like to be famous for.

Part Three

Science and Nature

A B C D E F G
H I J K L M
N O P Q R S T
U V W X Y Z

THE WONDERFUL ALPHABET

Did you know that one of the most wonderful inventions in the world is our alphabet? Who would ever imagine that these twenty-six little letters could be so important?

Do you think you could write a letter to a friend inviting him to visit you if you could not use the alphabet? Perhaps you could do it with pictures, but it wouldn't be very easy. Your friend might even misunderstand the letter and think that you were coming to visit him!

Yet thousands of years ago, people did write with pictures because no alphabet had been invented. Instead of writing "sun," they would draw a circle. A few straight lines might

---

WORDS TO WATCH

misunderstand	Phoenician	German
Chinese	Spanish	Roman
alpha	French	Russia
beta		

106

mean "trees" or "forest." A few wavy lines might mean "water," or "lake," or "ocean." This is writing the hard way, and many ideas were not easy to write with pictures. For example, it would be hard to say with pictures, "the boys looked like good boys but were really bad boys."

The ancient Egyptians could do many amazing things, but they also used picture writing because they did not have an alphabet. So did many Indian tribes in America.

Some of the peoples of the world wrote with signs instead of pictures. Sometimes the signs looked a little bit like the thing they stood for. In Chinese, for example, the sign for

man is 人 , which looks a little bit like a man walking;

and 木 , which means "tree" or "wood" in Chinese,

looks a little like a tree with some branches. But in Chinese and some other languages like Chinese, there are thousands and thousands of these signs, all different. Most of them don't look at all like the things they stand for.

Did you ever stop to think how our alphabet was invented? The word "alphabet" comes from the words "alpha" and "beta," which are the Greek letters for A and B. But the Greeks did not invent our alphabet. The Phoenicians invented it. The Phoenicians lived a long time ago and were great sailors and traders. They traded with many countries across the seas, and in buying and selling, they needed a fast way of writing things down. So they invented signs that stood for the sounds of their language. In this way our alphabet began. The Greeks learned the alphabet from the Phoenicians, and the people of western Europe learned it from the Greeks.

Today most languages have alphabets. Many alphabets are quite different from ours, but they are just as useful. In recent years, the Chinese have made their own alphabet. People in Russia, Iran, India, and elsewhere each have their own alphabets. The alphabet of English and Spanish and French and German and many other languages is called the Roman alphabet because it hasn't changed much since the days of ancient Rome.

In German the word "tree" is written "Baum"; in French it is written "arbre"; and in Spanish it is "árbol," but the letters are written the same way that they are in English.

But no matter what the language may be, if it has an alphabet, it is easier to write the word for tree than to draw a picture.

QUESTIONS

1. How did people write before an alphabet was invented?
2. Where does the word "alphabet" come from?
3. How was our alphabet invented?
4. Name some languages that have the same letters as English.
5. Name some languages that have letters different from English.
6. Would you rather write with pictures or with the alphabet? Why?
7. Write a sentence using only pictures, and see if the rest of the class can read what you wrote.

The Invention of Printing

Hundreds of years ago there were no printed books like the one you are reading now. In olden times books were written in "manuscript," which means that they were written by hand.

The books were copied carefully and were very beautiful. It often took a person two to three years to finish one hand-written book. Therefore books were expensive, and only a few people could buy them and learn about the world the way you can today.

Though the people of Europe didn't know it, printing had been invented by the Chinese. The Chinese would carve the symbol for a word on a block of wood. This symbol had to be carved backwards. Then the wood was dipped in ink or paint, placed on a piece of paper, and pressed down. When the block was raised, the word would be on the paper—right side around.

WORDS TO WATCH		
Johann Gutenberg	expensive	printing press
manuscript	movable type	improvement

Years later in Europe, printers would carve an entire page on wood. Every letter, word, and sentence had to be backwards! Then the whole page was covered with ink. Large machines worked by hand were built to hold these wooden pages and to press them to paper. These machines are called printing presses.

Different printers began making small, separate blocks for each letter of the alphabet. The letters were then put together to spell words. If enough letters were made for the words on a page, the whole page could then be inked and printed. By using more ink, many copies of a page could be printed. Then each letter was removed and used over again to form new words for another page of a book. Books were now much easier and cheaper to make.

In time, the letter blocks were made of metal. We call these blocks "type." What these printers were using was "movable type"—just as the Chinese had been doing for years.

A German named Johann Gutenberg was one of the first printers in Europe to use movable type and the printing press. Some of the oldest printed material in Europe was made by

him. He is often thought of as the inventor of the printing press, mainly because we don't know the names of many other early European printers.

The first book that we believe Gutenberg and his helpers printed was the Bible. It is a very beautiful example of the printer's art. Today a copy of the Gutenberg Bible is very valuable.

Soon books were printed all over Europe. For the first time, many people could read about faraway places, and the poets and thinkers of long ago were brought back to life.

The Gutenberg Bible was printed a little before Columbus discovered America. Since then, many improvements have been made on printing presses. Today printing presses can print thousands of books in an hour. Books, magazines, and newspapers are all printed on printing presses.

For very little money, you can buy enough newspapers and magazines and books to keep you busy reading for a whole week. And for nothing at all, at your public library you can read books on every subject you can think of.

Did you ever think that one invention could be so important?

QUESTIONS

1. How were books made before the printing press was invented?
2. What is movable type?
3. Why was the invention of the printing press important?
4. How could the printing press bring the poets and thinkers of long ago back to life?
5. Did you ever visit a library to see all the interesting books?
6. Why is the letter on a piece of type backwards?

The International System of Units
(Metric System)

I. Read and Spell

Length	Weight (Mass)	Volume
millimeter	milligram	milliliter
centimeter	centigram	centiliter
decimeter	decigram	deciliter
meter	gram	liter
dekameter	dekagram	dekaliter
hectometer	hectogram	hectoliter
kilometer	kilogram	kiloliter

II. Find Out and Answer

1. What does the prefix *milli-* mean? What does the prefix *kilo-* mean? What do they both mean in the Metric System?
2. What do the prefixes *centi-, deci-, deka-,* and *hecto-* mean? What meaning do they have in the Metric System?
3. How many cents are there in a dollar?
4. How many centigrams are there in a gram? Centimeters in a meter? Centiliters in a liter?
5. How many meters are there in a kilometer? How many grams are there in a kilogram?
6. What does the word *decathlon* mean? What does the word *millipede* mean?
7. Why is the Metric System of Units easy to use?

Copernicus and Galileo

On the morning of a clear day, you can see the sun rising in the east; and in the evening, you can see it going down in the west. This makes you think that the sun is going around the earth. And this is why, long ago, most people used to think that the sun went around the earth. They thought that the stars and the planets moved around the earth in big circles. They thought that our earth was the center of these circles.

WORDS TO WATCH		
planet	movement	telescope
Copernicus	Galileo	

But a man named Copernicus did not believe that the sun went around the earth. He traveled from university to university and studied mathematics, geography, astronomy, and as much as he could about the heavens. He observed very closely the movement of the sun, the planets, and the stars. Like certain ancient Greeks, he believed that the earth and the planets went around the sun.

After studying the movements of the sun, the planets, and the stars for a long time, he told other people that the earth goes around the sun. They did not believe him. They said, "If you are right, then why does the sun rise in the east and set in the west?"

Copernicus replied, "Because the earth spins like a top, and the sun stands still. It only seems that the sun is moving."

Copernicus explained his ideas in books for everyone to read, but people still would not believe him.

Another very wise man named Galileo helped prove that this new idea was right. He improved the telescope, so that at last people could see the sun, the planets, and the moon much better. He was the first man to see the moons circling around Jupiter and many other interesting things. He wrote a book about his new discoveries. He explained why Copernicus was right, even though many people still thought the sun went around the earth.

Today we have bigger and better telescopes to look at the stars, and we know that Copernicus and Galileo were right. These men were great men because they believed what they observed instead of what other people said. They did not discover a new world on earth as Columbus did, but they learned many things about other worlds in the sky that nobody had known about before.

Today, even though we know that the earth moves around the sun, we still talk about the sunrise and the sunset.

QUESTIONS

1. Why does the sun seem to be moving around the earth?
2. What did Copernicus try to show in his book?
3. Why could Galileo find out more than Copernicus about the sun, the planets, and the moon?
4. Why were Copernicus and Galileo great men?
5. Find out who Johannes Kepler was and what he did.
6. Who was Sir Isaac Newton?
7. Find out more about the movement of the earth, the moon, and the planets.
8. What is a solar system? A galaxy?

THE MOON

People have always liked to look up at the moon on a clear night. When the moon is full, sometimes it looks like a giant lantern that lights the night sky. Sometimes there seems to be a person in the moon looking down on us, and sometimes there seems to be a witch or a donkey in the moon.

Since olden times, people have sung songs and told many different legends about the moon, for it was the most popular of all the heavenly bodies. Above all, people have wondered at its beauty and wondered why it is forever changing. They thought that these changes had something to do with the birth, growth, death, and rebirth of many things on Earth. That is why people of olden times were careful to see whether the moon was in the right spot in the sky before they were going to do something important. They wanted the moon to bring them good luck.

Long ago people did not have calendars, but they wanted to count the days in some way. They noticed that about once every twenty-eight days there was a *new* moon, so they called this length of time a *moonth.* In some places a man would blow a trumpet when he first sighted the *new* moon so that everyone would know a new *moonth* (or month) had begun.

WORDS TO WATCH

Soviet	*Eagle*	manned spacecraft
calendar	orbit	Honolulu
Tranquility Base	moon rocks	telescope
mankind	rebirth	heavenly bodies

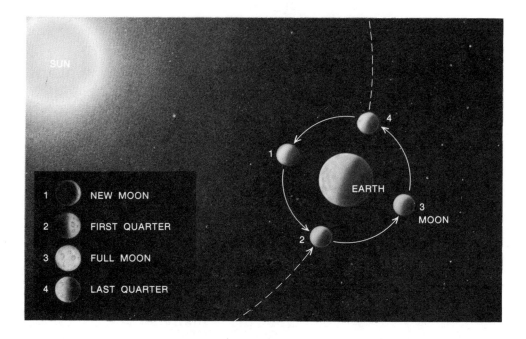

In the last few hundred years, people have looked at the moon through telescopes and learned more about it than ever before. We know that the moon is not changing its shape each night, as people used to think, but that it is traveling around the earth, and that the sunlight shines on it a little differently each night.

It is a *new* moon when the moon is between the earth and the sun so that we can hardly see the side that the sun is shining on. It is a *full* moon when the moon moves to the other side of the earth. Then the moon is on one side of the earth, and the sun on the other side so that we can see all of the moon that the sun is shining on.

Because of the way in which the earth and moon move, one side of the moon always faces earth. Until 1959 when a Soviet spacecraft traveled around the moon and took pictures, no one knew what the other side looked like. Since then, men too have traveled around the moon.

On Sunday, July 20, 1969, one of humanity's oldest dreams came true. On that day at 4:17 p.m. Eastern Daylight Time, Neil Armstrong and Edwin (Buzz) Aldrin safely landed America's manned spacecraft *Eagle* on the moon. Eight hundred million people were thrilled to hear Neil Armstrong's now-famous words: "Tranquility Base here. The *Eagle* has landed." And 800 million people watched, by television, one of the most exciting adventures in history; the first human step onto the surface of the moon. No one who watched will ever forget the moment when Neil Armstrong's ghostly white figure appeared outside *Eagle,* when his heavy-booted foot made the first human footprint on the moon, and when his voice was heard once again, "That's one small step for man, one giant leap for mankind."

After two hours and twenty minutes of exploring and gathering moon rocks, the men climbed back into *Eagle.* They guided their spacecraft back to the waiting mother ship *Columbia* in which Michael Collins, the third man of the team, had orbited the moon. Together they returned to earth exactly as planned, splashing down 950 miles west of Honolulu on July 24.

When we look up at the moon now, it somehow does not seem so far away and strange any more. We know that somewhere on its surface stands our flag and, not far from it, on the historic landing spot, a plaque signed by the astronauts and President Nixon which reads:

HERE MEN FROM THE PLANET EARTH FIRST SET FOOT UPON THE

MOON JULY 1969, A.D. WE CAME IN PEACE FOR ALL MANKIND

The Man in the Moon

Anonymous

The Man in the Moon, as he sails the sky,
Is a very remarkable skipper.
But he made a mistake
When he tried to take
A drink of milk from the Dipper.
He dipped right into the Milky Way
And slowly and carefully filled it.
The Big Bear growled
And the Little Bear howled,
And frightened him so, he spilled it.

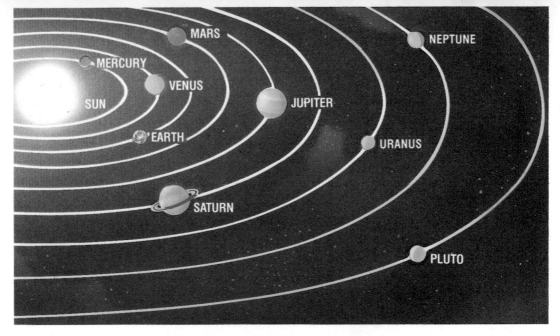

The Nine Wanderers

The word *planet* comes from the Greek language, and it means "wanderer." At night, when the people of long ago looked up into the sky, they noticed that these planets had wandered to a new spot. They could see five of them with their naked eyes, and they named them after their gods.

These five planets that were known long ago are Mercury, Venus, Mars, Jupiter, and Saturn. Most people did not know where these planets wandered. Then, hundreds of years later,

---

WORDS TO WATCH

Mercury	Uranus	planet
Venus	Neptune	god
Mars	Pluto	goddess
Jupiter	Saturn	telescope
Copernicus	sun	North Pole
Galileo	moon	Earth

Copernicus and Galileo proved that they wandered around the sun. They knew that Earth was a planet and that it also wandered around the sun. That made six planets.

Later, three more planets were discovered. They were also given the names of the ancient people's gods: Uranus, Neptune, and Pluto. Today we know that there are at least nine planets all traveling around the sun, and that Earth is one of them.

The sun and the stars are like giant fireballs with giant flames leaping out from them. But planets are not like fireballs.

The smallest planet is Mercury. Because it appears to travel faster than the other planets it was named for the god that carried messages swiftly. It travels closer to the sun than any other planet.

Venus was named for the goddess of beauty. At night it shines brighter than any star in the sky. It is called the Evening Star when it shines in the western sky after the sun sets. And it is called the Morning Star when it shines in the eastern sky just before the sun rises.

Mars was named for the god of war. It looks like a red star in the sky. If you look at Mars through a telescope, you can see that it has poles with white caps, like the North Pole and the South Pole of our earth. Of all the planets besides Earth, Mars has an environment that seems most likely to be able to support forms of life.

Jupiter was king of the gods, and the planet named Jupiter is the largest of all the planets. More than one thousand planets the size of Earth could fit into Jupiter if it were hollow inside. There is only one moon that goes around the earth, but thirteen or more moons go around Jupiter.

Saturn looks different from other planets because it has rings around it. Our earth takes only one year to travel around the sun. But Saturn takes about thirty of our years to go completely around the sun. If you lived on Saturn, you would have to wait about thirty years before you could have a birthday.

Uranus, Neptune, and Pluto are so far away that you cannot see them without a telescope. People did not know about these planets before the telescope was invented. Nobody can live on these planets because the temperature is much too cold. On Pluto you would have a birthday only once in every 248 years.

The more you learn about other planets, the happier you will be that you live on this one.

QUESTIONS

1. Why are planets thought of as "wanderers"?
2. How many planets are there? Name them.
3. Which planets did the ancient Greeks know about?
4. Which planet besides Earth is most likely to support life?
5. Read and spell the names of the planets listed on the next page and tell what you know about each planet.

Astronomy

I. Read and Spell

sun	moon	star
planet	Earth	Mercury
Venus	Mars	satellite
cosmic ray	Neptune	observatory
Saturn	meteor	galaxy
Pluto	telescope	Jupiter
the Milky Way	the Big Dipper	comet
North Star	constellation	the Little Dipper
light year	Orion	eclipse

II. Find Out and Answer

1. Find out about one of these, and tell the class about it.
2. What is the difference between a star and a planet?
3. What is the difference between a comet and a meteor?
4. Why do you think astronomy is important?

III. Write

1. Write a story about why you like to see the stars at night.
2. Write a story about a subject listed in Part I.

Stopping by Woods on a Snowy Evening

Robert Frost

Whose woods these are I think I know.
His house is in the village though;
He will not see me stopping here
To watch his woods fill up with snow.

My little horse must think it queer
To stop without a farmhouse near
Between the woods and frozen lake
The darkest evening of the year.

He gives his harness bells a shake
To ask if there is some mistake.
The only other sound's the sweep
Of easy wind and downy flake.

The woods are lovely, dark and deep.
But I have promises to keep,
And miles to go before I sleep,
And miles to go before I sleep.

QUESTIONS

1. Why did the driver stop his horse?
2. How does this poem help explain the difference between a man and a horse?

Marie Curie

Anonymous

Today scientists use modern equipment in their work. Special tools help scientists to find new things and to learn new facts.

In 1898, Marie Curie used huge iron kettles to melt tons of ore. Her work took four long years. At the end of all that time, she had a few grains of something that looked like table salt, but glowed in the dark. Yet those few grains gave doctors a way of saving the lives of thousands of people suffering from cancer. Studying them led to atomic power.

Marie Curie's long search began while she was studying in Paris, France. She read that uranium compounds had been found to give off strange rays. Scientists could not explain what these rays were. The rays acted something like X-rays. They could not be seen, but they left marks on camera film.

Marie wanted to learn more about the strange rays. Her husband, Pierre Curie, who taught physics, said that he

WORDS TO WATCH		
Marie Curie	compound	ore
radium	Pierre Curie	element
uranium	Nobel Prize	physics
radioactive	thorium	Irène
exposed	diseased	chemicals

would like to help her on this project. They both wanted to solve the mystery of the rays.

They had very little money, so they could not afford a real laboratory. But a school agreed to let Marie use an old shed. The roof leaked. The shed was full of machinery and lumber, but there was room for the equipment she needed. She started to work.

She knew that uranium compounds gave off rays all the time. The rays never stopped. Marie tried using light and heat on these compounds. She mixed them with other chemicals. But nothing stopped or changed the rays. Pierre invented a machine that Marie used to measure the strength of the rays.

Uranium is an element. Elements are the simplest forms of matter. Iron, gold, and lead are elements. Two or more elements go together to make compounds. Salt, sugar, and rust are compounds. Scientists had found 80 elements in 1896. Marie wondered if any other elements had the power to send out these rays.

Patiently Marie tested every element known, either by itself or as a compound. Only thorium compounds gave off rays the way uranium compounds did.

Marie made up a new word—*radioactive*—to describe the chemicals that gave off rays all the time. And she called the rays *radioactivity*.

She decided to test minerals and ores. At first she found what she expected. Only those ores that contained uranium or thorium gave off the rays. If the ores contained a lot of uranium, they gave off many rays. If they had only a little uranium, they gave off only a few rays.

One day, Marie found an ore that gave off many rays. She measured the uranium in it. There was only a small amount. She thought that she made a mistake. But when she did the test over, she knew she was right. The ore gave off more rays than it would if the uranium were the only radioactive element in it. There could be only one answer. Some unknown element, one that was far more radioactive than uranium, had to be in the ore.

She wrote about her discovery. Some scientists agreed that there must be a new element they didn't know about. Other scientists didn't believe her. They said they knew exactly what elements were in the rocks. If there was another element there, Marie would have to show it to them.

Marie said that she would. Pierre was so excited that he gave up his own studies to work only with Marie.

They knew that the element would be very hard to find, because it had never been found before. They knew there was very little of it in the ore, so they would need a lot of ore. Uranium ore was very expensive, and they did not have enough money to buy all they needed.

One day they realized that the element they were looking for must still be in the ore after the uranium had been taken out. The used ore was just dumped in piles, because nothing could be done with it. The Curies were given a ton of the used ore for their work.

When the big sacks of ore arrived they were piled in the yard outside the shed. There was no room inside for the huge iron pots needed to melt it, so they were put outside too. Marie stood in the yard stirring the melting ore with a large

iron rod. After the ore melted, Marie added other chemicals that helped her find the new element.

For months Marie and her husband worked. They got more ore. They borrowed some money and got more equipment. After four years of hard work in the leaky shed, Pierre became sick. He had to give up for a while. Marie worked on alone.

In 1902, she succeeded. In the bottom of a test tube were a few tiny grains containing an element no one had ever seen before. Marie named the element radium.

It was an amazing element. It was five million times more radioactive than uranium. The rays could pass through wood and even steel. Only a thick screen of lead could block them.

They could act on a person's body. Marie's fingers had been badly burned by them. Pierre had purposely exposed himself to the rays, to see what would happen.

When doctors heard of these new rays, they wondered whether the rays could destroy diseased cells in the human body. They tried and found that the rays could. And after the diseased cells were destroyed, healthy cells often grew in their place. Because the rays worked this way, they could be used to treat some kinds of cancer.

At once, radium was wanted all around the world. Only the Curies knew how to get it out of the ore. The secret belonged to them. They could sell the secret in countries everywhere. They could become rich.

A letter came from America. People wanted to produce radium there. Pierre asked Marie what she wanted to do. Did she want to sell their secret, or did she want to give it away free?

"We did our work so scientists would have more knowledge," Marie said. "It would be wrong to sell what we know."

Pierre nodded. "You're right," he said. "I'll write back tonight and tell them everything they want to know."

Although the Curies chose not to profit from their work, they could not avoid fame. News of their discovery went everywhere. When she and Pierre were awarded the Nobel Prize in 1903, Marie Curie became world famous. When Pierre died in 1906, Marie was asked to take Pierre's place as a teacher. It was the first time that a woman had held this job.

Marie still worked on the radium compounds. She wanted to take radium out of the compounds and see it by itself. In 1910, she succeeded. Again she had done something so important that the news went everywhere. And in 1911 she was awarded another Nobel Prize. She was the first person to receive this famous award twice.

In 1921, Marie Curie visited the United States. She was asked what gift she would like most. Her reply was, "A gram of radium that would be mine to use." So the women of the United States raised $100,000 and bought a gram of radium. They gave it to Marie Curie.

Marie died in 1934, just one year before her daughter Irène was to receive a Nobel Prize. Irène had gone on with her mother's work on radioactive chemicals.

Robinson Crusoe

Adapted from Daniel Defoe

Robinson Crusoe was an English sailor who loved the sea. One time as he was sailing near South America, his ship struck a reef during a storm and was shipwrecked. The sailors climbed into a lifeboat, but that was soon dashed to pieces on the rocks. Everyone was drowned except Robinson Crusoe, who was luckily washed to the shore of a deserted island. There was no one to help him find food or shelter, and there was no way to leave the island.

But Robinson Crusoe knew how to do things for himself. He swam out to the broken ship, which was stuck in shallow

WORDS TO WATCH		
Robinson Crusoe	shelter	barley
South America	ammunition	diary
reef	crew	Bible
shore	lumber	savages
island	racks	cannibals

133

water. From the ship he took food, guns, ammunition, water, clothes, tools, sailcloth, and lumber. Then he built a crude raft and returned to the island. He was able to make twelve trips to the ship before another storm destroyed it.

With the sailcloth he made a tent on the side of a small hill. Then he built a fence with sharp-pointed stakes to protect himself against enemies that might come to the island. He did not have much food, but with his guns he killed birds and small animals which he could cook and eat. He also found several springs on the island which gave him all the water he needed.

After a while, he made a bigger and stronger shelter in a cave that he found near the tent. The cave protected him from bad weather. He built shelves and racks for his guns, and he built a table and a chair.

He was able to grow corn and rice and barley so that he could make bread. He carefully saved the new kernels so that he could plant more grain the next year. He also found some wild goats on the island. He tamed the goats, and they gave him all the milk and meat he could eat.

On the ship he had found a pen and some ink, and he kept a diary of what he did every day. The diary also helped him keep track of the days and months and years. He also had found three Bibles on the ship, and he read them carefully. Every day he thanked God for all that he had.

One day he took a walk along the shore of the island. Suddenly he saw some strange footprints in the sand, and he became frightened. Someone else must be on the island! He went back to his shelter and prepared for an attack, but no one came. He searched the island, and he could find no one.

Some time later as he was looking around the island, he found many bones lying on the sand. They were human bones! Robinson saw where a fire had been made, but the men who had made it had left.

Robinson Crusoe lived alone on this island for twenty-four years. Many times he felt lonely, and he wanted someone to talk to, but no one came to visit him.

Then one time Robinson saw on the beach a group of savages from another island. They were cannibals who were preparing to eat their prisoners.

When Robinson Crusoe saw what was happening, he shot some of the cannibals, and the rest ran away. He was able to rescue one of the prisoners, and they became friends. Now Robinson Crusoe had someone to talk to. He called his new friend Friday because Friday was the day on which he had found him. He taught Friday to speak English, and Friday became his faithful companion.

Four years later, a ship passed near the island, and Robinson Crusoe and Friday were rescued. Together they sailed back to Robinson Crusoe's home in England.

The Umbrella

Two sages of Chelm went out for a walk. One carried an umbrella, the other didn't. Suddenly, it began to rain.

"Open your umbrella, quick!" suggested the one without an umbrella.

"It won't help," answered the other.

"What do you mean, it won't help? It will protect us from the rain."

"It's no use, the umbrella is as full of holes as a sieve."

"Then why did you take it along in the first place?"

"I didn't think it would rain."

Important Inventions

I. Read and Pronounce

wheel	rocket	radar
alphabet	airplane	gunpowder
printing press	automobile	compass
telephone	camera	electric motor
radio	steam engine	telescope
telegraph	gasoline engine	microscope
phonograph	electric light	typewriter
television	motion pictures	thermometer

II. Find Out and Answer

1. Why do you think each of these inventions is important?
2. Find out who invented these things:
      the radio   the steam engine   the electric light
3. Name some other important inventions.
4. Why do people say, "Necessity is the mother of invention"?

III. Write

Write a little story about an invention and why you think it is important.

I. A. You have read these stories about science and nature in Part Three of your book. Write or tell what each story is about.

> The Wonderful Alphabet
> The Invention of Printing
> Copernicus and Galileo
> The Moon
> The Nine Wanderers
> Marie Curie
> Robinson Crusoe

B. Write or tell the class which story you liked best and why you liked it.

II. A. Write or tell the class which story you like best in the whole book and why you like it.

B. Which poem did you like best in the whole book? Why?

III. A. Memorize a poem in this book and recite it to your class.

B. Write a short poem of your own.

Part Four

For Readers
Brave and Bold

The Night Before Christmas

Clement C. Moore

'Twas the night before Christmas, when all through the house
Not a creature was stirring, not even a mouse;
The stockings were hung by the chimney with care,
In hopes that St. Nicholas soon would be there.
The children were nestled all snug in their beds,
While visions of sugar-plums danced in their heads;
And Mamma in her 'kerchief, and I in my cap,
Had just settled our brains for a long winter's nap,
When out on the lawn there arose such a clatter,
I sprang from my bed to see what was the matter.
Away to the window I flew like a flash,
Tore open the shutters and threw up the sash.
The moon on the breast of the new-fallen snow
Gave the luster of midday to objects below,
When, what to my wondering eyes should appear,
But a miniature sleigh, and eight tiny reindeer,
With a little old driver, so lively and quick,
I knew in a moment it must be St. Nick.
More rapid than eagles his coursers they came,
And he whistled, and shouted, and called them by name,
"Now, Dasher! Now, Dancer! Now, Prancer and Vixen!
On Comet! On, Cupid! On, Donder and Blitzen!
To the top of the porch! To the top of the wall!
Now dash away! Dash away! Dash away all!"
As dry leaves that before the wild hurricane fly,
When they meet with an obstacle, mount to the sky,

So up to the housetop the coursers they flew
With the sleigh full of toys, and St. Nicholas, too.
And then, in a twinkling, I heard on the roof
The prancing and pawing of each little hoof.
As I drew in my head, and was turning around,
Down the chimney St. Nicholas came with a bound.
He was dressed all in fur, from his head to his foot,
And his clothes were all covered with ashes and soot;
A bundle of toys he had flung on his back,
And he looked like a peddler just opening his pack.
His eyes—how they twinkled! His dimples how merry!
His cheeks were like roses, his nose like a cherry!
His droll little mouth was drawn up like a bow,
And the beard on his chin was as white as the snow;
The stump of a pipe he held tight in his teeth,
And the smoke it encircled his head like a wreath;
He had a broad face and a little round belly
That shook, when he laughed, like a bowlful of jelly.
He was chubby and plump, a right jolly old elf,
And I laughed when I saw him, in spite of myself;
A wink of his eye and a twist of his head
Soon gave me to know I had nothing to dread;
He spoke not a word, but went straight to his work,
And filled all the stockings; then turned with a jerk,
And laying his finger aside of his nose
And giving a nod, up the chimney he rose;
He sprang to his sleigh, to his team gave a whistle
And away they all flew like the down of a thistle.
But I heard him exclaim, ere he drove out of sight,
"Happy Christmas to all, and to all a good night."

Winter in the Mountains

Johanna Spyri

Suddenly a lot of snow fell during the night, and in the morning the whole meadow was white with snow. Not one single green leaf could be seen anywhere. Heidi was amazed as she looked through the little window, for now it started to snow again, and the heavy flakes fell on and on, until the snow was so high that it reached up to the window and then still higher so that you could not even open the window.

Heidi thought this was so funny. She ran from one window to the other, wondering whether the snow might soon cover the whole hut so that they would need to light candles in the middle of the day. Finally it stopped snowing, and the next day Grandfather went outside and shoveled around the whole house, making big piles of snow. The hut looked as if it were surrounded by snow-capped mountains. The windows and the door were cleared once again, and this was good, for in the afternoon a visitor was coming.

143

Heidi and Grandfather were sitting by the fire, when all of a sudden they heard a loud thumping and something rapping against the door again and again. Finally the door opened, and in came Peter. It was not out of naughtiness that he had rapped against the door, but to get the snow off his boots, which were still all covered. All of Peter was covered with snow, because he had to battle through high drifts on his way up. In the bitter cold, big chunks of snow had frozen onto his coat and pants. But he did not give up. Today he wanted to visit Heidi, whom he had not seen for a whole week.

"Good evening," he said as he came in, and he stood by the fire as closely as possible, not saying another word. His whole face beamed with pleasure that he was there. Heidi looked at him in amazement, for as he was now so close to the fire, everything on him started to thaw, so that all of Peter looked like a small waterfall.

Grandfather got up and brought the supper out of the cupboard, and Heidi moved the chairs to the table. Peter opened his round eyes wide when he saw the big piece of good dried meat which Grandfather put on his thick slice of bread. Peter had not had it so good for a long time.

When the cheerful meal was over, it started to get dark and Peter had to think of going home. He said "Good night" and "God thank you" and was already outside when he came back once more. "Next Sunday I'll be back again, a week from today," he said. "And my Grandmother told me that you should come and visit her sometimes."

Now this was a completely new idea for Heidi, that she should visit someone. But she liked the idea very much, and the very next morning Heidi's first words were, "Grandfather, now I surely will have to go down to Grandmother; she is expecting me."

"There is too much snow," Grandfather replied. But Heidi was determined to go, because Grandmother had given her the message to come, so it had to be. She had to do it. Not a single day passed but that Heidi would say five or six times, "Grandfather, now I will have to go for sure; Grandmother is waiting for me!"

On the fourth day when it was so cold outside that every step creaked and crunched and the whole big blanket of snow all around was frozen hard, the beautiful sun peeked into the window just onto Heidi's big chair, where she was eating her lunch. Then she started her little story again. "Today I really have to go to see Grandmother. Otherwise she just will have to wait too long." Then Grandfather got up, climbed up into the hayloft, brought down the heavy sack which was Heidi's blanket, and said, "So come now!"

Heidi jumped for joy and skipped out after him into the sparkling snow. Now it was very quiet in the old fir trees. The white snow covered all their branches, and all trees glittered and sparkled in such splendor that Heidi jumped with delight and shouted again and again, "Come out, Grandfather, come out! There is nothing but silver and gold on the fir trees!"

Grandfather had gone into the shed and now came out with a wide sled: it had a board fastened to one side, and you could sit on the sled. Putting down your legs on both sides, you could steer it by dragging your feet in the snow. Grandfather sat down on it, after Heidi and he had looked at the glistening fir trees all around. He took the child on his lap, wrapped the heavy blanket around her so that she would be nice and warm, and held her closely with his left arm. This was necessary for the coming trip. Then he held onto the sled with his right hand and gave a jerk with both his feet. Right away the sled shot down the mountain with such speed that Heidi thought she was flying in the air like a bird, and she shouted loudly for joy.

All of a sudden the sled came to a stop just in front of Peter's hut. Grandfather lifted Heidi off the sled, unwrapped the blanket, and said, "Now, go inside, and when it begins to get dark, come out again and start back home!" Then he turned around with his sled and pulled it back up the mountain.

This story is from a book called *Heidi* written by Johanna Spyri. Heidi had a quiet and happy life with Grandfather on the mountain, but something happened to change her life. You can read more about Heidi if you borrow the book from your library.

QUESTIONS

1. Why was Heidi amazed when she looked out of the window of the hut?
2. What happened after it stopped snowing?
3. What did the visitor look like, and why did he come?
4. Did Heidi like the invitation? Why?
5. How did the fir trees look in the sunshine?
6. Tell how Heidi and Grandfather got down the mountain.

The Dead Tree

Alvin Tresselt

It stood tall in the forest. For a hundred years or more, the oak tree had grown and spread its shade. Birds nested in its shelter. Squirrels made their homes in bundles of sticks and leaves held high in the branches. And in the fall they stored their winter food from acorns that fell from the tree.

Tucked under its roots, small creatures were safe from the fox and the owl. Slowly, slowly, over the years the forest soil grew deeper as the dry brown leaves, brought down by the autumn winds, decayed under the snow.

But even as the tree grew, life gnawed at its heart. Carpenter ants tunneled through the strong oak. Termites ate out hallways from top to bottom. A broken limb let a fungus enter the heartwood of the tree. A rot spread inside the healthy bark.

Year by year, the tree grew weaker as its enemies worked inside it. Each spring fewer and fewer leaves unfolded. Its great branches began to turn gray with death. Woodpeckers covered the limbs with holes, looking for the tasty grubs and beetles that had tunneled the wood. Here and there they dug bigger holes to hold their babies.

In winter storms, one by one, the great branches broke and crashed to the floor of the forest. Then there remained only the proud trunk holding its broken arms up to the sky.

Now it was the autumn weather. The days were long and lazy. Yellow-gray and misty mornings, middays filled with false summer warmth, and sharp frosty nights.

Then came a day of high wind and slashing rain. As the fierce wind shrieked through the forest, the tree split off and crashed to the ground. There it lay in pieces, with only a jagged stump to mark where it had stood for so long.

The cruel days of winter followed. A family of deer mice settled into a hole that had once held a long branch. A rabbit found shelter from the cold wind in the rotted center of the trunk. The ants and termites, the sleeping grubs and fungus waited out the winter weather, under the bark and deep in the wood.

In the spring the sun warmed the forest floor. Last year's acorns sprouted to replace the fallen giant. Now new life took over the dead tree.

Old woodpecker holes made snug homes for chipmunks. A family of raccoons lived in the hollow center of the trunk. Under the bark, the wood-eating fungus spread a ghostlike

and sulphur-yellow coat. And deep inside, the carpenter ants and the termites continued their digging and eating.

On the underside, where the trunk lay half buried in the damp leaf loam, the mosses formed a soft green carpet. Fragile ferns clustered in its shadow. Mushrooms popped up out of the decaying mold. Scarlet clumps of British soldiers sprinkled the loose bark.

The years passed. The oak's hard wood grew soft. A hundred thousand grubs and beetles crawled through it. Many-legged centipedes, snails, and slugs fed on the rotting wood. And earthworms made their way through the feast. All these creatures helped to turn the tree once more into earth.

Pale shelf fungus grew on the stump like giant clamshells, eating away and growing as the tree decayed.

A skunk came by with her babies. Sniffing at the wood, she ripped into the softness to uncover the scrambling life inside.

Eagerly the skunk family feasted. Quiet forest birds scratched and picked for grubs and worms, pulling the tree apart bit by bit. The melting winter snows and soft spring rains helped to speed the rotting of the wood.

In this way, the great oak returned to the earth. There remained only a brown ghost of richer loam on the ground where the proud tree had come to rest. And new trees grew in strength from acorns that had fallen long years ago.

QUESTIONS

1. What did the *living* oak tree provide for other living things? How?

2. What did the *dead* oak tree provide for other living things? How?

3. Why was the dead, decaying tree as important to nature as the living tree?

The Judgment of Solomon

The Bible

A long time ago a great king named Solomon ruled over Israel. When he first became king, God appeared to him in a dream and said, "Solomon, you are a good man. What gift would you like most to have?"

"I would like most of all the gift of wisdom to rule my people well," said Solomon.

God was pleased that Solomon asked for great wisdom rather than great wealth or great power, and he said to Solomon, "You shall be wiser than any man on earth, and you shall be richer than any other king."

WORDS TO WATCH		
Solomon	wisdom	Israel
ruled	complaints	judgment
spare		sword

151

In those days kings often listened to the complaints of their people, and then the kings would judge who was right and who was wrong. One day two women came before Solomon. They told Solomon that they both lived in the same house. Each of them had a very young child. In the night one of the children died. The mother took her dead child and put it in the bed where the living child was sleeping and took the living child away with her.

When morning came the other awoke and saw what had happened. She tried to get her living child back, but the woman who had stolen it would not give it back. So both women went before King Solomon, and each said that the living child was hers.

Solomon had to decide who was the real mother. He ordered a servant to bring him a sword. Then he ordered some other servants to cut the living child in two with the sword and give each woman half.

The woman who stole the child did not object to this plan. But the real mother of the child cried out, "Give the child to this woman, but spare its life!"

Then the wise Solomon knew that the mother who cried out was the real mother. He knew that she loved the child so much that she would rather give it to the other woman than to see it killed.

Solomon said to the servants, "Give the child to her, for she is the real mother."

When the people of Israel heard about this judgment of Solomon, they knew that he was the wisest of men.

1. When God asked Solomon what gift he would most like to have, what did Solomon ask for?
2. Why was God pleased with Solomon's answer?
3. What did one of the mothers do that was bad?
4. How did Solomon decide who was the real mother?
5. Why was this judgment of Solomon a wise judgment?

Puss-in-Boots

Charles Perrault

There was once an old miller who had three sons. When the old miller died, he had nothing to give to his sons except his mill, his donkey, and his cat. The oldest son took the mill, the second son took the donkey, and the youngest son had to take the cat.

This made the youngest son feel very sad. "What am I to do?" he said. "My oldest brother can grind wheat with his windmill, and my other brother can carry sacks of flour from the mill on his donkey. But what can I do with a cat? I can eat him and sell his skin, but then what will I do? I shall die of hunger."

WORDS TO WATCH

miller	mowers	ogre
reapers	Marquis of Carabas	partridges

The cat heard these words and looked up at his master. "Do not worry," he said. "You will not have to eat me. Only give me a bag and get me a pair of boots, and I will show you how we can live very well."

The young man did not see how the cat could help him to live, but he knew the cat was clever. Besides, what else could the young man do?

So he got the cat a bag and a pair of boots. Puss put on the boots and tied the bag around his neck. Then he set off for a place where there were some rabbits.

He filled the bag with grain and left the mouth of the bag open. Then he lay down and pretended to go to sleep. Soon a young rabbit smelled the grain and saw the open bag. He crawled into the bag to eat the grain. Quickly the cat drew the strings of the bag closed and caught the rabbit.

Puss now went to the palace and asked to speak to the king. The guards took him to the king. He made a low bow and said, "Sire, this is a rabbit which my master asked me to give to you."

"And who is your master?" said the king.

"He is the Marquis of Carabas," said the cat, bowing low.

"Tell your master that I gladly accept his gift," said the king with a smile. "Here are some coins for your master to show him that I like his gift. And before you go, get something for yourself in my kitchen."

Puss returned home and gave the coins to his master and said, "Now you need not go to bed hungry or sleep on the ground. And I have something else for you too."

"What can that be?" said the young man, amazed.

"A new name," said the cat. "From now on you are to be the Marquis of Carabas."

The young man thought this very amusing, and he burst out laughing.

The next day Puss took his bag and hid himself in a cornfield. This time he caught two partridges and took them to the king. The king thanked him as before and gave him more money.

Many times Puss caught birds and small animals, and each time he took them to the king, and the king gave him more money. And so Puss and his master always had plenty to eat and a good place to live.

One day Puss heard that the king and his daughter were going to take a drive along the banks of the river. Quickly he ran home to his master and said, "Do just as I tell you, and your fortune will be made. You need only go and bathe in the river at a certain spot and leave the rest to me."

"Very well," said his master. He did as the cat told him, but he did not understand what Puss was going to do.

While he was bathing in the river, the king and the princess

drove by. Puss jumped out of the bushes and cried, "Help! Help! The Marquis of Carabas is drowning! Save him!" The king heard the cry and looked out of his carriage. Then he saw the cat that had brought him so many birds and animals. The king ordered his men to run and help the Marquis. When he was out of the river, Puss explained to the king what had happened.

"My master was bathing, and some robbers came and stole his clothes. I ran after them and cried 'Stop thief!' but they got away. My master swam out into the deep water and would have drowned if you had not saved him."

The king felt sorry for the Marquis, and he ordered his servants to bring back a fine suit of clothes for him. The servants brought back a new suit, and soon the Marquis was dressed more finely than he had ever been before in his life. He looked so handsome that the king invited him to ride in his carriage beside the princess.

Puss-in-Boots ran on in front of the carriage and soon came to a meadow. Some men were mowing grass. Puss came up to them and said, "I say, good folks, the king is coming this way. Be good enough to tell him that these fields belong to the Marquis of Carabas."

The mowers agreed.

Soon the king's carriage came down the road. The king stuck his head out and said, "This is good grassland. Who owns it?"

"The Marquis of Carabas, sire," they all said.

"You have a fine estate, Marquis," said the king to the young man.

"Yes, sire," replied the Marquis, "it pays me well."

Puss ran on farther and soon came upon some reapers who were cutting grain.

"I say," he cried, "the king is coming this way. If he asks whose grain this is, be good enough to tell him that it belongs to the Marquis of Carabas." The reapers agreed.

Soon the king came by, and when he asked the reapers who owned the grain, they replied, "The Marquis of Carabas, sire."

The new Marquis liked to pretend that he owned all this land and grain, and the king and princess were amazed.

Soon the carriage came toward a large castle. In this castle lived an ogre, and this ogre was the real owner of all the land the carriage had been passing through.

Again Puss-in-Boots ran on ahead of the carriage. He asked to speak to the ogre. A servant led Puss into a large room where the ogre was sitting. Puss stood a safe distance away and said, "I have heard that you can change yourself into any kind of animal you wish. But I do not believe that you can do it. Can you change yourself into a lion?"

"Of course I can change myself into a lion," roared the ogre. "Just watch me."

In no time at all the ogre became a lion, and now he roared louder than ever.

When Puss saw the ogre become a lion, he almost jumped out of his boots.

"Wonderful! Marvelous!" he exclaimed. "But I do not think that you can change yourself into a mouse, for a mouse is very small."

The ogre changed himself back into his own ugly shape and said, "Just watch me. I can become a mouse as easily as I can become a lion."

And quick as a wink the ogre became a mouse, and quicker than a wink the cat gobbled up the mouse. And that was the end of the ogre.

By now the king's carriage was in front of the castle. When Puss-in-Boots heard the noise of the carriage wheels, he ran outside and met the king at the gate.

"Welcome, your majesty, to the castle of my master, the Marquis of Carabas," he said.

"What!" said the king, turning to the young man. "Does this castle also belong to you? I have never seen such a fine castle."

They all went inside and found that a great feast was waiting for them. The cat invited them to sit down, and they all ate until they could eat no more.

After the meal Puss whispered in his master's ear, "This castle really does belong to you. When your grandfather lived, he was the true Marquis of Carabas. He was driven from his castle and his lands by an ogre, but I am happy to say that the ogre will harm you no more. It is right that you be called the Marquis of Carabas from now on. You are the true owner of this castle and these lands."

When the young man heard these words, he jumped for joy. Soon afterward he asked the princess to marry him, and the princess accepted. Now everybody was happy, including Puss-in-Boots, who did not run after mice any more except for fun.

QUESTIONS

1. What did Puss-in-Boots's master have at the beginning of the story? What did he have at the end of the story? Why did he have more at the end of the story?
2. What are some of the things Puss-in-Boots did that show he was clever?
3. Why did the castle really belong to Puss-in-Boots's master?
4. Do you feel sorry for the ogre? Why?

Doña Felisa

On Wednesday mornings the city hall in San Juan, Puerto Rico, became the house of the people. Every week on that day, the mayor of San Juan, Felisa Rincón de Gautier, held open house. Wearing one of the astonishing hats that were her trademark, she came into the council room where hundreds of people waited. She wished a good day to these people, her friends—"*Buenos días, amigos.*" They answered, "*Buenos días, Doña Felisa.*" Then she took her seat at a simple table. One by one the people came up for a few moments of quiet talk. She helped them to get whatever it was they needed—school shoes, medical care, or a place to live. Perhaps just comfort and advice were needed. She would not leave the room until she had talked with everyone there.

The story of how Doña Felisa became mayor of the capital city of Puerto Rico is partly a story of changing ideas about the place of women in public life.

Felisa was the eldest of eight children in a well-to-do family. When she was twelve years old, her mother died. After a time, her father decided that he needed his eldest daughter to run the household. So Felisa, who had hoped to become a

---

WORDS TO WATCH

San Juan	*barrios*	Felisa Rincón de Gautier
amigos	poverty	Puerto Rico
Doña	population	*buenos días*
trademark	Don Jenaro	political party
reform	open house	Luis Muñoz Marín

doctor, had to leave high school. It would have been very hard for a young girl, brought up in the old Spanish way, to argue with her father. Even about her own future.

Felisa went on being an obedient daughter. Her father decided that he would move his family to the country and spend only weekends with them. Although she missed the city, Felisa had to go to the country to take care of her younger brothers and sisters and to run the family farm. She became an able manager.

At last a time came when Felisa could no longer bow to every wish of her father. In 1917, Congress had passed a law making Puerto Ricans citizens of the United States. In 1920, it had passed another law giving women on the mainland the right to vote. After some years, Puerto Rico also gave women that right. Felisa wanted to register to vote, but her father objected. This time, however, she would not give in. She won her father's consent and was proud to be among the first women to sign the voting register.

When she registered to vote, she joined the political party of Luis Muñoz Marín. From that day on, Felisa made herself useful to her political party. Her special job was to bring the party's promise of reform to the poor people in the *barrios* of San Juan. She made friends with these people. She saw that their poverty and hunger were growing, as were their numbers. Luis Muños Marín was to become the governor of Puerto Rico for many years. His famous ''Operation Bootstrap'' was a program to build wealth and independence of Puerto Rico. Felisa was determined to do whatever she could to help.

After years of party work, Doña Felisa was well-known and loved in the city. Her party then asked her to run for mayor. Now it was her husband, Don Jenaro, who objected. Once again, she bowed to the wish of a man she loved. But she was not happy about it. When she had a second chance to become mayor, she accepted. This time Don Jenaro agreed.

Doña Felisa was elected then and many other times. She was mayor of San Juan for twenty-two years in all. During that time she cleaned up the city. She built a chain of nursery schools and improved the hospitals. She made sure that the poor children of the city had shoes and clothes and toys at Christmas. And she encouraged Puerto Rican women to be active in public life. But perhaps she is best remembered for her Wednesdays—those days when she held open house and the city hall became the house of the people.

QUESTIONS

1. What did Doña Felisa do on Wednesdays when she was mayor?
2. In what ways did Doña Felisa help the people of San Juan?
3. How long did Doña Felisa serve as mayor of San Juan?
4. On a map, find Puerto Rico and San Juan.

Ludwig van Beethoven: A Song in a Silent World

Wherever he went, Ludwig van Beethoven heard music. He heard music when the wind whispered through the leaves, or went sssshh-sssshh-sssshh across the grass, or roared from the sky to bend trees and break branches.

Music filled Ludwig's home, too. His father was a singer in the royal choir that sang in the palace of the Elector (a German prince). Ludwig's neighbors played many instruments and every night they gave a concert, singing and playing music that could be heard for miles, all the way up to the sky.

In fact, Ludwig's whole life was music. When he was four years old, he began taking piano lessons from his father. Soon he played the violin. Outdoors, his friends played hide-and-seek, but Ludwig's father kept him indoors, practicing. "You will be a great musician," his father said. "You will give concerts and bring us extra money."

There was never enough money in Ludwig's house. His father did not earn enough to feed Ludwig and his brothers and mother, or to buy wood for the fireplace and clothes for

WORDS TO WATCH		
Ludwig van Beethoven		concertos
Elector	violin	symphonies
concert	viola	orchestra
Herr Pfeiffer	cello	quartets
musicians	chorale	Vienna

everyone to wear. Ludwig's mother sold their silver and even some of their furniture to get money for food.

So Ludwig knew he had to do something to help his family, and to fill his own empty stomach.

When he was seven, Ludwig gave his first concert in the palace where his father was a singer. All the seats were filled with rich people. Ludwig looked at their waiting faces, took a deep breath, put his strong fingers on the piano keys, and began to play.

"Bravo! Bravo!" shouted the audience when he finished. "Again! Again!" So Ludwig played again. His father was very proud. And Ludwig was given money by the Elector who lived in the palace.

But playing the piano and violin wasn't enough for Ludwig. There was different music inside his head. Sometimes it was so loud, it was all he could hear. He wanted to write it down, so a whole orchestra could play it.

Ludwig asked his new teacher, Herr (Mr.) Pfeiffer, to teach him to write music on paper. But as soon as Ludwig learned, he became so busy that he hardly had time to write any music.

Part of the time he was in school learning arithmetic and Latin. He practiced the piano, the violin, and now the organ, too, every day. He gave concerts at the palace. Soon he was playing the organ for church services every morning at six o'clock.

But Ludwig did write music, more and more each year. "I won't just play *other* people's music," he thought. "I want to write my own and play it. I want the whole world to be in my music."

And the whole world *was* in his music. Ludwig wrote music with thunderstorms, and music with dancing. Some of his music sounded like armies marching to war and fighting battles in ruined cities. Then his music sounded like funerals of men killed in fighting.

He wrote music for voices, for piano, for violin, for piano and violin together, for many violins, for whole orchestras. He tried every combination he could think of. He loved them all.

Soon Ludwig's music was played everywhere. He became famous and moved to Vienna, a town filled with music-loving people and with musicians like himself.

He was grown up, but in many ways he was still a young boy, playing the piano all day and most of the night. His manners were rough, his clothes often untidy or dirty. But his wonderful music made him important friends—great musicians and great noblemen.

One day he heard a new sound—a strange sound. What was it? A buzzing, an odd buzzing in his ears. Ludwig frowned. The buzzing bothered the music in his head. He shook his head back and forth but the buzzing was still there.

The buzzing became such a roar that Ludwig was frightened. "I cannot hear my music!" he shouted. He went to his doctor. "My ears, my ears," he said. "And my music." He shook all over. He wanted to play music, but all he could hear was a buzzing and a roaring in his head.

The doctor looked into Ludwig's ears and held Ludwig's head and looked again into his ears. "Well?" said Ludwig. "Make the noise go away!"

Slowly, sadly, the doctor shook his head. "No, my friend," he said. "Your ears are sick. The noise will stay for a while. But when it does go away, you will not hear anything."

Ludwig stared at the doctor. *"Anything?"* he whispered.

"You will be deaf," said the doctor.

"But I can't be deaf!" shouted Ludwig. "I must hear my music!" He ran from the doctor's office. When he got home, he slammed the door and for days no one saw him. He sat in his room, his head in his hands, trying to think. "My music," he said. Again and again, "My music, my music."

But a strange thing happened. When the buzzing and roaring stopped, the music came back into Ludwig's head. The world was silent—he couldn't hear anything around him. He couldn't hear children shouting and people singing; he couldn't hear birds or the wind or the clatter of horses' hooves on the street. When people moved their lips, there were no voices for him to hear. But he heard all the music in his head.

He wrote and wrote. Eight symphonies for orchestra. Five concertos for piano and one for the violin. An opera. Sixteen quartets for chamber groups—two violins, a viola, and a cello. And hundreds of other works for all instruments.

One day Ludwig began a new symphony. When he came to the fourth part of the symphony (the fourth movement), the instruments were not enough for him. He added new "instruments"—people singing. The fourth movement of his symphony was a giant song. It was called the "Ode to Joy." He wrote it about friendship and joy in the world, no matter what problems people had, like his own deafness, or another person's blindness, or another's lameness, or even poverty or sickness.

The symphony was finished. Ludwig's friends played parts of it on the piano. Word of the symphony spread from town to town. "A great symphony," it was called. "So beautiful," people said. "No symphony like it has ever been heard." But some people hated it, because it was so huge and hard to play. It was called *The Chorale,* or Beethoven's Ninth. Later it was known simply as the Ninth, for no other symphony was like it.

From the time he finished the Ninth Symphony until the end of his life four years later, Beethoven was troubled by sickness and worry. He was completely deaf and very poor. But in those years he wrote some of his greatest music. He seemed to enter a new world where no one had ever been before. His music was like none ever written. And every composer who came after Beethoven has looked up to him and learned from him.

QUESTIONS

1. Would it be hard to compose music if you were deaf? Why or why not?
2. Vienna is often called "the city of music." Find out the names of three other great composers who lived there.
3. Find out the name of the city Beethoven was born in.

Rachel Carson

When Rachel Carson was a little girl growing up in a small town in Pennsylvania, her mother taught her to take pleasure in the outdoors and in birds, insects, and fish. Young Rachel's two loves were nature and writing. It was no surprise to those who knew her that she grew up to be a scientist and a writer about nature.

Above all, she came to love the sea. She wanted to learn about the different kinds of living things that swim in the oceans, fly above them, and move on their shores. She studied marine biology, and worked during the summers at the Woods Hole Marine Biological Laboratory on Cape Cod. Finally, she went to work for the U. S. Fish and Wildlife Service. Part of her job was to write about how to protect our country's birds, fish, and other forms of wildlife.

Then she began to write for the public. In her most famous book, *The Sea Around Us,* she tells of the gray beginnings of the sea and of its storms and tides. She writes about the many strange creatures that live in the sea. Her book was widely

WORDS TO WATCH		
marine	eternal	balance of nature
biology	creatures	Marine Biological
public	environment	Laboratory
ebb	sprays	
marsh	generation	

enjoyed because she was able to make people understand both the science and poetry of the sea. In *The Sea Around Us,* she writes:

> To stand at the edge of the sea, to sense the ebb and flow of the tides, to feel the breath of a mist over a great salt marsh, to watch the flight of shore birds that have swept up and down the surf lines of the continents for untold thousands of years, . . . is to have knowledge of things that are as nearly eternal as any life can be.

Later, Rachel Carson's interest in living things and their environments made her turn to a new subject. She wrote a book called *Silent Spring,* which many people read and talked about. In this book she told how certain chemicals used to kill insects could be unhealthy for other living things—including people. She called the spring "silent" because already, in some places in America, the birds which used to sing in the springtime were not returning to their nests. Their insect food had been poisoned by sprays meant only to protect crops for people. The birds that did come back laid fewer eggs. The eggshells were thin and broke easily. She wrote about the *balance of nature*—the way in which all living things depend on one another. She showed how important it is not to upset this balance.

The ideas in *Silent Spring* were questioned by other scientists. These people knew that some chemicals upset the balance of nature. But they also knew that today's growing population could not live unless chemicals were used to kill harmful insects and weeds. They believed that they could find new ways to kill these pests.

Even though she was very shy, Rachel Carson defended her ideas with spirit. She started many people thinking about how important it was not to damage nature, which is very delicately balanced by many unseen and unknown forces. "I deeply believe that this generation must come to terms with nature," she said. Rachel Carson worked very hard to protect the lives of many of earth's creatures. Her efforts led many others to work for the same ends. Her success must have given Rachel Carson a deep feeling of joy as she went about her quiet life among her friends and pets, which were not fish and birds, as one might think, but cats.

QUESTIONS

1. Why are plants and animals important to human life?
2. What is your environment?
3. Find out more about the sea and some of the plants and animals that live in it.

Margaret Bourke-White

Helen Webber

Margaret Bourke-White was a photographer who could tell an exciting story in pictures. She was a pioneer in the art of photojournalism. Some pictures she took while lying in the snow and others while hanging out the door of an airplane. Some she took from the top of freight cars and some from the rafters of buildings. She photographed everything from the rural South to the frozen Arctic, from gold mining in South Africa to the bombing of Moscow in the Second World War. No conditions were too hard or dangerous for her to work under, no place too far away to travel to. People said of her, "Maggie won't take no for an answer."

Some of the picture-stories that Margaret Bourke-White liked best to tell were about industry. When she was a girl, she often went with her father, an absent-minded inventor, to visit factories. These trips were great adventures for her. She said later that the sudden magic of flowing metal and flying sparks had shaped her life's work. Yet photography was not her first idea for a career. In college she studied snakes and

WORDS TO WATCH		
photojournalism	torpedoed	fiery
rural	abilities	reptiles
studio	rafters	correspondent
industrial	career	crippling
furnace	factories	operation

Margaret Bourke-White photographing New York City (facing)

other reptiles. Not until she began taking pictures of the college and selling them to pay for her schooling did she think of photography as a career. In later years, she kept two pet alligators in her studio on the sixty-first floor of a New York skyscraper as a reminder of her earlier studies.

Margaret Bourke-White's industrial photographs were of factories, smoke stacks, bridges, water tanks, mines, and dams. This part of her work began at steel mills in Cleveland, Ohio, when she was a beautiful young woman of twenty-one. She had to show the factory owners that her strange desire to photograph a steel furnace was in fact a serious business. The first night that she was allowed to take pictures inside the steel mill was heaven to her. She was not dressed for the task. She had on a pretty dress and high-heeled shoes. And there she was, dancing on the edge of a fiery furnace, taking picture after picture and singing for joy. Later, Maggie learned to dress to suit her task, but she never stopped singing for joy.

Her later career took her to dozens of countries. She photographed famous leaders all over the world. She was a war correspondent and often went along on bombing flights. Once she was on a ship that was torpedoed, and all the passengers had to take to the lifeboats. Another time, the little airplane in which she was traveling had to land in heavy fog on a tiny island in the Arctic Ocean. And always she kept her cameras ready to record whatever adventure came her way. Her pictures were printed in magazines and collected in books. As time went on, she also wrote about her work and made speeches. She often said in her speeches that a photographer needed to be healthy and strong and able to do hard work.

Fort Peck Dam, Montana, 1936

South African gold miners, 1950 (facing)

Mahatma Gandhi, India, 1946

Steel worker and 200-ton ladle of molten steel, Otis Steel Mill (facing)

At the height of her powers, Margaret Bourke-White's health and strength failed her. A crippling illness struck her down and took from her the abilities she needed in her work.

But she was a fighter, and she fought back. After two brain operations and years of physical training, she was able to rise above her illness for a time. She took her usual keen interest in the war against her illness, and she allowed some of her photographer friends to record her progress in pictures. Margaret Bourke-White had once said, "I knew I would never run out of subjects that interested me while on this earth"—and she never did. She was a gifted and gallant woman who lived her life to the fullest.

QUESTIONS

1. If you were a photojournalist, what would you take pictures of?
2. Why is taking pictures hard work?
3. Where would you keep a pet alligator?
4. Find out about other photojournalists.
5. Find out about the development of the camera and photography.

Part Five

On Your Own

A Voyage to the Moon

Cyrano de Bergerac

People thought about flying long before the airplane was invented. They even thought about going to the moon for hundreds of years before space exploration began.

In the 1600s, many authors and scientists wrote about flying. Some of them wrote stories about flying to the moon. They thought there were four ways people might fly. One way was in a flying chariot. Other ways were with the help of spirits, by wings fastened to the body, or with the help of birds.

In 1638 an English bishop wrote a book called The Man in the Moon. *In this book, a Spaniard, Domingo Gonsales, flies to the moon. Gonsales makes the journey in a flying machine carried by wild geese. Bishop Godwin's book was read by many people, including Cyrano de Bergerac.*

Cyrano de Bergerac was a famous French soldier, swordsman, and writer. He too was interested in flying to the moon. He wrote a book called The Voyage to the Moon. *His book was published in 1657. This tale was funny and showed imagination. It also showed some of the ideas people had about science at that time. Parts of the tale are retold here, so you can judge it for yourself.*

One night about nine o'clock I was walking home with some friends from a party. The air was quiet. Our eyes fixed upon the full moon. We each spoke about it. One friend said that he thought the moon was a window of heaven. Another believed it to be the sun itself, who at night peeped through a hole to see what was happening in the world during its absence. "As for me, friends," I said, "I think the moon is a world like ours to which our earth is likewise a moon." The response to my statement was loud laughter. Still I continued to think about my idea all the way home.

When I entered my room, I noticed a book open on the table. That was strange, because I had not put it there. I glanced at the page. My eyes fell upon a passage in which a philosopher told of two tall old men who appeared before him one night. They had entered through the closed door of his room. He asked them many questions. Finally they said they were people of the moon. Then they disappeared.

Imagine my surprise to see the book on the table, opened to that passage! Perhaps it was a sign that I should visit the moon. This I made up my mind to do.

So I shut myself up in a house in the country and made plans. I thought of many ways to get to the moon. I decided on the best way and got ready for my journey.

I hung a great many bottles filled with dew around my body. I thought that since the heat of the sun draws up the morning dew, it would also attract the bottles of dew. As they rose in the air, I would rise with them.

This plan worked so well that soon I was high above the clouds. Here the sun's attraction was even stronger. My ascent became too rapid. I was being pulled closer to the sun and away from the moon. I broke some bottles and immediately began to descend. But I had broken too many, and fell to the ground.

Figuring time from the hour I had set out, it should have been about midnight. Yet the sun was overhead and it seemed to be noon! What puzzled me more was that the countryside was quite strange. It seemed to me that since I had risen straight up I should have fallen back to the same place I had left.

Still dressed in my bottles, I started toward some smoke I saw in the distance. Soon I came upon a fort. From the soldiers there I learned that I was, in a way, in France. But it was New France, or Canada. It came to me then that the earth must have turned below me during my flight.

With much laughter at my strange dress, the soldiers led me to the governor. Since I, too, was a Frenchman, he offered me the services of the fort.

For some days I rested and enjoyed talking with the governor. But at last my thoughts again turned to finding a way to reach the moon. On a hill behind the fort I built a flying machine. It had artificial wings and a spring. I thought my machine would carry me as high as I wished to go. I climbed in and pushed myself off a cliff into the air. But something went wrong, and I fell with a bang to the ground below.

I was full of bruises, but not ready to give up. I returned to my room at the fort. There I rubbed myself with beef marrow to heal my wounds. I rested for a while. Then I went back to look for my machine.

It was gone! Some soldiers, looking for wood for a bonfire, had seen the machine and carried it to the fort. When they had discovered the spring, some said that they ought to fasten rockets to the machine. The rockets would lift it high in the air and the spring would make its wings flap. The blazing fireworks would make it look like a fiery dragon.

I reached the machine just as the soldiers were lighting the rockets. My grief over the fate of my invention was so great that I ran toward the man who was setting fire to the rockets. I grabbed the match from his hand and jumped into the machine. I wanted to break off the fireworks around the machine. But it was too late. The rockets exploded and carried me high above the clouds. I rose very fast, with more and more rockets exploding all around me.

At last, the fireworks were used up. I expected to hit my head against a mountaintop. Instead the machine fell back towards the earth, while I continued to rise. At first I couldn't see how this was possible. Then I remembered that I had rubbed my body with beef marrow. Of course! The moon was waning! And at such times it sucks up the marrow of animals. Therefore, I was being pulled steadily and surely toward the moon.

When I had traveled about three-quarters of the way between the earth and the moon, I was suddenly turned upside down. Then I began falling towards the moon. This happened, I judged, when I passed out of the earth's attraction and into the moon's. Actually I appeared to be between two moons. But I was certain that my world was the larger of the two, since I did not fall toward the moon until I was past three-quarters of the way.

I was a very long time in falling. The hardness of my landing kept me from knowing just how long it took. But at last I found myself under a tree. I was tangled up in three or four branches that my fall had broken off. When I was able, I decided to march forward.

Good fortune was with me. Within a quarter of a mile I came upon two huge animals. One stopped in front of me, but the other ran back to its den. At least I thought so, until it returned with seven or eight hundred of its own kind.

Now I could tell that they were shaped like people, but they were twenty feet tall. They were really twenty feet *long* because they walked on all fours. When these people saw that I was so little and walked on only two legs, they could not believe me to be a human. They said that since nature had given people and beasts two legs and two arms, both legs and arms should be used for walking.

At length one of these beastlike people picked me up by the neck as wolves do when they go off with sheep. It tossed me over its shoulder and carried me straight to the Town House. There I watched the people trying to decide what sort of creature I might be. Finally one, who was the keeper of strange animals, asked that I be placed under his care. This the people agreed on, and I was carried to his

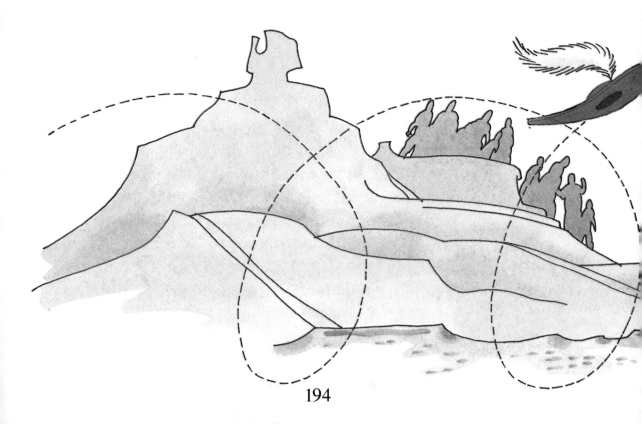

house. There the animal keeper taught me to tumble head over heels and perform a hundred other tricks. In the afternoons people came to watch me.

I could not get used to the manner in which these people lived. They ate by breathing the steam of cooking foods. And they used rhymes and verses for money.

One day the keeper took me to the palace where, tied to a rope, I was made to skip and leap about. There I met another man of my own build who was also kept as a monkey. The man spoke to me in Spanish, and I answered him as best I could in the same language. He told me he was from Spain and that he had come to the moon by means of birds. The queen had found him and taken him for a monkey too.

Seeing that we were friendly, the keeper let us stay together in the same cage. We spent many happy hours there talking about life on earth.

It really was not unfair for us to be treated as monkeys. If anyone from the moon had come to the earth and called himself or herself a person he or she would have been destroyed as a monster.

I had many talks with my keeper and with other moon people. I learned about their ways and ideas.

I tried to convince the people that they lived on the moon instead of the earth as they thought. It was *my* people, I told them, that lived on the real earth, the one they could see turning on its axis in the sky. They were greatly shocked by this statement. I was put on trial for having said this and found guilty of holding dangerous beliefs. I was driven from town to town in a chariot. The chariot stopped at every crossroads. People gathered around. I said what I had been ordered to say.

"Listen, good people, while I assure you that this moon is not a moon but a world. And the world you see in the sky is a moon. This is what the Council wants you to know."

I was then returned to my cage where I tried to think of some plan by which I could return home. Finally a moon spirit took pity on me and agreed to return me to my world. But first I had to tell the Council of my wish. They agreed that I could leave, but made me promise to tell everyone at home what I had seen on their world.

Then the spirit picked me up and rose like a whirlwind. With no trouble at all it crossed that wide space between the worlds in a day and a half. As we neared the earth I could see the outlines of Europe, Asia, and Africa. Then I smelled the fire of a volcano and fainted. When I awoke I was lying on a hill next to some shepherds who spoke Italian. They led me to a village where I rested.

Finally I made my way back to France, where I am writing of my adventures as I promised the moon Council.

Glossary

a_, ă_	apple, tan		ea	eat, leap, tea
ā	acorn, table		_ĕa_	head, bread
à	alone, Donna		ee	eel, feet, see
â	air, care		er	herd, her
ä	father, wand		_ew	few, blew
ạ	all, ball		f	far, taffy, off
a_e	ape, bake		g	gas, wiggle, sag
ai_	aim, sail		ġ	gem, giant, gym
àr	calendar		gh_	ghost
är	art, park, car		_gh	though, thought (silent)
au_	author, Paul		h_	hat
aw	awful, lawn, saw		i_, ĭ_	it, sit
_ay	say, day		ī	pilot, pie
b	bat, able, tub		_ï	babies, machine, *also*
c	cat, cot, cut			onion, savior, familiar
ce	cent, ace		i_e	ice, bite
ch	chest, church		_igh	high, bright
c̄h	chorus, ache		ir	irk, bird, fir
c̲h	chute		j_	jam
ci	cider, decide		k	kite, ankle, ink
_ci_	special		kn_	knife
_ck	tack, sick		l	lamp, wallet, tail
cy	bicycle		_le	table, ample
d	dad		m	man, bump, ham
_dge	edge, judge		_mb	lamb, comb
e_, ĕ_	elf, hen		n	no, tent, sun
ē	equal, me		_ñ_	uncle, anger
ė	moment, loaded		_ng	sing, ring

1. If a word ends in a silent *e,* as in **face,** the silent *e* is not marked. If a word ends in -*ed* pronounced **t,** as in **baked,** or **d,** as in **stayed,** no mark is needed. If the ending -*ed* forms a separate syllable pronounced **ĕd,** as in **load'ėd,** the *e* has a dot.

2. If there are two or three vowels in the same syllable and only one is marked, as in **beaū'ty, friĕnd, rōgue,** or **breāk,** all the other vowels in the syllable are silent.

o_, ŏ_	odd, pot	_ti_	nation, station,
ō	go, no, toe		*also* question
ȯ	come, wagon	ṭu	congratulate
ô	off, song	u_, ŭ_	up, bus
oa_	oat, soap	ū	use, cute, *also*
o_e	ode, bone		granulate
oi_	oil, boil	ṵ	truth, true
o͝o	book, nook	u̇	nature
o̅o̅	boot, zoo	ṷ	pull, full
or	order, normal	ur	urge, turn, fur
ȯr	motor, doctor	ūr	cure, pure
ou_	out, hound	v	voice, save
ow	owl, town, cow	w_	will, wash
_ōw	low, throw	wh_	white, what
_oy	boy, toy	wr_	write
p	paper, tap	_x	extra, ax
ph	phone, elephant, graph	_x_	exist, example
qu_	quick, queen	y_	yes, yet
r	ram, born, ear	_y	baby, happy (when
s	sun, ask, yes		it is the only
_s	toes, hose		vowel in a final
_ş_	vision, confusion		unstressed
sş	fission		syllable)
sh	show, bishop, fish	_y̆_	cymbal
t	tall, sets, bit	_ȳ	cry, sky
th	thick, three	ẏ	zephyr, martyr
<u>th</u>	this, feather, bathe	z	zoo, nozzle, buzz
_tch	itch, patch		

3. The Open Court diacritical marks in the Pronunciation Key make it possible to indicate the pronunciation of most unfamiliar words without respelling.

a·bil·i·ty *n.* The skill or power to do things.

Ac′cra *n.* The largest city and capital of Ghana.

Ac′ti·um *n.* A sea town in ancient Greece, site of the 31 B.C. naval battle between Octavian's fleet and the fleets of Mark Antony and Cleopatra.

A.D. The abbreviation for *anno Domini,* the Latin words meaning ''in the year of our Lord,'' used with dates.

Af′ri·ca *n.* The second-largest continent.

Af′ri·can *n.* A person who lives in or comes from Africa.

Al·ex·an′der III *n.* A king of ancient Greece who conquered most of the world known in his time (also known as Alexander the Great).

Al·ex·an′dri·a *n.* A city in Egypt at the mouth of the Nile River.

al′pha *n.* The first letter of the Greek alphabet.

Alt′dôrf *n.* A small town in Switzerland.

a·mi′gōs *n.* The Spanish word for ''friends.''

am·mu·ni′tion *n.* Supplies for a gun, such as bullets and powder.

ar′rant *adj.* Downright; out-and-out; thorough.

A′sia Mi′nor *n.* The peninsula bordered by the Black, Aegean, and Mediterranean seas.

as·ton′ish *v.* To surprise; to amaze.

Aus′tri·a *n.* A mountainous country of central Europe.

bal′ance of na′ture The way that all living things depend on one another.

ban′ish *v.* To send away forcefully; to exile; to drive away.

ban′ner *n.* A flag; a pennant.

bär′ley *n.* A kind of grain used for food.

bär′riôs *n.* parts of a Spanish town or city; neighborhoods of Spanish-speaking people

bat′ter·ing ram *n.* A heavy device used to knock down gates, doors, and walls.

bawl *v.* To yell loudly; to cry continuously.

B.C. The abbreviation for ''before Christ,'' used with dates.

Beethoven, Ludwig van (lud′wig van bä′tō·ven) *n.* A German composer of music, especially known for his symphonies and sonatas.

be·head′ *v.* To cut off the head.

beta (bā′ta) *n.* The second letter of the Greek alphabet.

Bī′ble *n.* The scriptures of the Christian church; the Old and New Testaments.

Big Bear *n.* Another name for the group of stars known as the Big Dipper.

bi·ol′o·gy *n.* The scientific study of life, both plant and animal.

black′ber·ry buck′le *n.* A kind of fruit dessert.

Bō·ad·i·ce′a *n.* The queen of the Iceni, who led an uprising against the Roman rulers in Britain at the time of Nero.

bound *n.* A leap.

boy'cott *n.* An organized refusal to do business with.

brass *n.* A mixture of copper and zinc.

Brit'ain *n.* The old name for Great Britain, an island that lies just west of Europe.

British soldiers (brit'ish sōl'jers) *n.* A lichen that grows on dead trees or dry soil in the eastern United States, having a green stem and a red tip.

Bū·ceph'a·lus *n.* The horse used by Alexander the Great in most of his wars.

buenos días (bwā·nòs dē'às) The Spanish words for ''good day,'' meaning ''hello.''

bur'nished *adj.* Polished.

but'ter·cup *n.* A wild plant with yellow, cup-shaped flowers.

bȳ'stand·er *n.* An onlooker; a spectator.

Caē'sar, Jul'ius *n.* A Roman general and statesman; the dictator of the Roman Empire from 49 to 44 B.C.

Caè·sâr'ï·òn *n.* The son of Julius Caesar and Cleopatra.

cal'én·dar *n.* A system of dividing time into days, weeks, months, or years.

can'ni·bàl *n.* A man-eating savage.

cà·reer' *n.* A profession.

cär'pen·ter ant *n.* Any of a group of large, black ants that build their nests in wood.

cast'ing on Putting yarn on a needle for knitting.

cat'a·pult *n.* A weapon once used to throw heavy objects at enemies.

Cath'ò·lic *adj.* Of or belonging to the Roman Catholic church.

cello (chel'lō) *n.* A stringed musical instrument like a large violin with a deep tone.

cen'ti·pēde *n.* Any of a group of many-legged creatures that have two poisoned claws used to kill other insects.

cham'pï·òn *n.* An able and valiant fighter.

Chelm *n.* A small town in Poland.

chem'i·càl *n.* A substance, especially one whose reactions are studied by a chemist.

Chī·nēse' *n.* The language of China.

cho·răle' *n.* A musical composition sung by a choir.

chunk *n.* A short, thick piece.

civ'il *adj.* Concerned with a nation; national.

Pronunciation Key

VOWELS: s**a**t, h**ă**ve, **ā**ble, f**ä**ther, **a**ll, c**â**re, **a**lone; y**e**t, br**ea**d, m**ē**, load**e**d; **i**t, pract**i**ce, p**ī**lot, mach**ï**ne; h**o**t, n**ō**, **ô**ff, wag**o**n; f**o͝o**t, f**o͞o**d; **oi**l, t**oy**; c**ou**nt, t**ow**n; **u**p, **ū**se, tr**u**th, p**u**ll; m**ȳ**th, bab**y**, cr**ȳ**, zeph**ỳ**r.

CONSONANTS: **c**ent, **c**ider, **c**y**c**le; **ch**orus, **ch**ute; **g**em; li**gh**t and thou**gh** (silent), **gh**ost; i**ñ**k; ele**ph**ant; toe**s**; **th**em; spe**ci**al, mea**s**ure, na**ti**on, na**t**ure.

Clē·ȯ·pa′trȧ *n*. The last of the line of Ptolemy kings and queens of Egypt.

clog *n*. A wooden shoe.

clus′ter *n*. A bunch; a group.

cob′ble·stone *n*. A round, flat stone once used for paving streets.

Cŏl′ches·tẻr *n*. A town in northeastern England that was burned by Boadicea's warriors.

Cȯl·lō′dï, Cär′lō *n*. An Italian author of children's books, including *The Adventures of Pinocchio*. His real name is Carlo Lorenzini.

cȯm·plaint′ *n*. A statement that something is wrong; a grumbling.

com′pound *n*. A substance formed by two or more elements.

con′cert *n*. A musical performance.

concerto (cȯn·chĕr′tō) *n*. A composition for one or more musical instruments to be played with an orchestra.

conqueror (coñ′ker·ȯr) *n*. One who overcomes an enemy by force.

con′tent *n*. All that is within.

cȯn·vēn′ïènt *adj*. Handy; easily reached.

Cȯ·per′ni·cus, Nĭc·ō·lā′us *n*. A Polish astronomer who said that Earth spins and that all the planets circle the sun.

cor·rė·spond′ènt *n*. A person employed by a magazine, newspaper, or the like to gather news and sometimes take pictures.

coŭn′try *n*. A land; a nation.

cow′ȧrd *n*. A person without courage; a timid, fearful person.

crēak *v*. To make a sharp, harsh noise.

crea′ţure *n*. A living, moving being, as a person or animal.

Crēte *n*. An island south of Greece in the Mediterranean Sea.

Crī·mē′ȧ *n*. A state in the southwestern part of the Soviet Union.

crim′sȯn *adj*. Deep red in color.

crip′pling *adj*. Disabling.

crôss′bōw *n*. A weapon that fires short arrows.

crunch *v*. To make a grinding noise, especially underfoot.

Crụ′sōe, Rob′in·sȯn *n*. In the novel by Daniel Defoe, a shipwrecked English sailor.

cupboard (cub′ėrd) *n*. A cabinet with shelves on which dishes or food is kept.

Curie, Irène (ē·ren′ cū′rïe) *n*. The daughter of Pierre and Marie Curie. She won the Nobel chemistry prize in 1935 with her husband, Frédéric Joliot-Curie, for their work with new radioactive elements.

Cū′rïe, Mȧ·rïe′ *n*. A Polish chemist who won the Nobel physics prize in 1903 with her husband for their work on radiation. She also won the Nobel chemistry prize in 1911 for the discovery of radium and polonium.

Curie, Pierre (pē·âr′ cū′rïe) *n*. A French chemist who won the Nobel physics prize in 1903 with his wife for their work on radiation.

curse *v*. To utter wishes that evil happen to a person or thing; to swear.

Daĕd′à·lûs *n.* A legendary architect and sculptor who built the Cretan labyrinth.

deer′mice *n.* White-footed and white-bellied mice of the North American woodlands.

dĕ·ter′mĭned *adj.* Resolved; decided.

dī′à·ry *n.* A daily record; a journal.

Dip′per *n.* A group of stars in the shape of a ladle or dipper; the Big or Little Dipper.

dĭs̲·ea̲s̲ed′ *adj.* Sick; not healthy; unwell.

dĭs·guī̲s̲e′ *n.* A costume that changes one's appearance.

Dȯ·lō′rès *n.* A village in central Mexico where Father Hidalgo began the Mexican Revolution.

Doña (dô′nyä) A Spanish title of respect used before a married woman's first name.

down′y *adj.* Like fine hair or feathers.

drĕad *v.* To fear greatly.

drŏll *adj.* Humorous in an odd way.

dun′g̣eȯn *n.* A cold, dark, wet underground prison.

dwạrf *n.* A short, stocky person with magical powers.

Ea′gle *n.* The name of the lunar module of the Apollo 11 spacecraft.

ėar′nèst·ly *adv.* Seriously; determinedly.

Ėarth *n.* The third planet from the sun in our solar system. —**ėarth** *n.* The planet on which we live.

ebb *n.* The flow of water back out to sea.

eb′ȯn·y *n.* A black, heavy, long-lasting wood.

Ē′g̣y̌pt *n.* Formerly a kingdom, now a republic, in northeastern Africa.

Ė·lec′tȯr *n.* Any of the German princes that helped elect the emperor of the Holy Roman Empire.

el′ė·mènt *n.* A substance that cannot be separated into other substances by chemistry.

em′per·ȯr *n.* The ruler of an empire.

en·dụre′ *v.* To bear; to put up with; to hold out.

Ėng′lànd *n.* A country on the island of Great Britain, just west of Europe.

enough (ė·nȯuf′) *adj.* Sufficient; ample.

en·ter·tain′ *v.* To amuse; to keep occupied.

en·vī′rȯn·mènt *n.* The surrounding things and conditions.

Pronunciation Key

VOWELS: s**a**t, h**ă**ve, **ā**ble, f**ä**ther, **ạ**ll, c**â**re, **à**lone; y**e**t, br**ĕ**ad, m**ē**, load**ė**d; **i**t, pract**ĭ**ce, p**ī**lot, mach**ĭ**ne; h**o**t, n**ō**, **ȯ**ff, wag**ȯ**n; f**ŏŏ**t, f**ōō**d; **oi**l, t**oy**; c**ou**nt, t**ow**n; **u**p, **ū**se, tr**ụ**th, p**ụ**ll; m**y̌**th, bab**y**, cr**ȳ**, zeph**ẏ**r.

CONSONANTS: **c**ent, **c**ider, **cy**cle; **ch**orus, **ch**ute; g̣**em**; li**gh**t and thou**gh** (silent), **gh**ost; i**ñ**k; **e**lephant; toe**s̲**; **th**em; spe**c̣**ial, mea**ṣ**ure, na**t̲**ion, na**ṭ**ure.

en′vy *n.* Jealousy.

e·ter′nal *adj.* Lasting forever; endless.

Eū′rope *n.* The second-smallest continent.

ex·pen′sive *adj.* Costing much; valuable.

ex·pose′ *v.* To uncover; to make open to attack.

fac′to·ry *n.* A building in which goods are made.

false′hood *n.* An untruth.

fash′ion *v.* To make; to shape.

fash′ion·a·bly *adv.* In a style popular at the moment.

fier′y *adj.* Flaming; burning.

fled *v.* To have run away.

flock *n.* A Christian congregation.

foo-foo *n.* A hot African dish.

fore·see′ *v.* To look ahead; to anticipate; to predict.

for·give′ *v.* To pardon; to excuse; to let off.

for′mu·la *n.* A mixture of milk and other ingredients for feeding a baby.

frag·ile *adj.* Easily broken; breakable.

French *n.* The language of France.

fum′ble *v.* To handle in a clumsy way; to bungle.

fuñ′gus *n.* A group of spongy plants, including mushrooms and molds, that live on other plants.

fur′nace *n.* A large oven used to melt metals.

Gal′i·le·ō *n.* An Italian astronomer and physicist, the first to use a telescope to study the heavens. His full name was Galileo Galilei.

gal′lop *n.* The fastest pace of a horse; a fast run.

Gautier, Felisa Rincón de (fe·li′sa riñ·cōn′ dā go·tyār′) *n.* The mayor of San Juan, Puerto Rico, from 1946 to 1968.

Gautier, Jenaro (hā·nä′ro go·tyār′) *n.* The husband of Felisa Rincón de Gautier.

gen·er·ā′tion *n.* All the people born at about the same time.

Ger′man *n.* The language of Germany, Austria, Luxembourg, Liechtenstein, and parts of Switzerland.

Ghana (gä′na) *n.* A country in western Africa.

ghōst′like *adj.* White and like a spirit.

gin′ger *n.* The hot, spicy root of the ginger plant, used in cooking.

glee *n.* Merriment; joy.

glisten (glĭs′en) *v.* To gleam; to glitter.

gnaw (naw) *v.* To grind on with the teeth.

god *n.* A male object of worship; a male idol.

god′dess *n.* A female object of worship; a female idol.

Go·lī′ath *n.* A giant, leader of the Philistines, who was killed by David with a sling and stone.

Greece *n.* A kingdom in southern Europe, on the Mediterranean Sea.

greed′y *adj.* Unsatisfied; always wanting more.

grim *adj.* Stern; foreboding.

groan *v.* To moan; to make a complaining sound. —*n.* A moan; a complaining sound.

grub *n.* A newly hatched insect; a maggot.

guĕst *n.* A visitor in one's home.

Gutenberg, Johann (yō'hänn gṳ'tĕn·berg) *n.* The German inventor of movable type for printing.

här'nĕss *n.* The leather straps and metal pieces used to fasten an animal to a plow or carriage.

haugh'ty *adj.* Full of pride; arrogant; snobbish.

hay'lôft *n.* The upper part of a stable or barn where hay is kept.

heärt'wŏod *n.* The hard, nonliving wood at the center of a tree trunk.

hĕav'ĕn·ly bŏd'y *n.* A star, planet, moon, or so on in the sky.

Hi·däl'gō, Mï·guĕl' *n.* A Mexican priest and patriot who began the revolt of Mexico against Spain.

Hon·ô·lṳ'lṳ *n.* The capital of the state of Hawaii.

hos'pi·tȧl *n.* A building for the care of the sick.

hushed *adj.* Quiet; silent.

Ic'ȧ·rus *n.* The son of Daedalus.

Ī·cē'nī *n.* A tribe of Celts who lived in England at the time of Nero.

im·pres'sĭve *adj.* Wonderful; striking; admirable.

improvement (im·prṳv'mėnt) *n.* A change for the better.

im'pū·dėnt *adj.* Disrespectful; rude.

In'dĭ·a rub'ber *n.* A springy rubber used to make bouncy balls.

in·dus'trĭ·ȧl *adj.* Having to do with manufacturing and other such businesses.

in'fi·nĭte *adj.* Limitless; immense.

in·jus'tĭce *n.* A wrong; an unfairness.

in'sult *n.* A scornful or disrespectful comment.

island (ī'lȧnd) *n.* A piece of land surrounded by water.

Israel (is̲'rē·ėl) *n.* The land of the ancient Hebrews at the southeastern end of the Mediterranean Sea, now a modern country formed as a Jewish state by the United Nations.

Israelites (is̲'rē·ėl·ites) *n.* The people of ancient Israel.

---

jag'gėd *adj.* Rough edged; notched.

jăve·lin *n.* A light spear used for throwing.

jerk *n.* A short, sharp movement; a twitch.

jȯur'nēy *n.* A trip; a voyage.

judġ'mėnt *n.* A decision in a case of law.

Jṳ'pi·ter *n.* The largest planet in our solar system, with thirteen or more moons and a small ring.

knelt *v.* To have rested or fallen on bent knees.

lab'ẏ·rinth *n.* A maze; a place with many winding turns.

language (lañ'gwȧġe) *n.* The speech of a person, nation, or race.

lär'der *n.* A place where food is stored; a pantry.

latch *v.* To fasten with a catch.

lī'ȧr *n.* One who tells falsehoods.

Lit'tle Beâr *n.* Another name for the group of stars known as the Little Dipper.

loam *n.* A fertile soil.

Lȯn'dȯn *n.* A city in southeastern England and the capital of the British Commonwealth.

lum'ber *n.* Sawed timber.

lus'ter *n.* A bright shine on a surface.

mȧ·hog'ȧ·ny *n.* A tropical tree with hard, reddish brown wood.

man·kīnd' *n.* The human race; humanity.

manned space'craft *n.* A spacecraft that is controlled by the people who occupy it.

man'ū·script *n.* A book or paper written by hand.

Marín, Luis Muñoz (lu·is' mū·nyôs' mä·rïn') *n.* The first governor of Puerto Rico to be elected by the people.

mȧ·rïne' *adj.* Having to do with the ocean.

Marine Biological Laboratory (mȧ·rïne' bī·o·loġ'i·cȧl lab'rȧ·tō·ry) *n.* A center for research and study at Woods Hole, Massachusetts.

Märk An'tȯ·ny *n.* A Roman general who hoped to succeed to Julius Caesar's position.

mär'kėt place *n.* An open place in a town where people gather to buy, sell, and trade goods.

Märs *n.* The planet in our solar system fourth-closest to the sun.

Marseilles (mär·say') *n.* A city in southern France; France's largest seaport.

märsh *n.* A swamp; a bog.

mĕad'ōw *n.* An open grassland, especially one used as a hay field.

mĕas̗'ȗre *v.* To find the size or amount of something.

Mer'cūr·y *n.* The smallest planet in our solar system and the hottest and closest to the sun.

mer'maid *n.* A creature that is half woman and half fish.

Mex'i·cō *n.* A country in North America, just south of the United States.

mid′day *n.* Noon.

Milk′y Way *n.* The name of our galaxy; the group of stars whose light looks like a pathway of milk.

mil′ler *n.* An owner of or worker in a grain mill.

mine *v.* To dig in the earth for metals, jewels, and so on.

Mī′nȯs *n.* In Greek mythology, the king of Crete and son of Zeus and Europa.

Min′ȯ·taur *n.* The monster, half man and half bull, kept in the labyrinth built by Daedalus.

Mi·ṉṵ′ An African word meaning "I do not understand."

mis·un·der·stand′ *v.* To misinterpret; to understand wrongly.

mock *v.* To make fun of.

Mont·gȯm′er·y *n.* The capital of the state of Alabama.

mōon *n.* The large natural satellite of the earth.

mōon rock *n.* A rock brought to Earth from the surface of the moon.

Mos′cow *n.* The capital of the Soviet Union.

mot′tō *n.* A wise saying.

mount *v.* To get onto a horse or cycle.

mōurn *v.* To grieve; to be sorry about.

mōurn′er *n.* A person who feels or shows sadness, as at someone's death.

movable type (mṵv′ȧ·ble tȳpe) *n.* Pieces of metal or wood used to print words directly onto paper.

movement (mṵv′mėnt) *n.* Motion.

mōw′er *n.* One who cuts grass to make hay.

mug *n.* A cup, usually with a handle and made of a heavy material.

mul′bĕr·ry *n.* A tree on whose leaves silkworms feed.

mū·ṣi′ciȧn *n.* A person who plays musical instruments.

naugh′tï·nėss *n.* Bad behavior; troublesomeness; mischievousness.

neighborhood (nā′bȯr·hŏod) *n.* A part of a town.

neighboring (nā′bȯr·ing) *adj.* Near to; adjoining.

Nep′tṵne *n.* The planet that is eighth from the sun.

Nile Rĭv′er *n.* The longest river on earth and a center of civilization at the time of Cleopatra.

Nō·bel′ Prize *n.* An annual international award given in chemistry, physics, medicine, literature, and for promoting peace.

Pronunciation Key

VOWELS: s**a**t, h**ă**ve, **ā**ble, f**ä**ther, **a̱**ll, c**â**re, **ȧ**lone; y**e**t, br**ĕ**ad, m**ē**, load**ė**d; **i**t, pract**ĭ**ce, p**ī**lot, mach**ï**ne; h**o**t, n**ō**, **ô**ff, wag**ȯ**n; f**ŏo**t, f**ōo**d; **oi**l, t**oy**; c**ou**nt, t**ow**n; **u**p, **ū**se, tr**ṵ**th, p**u̱**ll; m**ÿ**th, bab**y**, cr**ȳ**, zeph**ẏ**r.

CONSONANTS: **c**ent, **ci**der, **cy**cle; **c̄**horus, **c**hute; **ġ**em; li**gh**t and thou**gh** (silent), **gh**ost; i**ñ**k; ele**ph**ant; toe**ṣ**; **th**em; spe**ci**al, mea**ṣ**ure, na**t**ion, na**t**ure.

209

non·vī′ó·lĕnce *n*. Purposely not using fighting in making a protest.

North Pole *n*. The northern end of the earth's axis.

nóur′ish·ing *adj*. Sustaining; strengthening; wholesome.

numb *adj*. Dulled; without feeling.

nurse *n*. One trained to take care of the sick.

nўmph *n*. A sea, wood, or water goddess.

Oc·tā′vĭ·ȧn *n*. The adopted son of Julius Ceasar who became the ruler and first emperor of Rome after Caesar's murder.

ogre (ō′ger) *n*. A man-eating giant; a monster.

ō′pĕn house *n*. An informal meeting in one's home with visitors coming and going as they will.

op·er·ā′tĭȯn *n*. Surgery.

op·pȯr·tṳ′nĭ·ty *n*. A good chance; a favorable time.

or′bit *v*. To circle a heavenly body, as in a spacecraft.

or′chĕs·trȧ *n*. A group of musicians that plays in concerts, operas, plays or at dances.

ore *n*. Rock, sand, or dirt that contains a mineral.

out′cast *n*. An exile; a vagabond.

out′skirts *n*. The outer parts of a city or town.

pace *n*. A step; a stride.

page *n*. A boy attendant.

pale *adj*. Light in color.

pär′tridġe *n*. A wild bird related to the chicken.

pas′sȧġe·way *n*. A hall; a corridor.

Paulinus, Suetonius (swi·tō′nĭ·us pau·lī′nus) *n*. The Roman general who was governor of Britain at the time of Nero.

pĕas′ȧnt *n*. A poor country person; a poor farm worker.

Phil′ip II *n*. In ancient Greece, the father of Alexander III.

Phi′lis·tīnes *n*. A people of the ancient Middle East who often had wars with Israel.

Phȯe·ni′cĭȧns *n*. An ancient tribe of people who lived on the eastern shore of the Mediterranean Sea and were sailors and traders.

phō·tō·joṳr′nȧl·ism *n*. A way of reporting news by using mostly pictures.

phўs′ics *n*. The science that deals with natural forces.

plain *n*. A stretch of flat country; a prairie.

plan′ĕt *n*. Any of the nine heavenly bodies, including Earth, that revolve around the sun and shine by reflecting its light.

plun′der *v*. To rob; to take goods or valuables by force.

Plṳ′tō *n*. The planet that is ninth from the sun.

pȯ·lit′i·cȧl pär′ty *n*. A group of people with similar political goals who work together to increase their strength in the government.

210

pop·ū·lā′tion   *n.* All the people in one area or group.

pov′er·ty   *n.* Need or want.

pow′er   *n.* Strength; control; mastery.

pranc′ing   *adj.* Springing; jumping around.

prĕ′cious   *adj.* Costly; loved; prized.

prïest   *n.* A person whose job is to perform religious rites.

print′ing press   *n.* A machine for printing from inked type, plates, and so on.

pris′on   *n.* A place where those accused of or sentenced for a crime must stay; a jail.

prò·ces′sion   *n.* A group of people marching in line; a parade.

prop′er   *adj.* Right; correct; suitable.

prop′er·ly   *adv.* Rightly; correctly; suitably.

Prot′ès·tant   *adj.* Of or belonging to the Christian churches that broke away from the Roman Catholic church.

Ptolemies (tol′é·mēs)   *n.* A line of kings and queens of Egypt, ending with Cleopatra.

pub′lic   *n.* The people; the community.

Puerto Rico (pwĕr′tó rï′cō)   *n.* An island in the West Indies that is self-governing but is protected by the United States.

pup′pet   *n.* A doll controlled by strings or by hand.

puz′zle   *v.* To confuse; to perplex.

quạr·tet′   *n.* A musical composition for four persons or instruments.

rā′cial   *n.* Of or concerning a group of people with the same inherited physical traits, such as color of skin or shape of body.

rack   *n.* A frame for holding or drying articles.

rā·dĭ·ō·ac′tĭve   *adj.* Giving off energy as rays or particles.

rā′dĭ·um   *n.* A metal that is very radioactive.

raf′ter   *n.* A roof beam.

raġe   *n.* Anger; passion; fury.

rap   *v.* To strike a sharp blow.

rēap′er   *n.* A person who cuts grain.

rēar   *v.* In animals, to rise on the hind legs.

Pronunciation Key

VOWELS: sat, hăve, āble, fäther, ạll, câre, ȧlone; yet, brĕad, mē, loadèd; it, practĭce, pīlot, machīne; hot, nō, ôff, wagȯn; fŏŏt, fōōd; oil, toy; count, town; up, ūse, trụth, pụll; mӯth, baby, crӯ, zephẏr.

CONSONANTS: cent, cider, cycle; c͞horus, c͟hute; ġem; light and though (silent), ghost; iñk; elephant; toeṣ; t͟hem; special, meaṣure, nation, naṭure.

rē·birth′ *n.* A renewal; a revival.

reef. *n.* A ridge of coral, sand, or rocks near the surface of the sea.

rė·form′ *n.* An improvement; a change for the better.

rė·fūṣe′ *v.* To decline; to reject; to say no to.

rė·lā′tiȯn *n.* A relative.

rė·märk′ȧ·ble *adj.* Unusual; extraordinary; worth noticing.

rep′tĭle *n.* A group of cold-blooded animals with scales that creep or crawl, including snakes and lizards.

rest′lėss *adj.* Unable to rest, be quiet, or relax.

Rō′mȧn *n.* Of or belonging to Rome.

Rome *n.* The capital of the Roman Empire at the time of Julius Caesar; now the capital of Italy.

rud′der *n.* The part of a ship or airplane by which it is steered.

rṳle *v.* To govern; to control.

rṳ′rȧl *adj.* Having to do with the countryside.

Rus′ṣiȧ *n.* A country in northern Europe and Asia.

saġe *n.* A wise man; a philosopher.

sąlt′cel·lȧr *n.* A small dish or shaker for salt.

San Juan (san wän) *n.* The capital of Puerto Rico.

Sat′urn *n.* The large planet sixth from the sun, noted for its system of rings.

sav′ȧġe *n.* An uncivilized person; a barbarian.

Scot′lȧnd *n.* A country in northern Great Britain.

Scots *n.* The people of Scotland.

scuf′fling *adj.* With noises made by moving the feet quickly back and forth.

scur′vy *adj.* Bad; worthless.

Scṳ′tä·rï *n.* The old name for the town of Uskudar, Turkey, where Florence Nightingale had her hospital.

sen′try *n.* A soldier on guard duty.

shelf fuñ′gus *n.* A mushroomlike fungus that grows on trees in the shape of brackets.

shel′ter *n.* Something that protects; cover.

shepherd (shep′ėrd) *n.* One who takes care of sheep.

shore *n.* The land near a large body of water; the coast.

shȯv′ėl *n.* A broad-bladed spade for lifting loose dirt.

shrïek *n.* A shout; a yell.

sïeve *n.* A mesh-bottomed container for separating fine from coarse matter or for draining; a sifter.

sigh *n.* A long, loud breathing out.

silk′wȯrm *n.* The larva of a moth that spins a silk cocoon.

sip *v.* To drink in small mouthfuls; to taste.

skip′per *n.* A boat captain or master.

slen′der·er *adj.* Slimmer; slighter.

sling *n.* A strap used for hurling rocks.

smȯth′er *v.* To suffocate; to choke.

Sol′ȯ·mȯn *n.* The king of Israel from 973 to 933 B.C.

South Ȧ·mĕr′i·cȧ *n.* The fourth-largest continent.

Sō′vi·et *adj.* Of or from the Soviet Union, or Russia.

Span′ish *n.* The language of Spain and many countries in Latin America.

spâre *v.* To avoid punishing or hurting someone.

splen′dor *n.* Grandness; magnificence.

spray *n.* Fine particles of a liquid.

stale *adj.* Dull and uninteresting.

stär′tle *v.* To frighten; to surprise; to astonish.

stout′ness *n.* Fatness; plumpness.

stu′di·ō *n.* An artist's or photographer's workroom.

sul′phur *n.* A yellow mineral with a sharp odor; brimstone.

sun *n.* The star at the center of our solar system that provides heat and light for the earth.

sway *v.* To move from side to side; to swing.

sweep *n.* A long, curving motion.

Switzerland (swit′ser·land) *n.* A mountainous country in central Europe.

sword (sōrd) *n.* A long, narrow-bladed weapon.

sym′pho·ny *n.* A musical composition to be played by an orchestra.

tel′e·scope *n.* An instrument that makes distant objects seem near.

tend *v.* To care for; to watch over.

ter′mite *n.* A white, antlike creature that eats wood.

thatched roof *n.* A roof covered with straw or similar material.

thō′ri·um *n.* A grayish metal that is radioactive.

thōugh *adv.* However.

thump *v.* To strike with a heavy, blunt instrument or the fist.

'tis A contraction of *it is*.

tor·pē′dō *v.* To hit with an exploding shell that travels underwater.

tow′el-horse *n.* A towel rack.

trade′märk *n.* A name or symbol that identifies someone or something.

trag′e·dy *n.* A disaster.

Tran·quil′i·ty Base *n.* The place on the Sea of Tranquility on the moon where the Apollo 11 spacecraft landed.

trot *n.* A slow run.

trudge *v.* To walk wearily and heavily; to plod.

twit′ter *v.* To make a series of high, sharp, light sounds like a bird's chirp.

ty′rant *n.* A cruel and severe ruler.

Pronunciation Key

VOWELS: s**a**t, h**ă**ve, **ā**ble, f**ä**ther, **a**ll, c**â**re, **a**lone; y**e**t, br**ĕ**ad, m**ē**, load**ĕ**d; **i**t, pract**ĭ**ce, p**ī**lot, mach**ī**ne; h**o**t, n**ō**, **ô**ff, wag**o**n; f**ŏŏ**t; f**ōō**d; **oi**l, t**oy**; c**ou**nt, t**ow**n; **u**p, **ū**se, tr**u**th, p**u**ll; m**ȳ**th, bab**y**, cr**ȳ**, zeph**ȳ**r.

CONSONANTS: **c**ent, **c**ider, **c**ycle; **ch**orus, **ch**ute; **g**em; li**gh**t and thou**gh** (silent), **gh**ost; i**ñ**k; ele**ph**ant; toe**s**; **th**em; spe**ci**al, mea**s**ure, na**ti**on, na**t**ure.

213

un·grate′fŭl *adj.* Unthankful; not showing appreciation.

un·latch′ *v.* To open; to unfasten.

un·wrapped′ *adj.* Undone; opened.

up′rīs·ing *n.* A revolt; a revolution.

ū·rā′nĭ·um *n.* A heavy, hard, white radioactive metal.

Ūr′ȧ·nus *n.* A large planet that lies seventh from the sun in our solar system.

val′ūe *n.* The worth of an object.

Vē′nus *n.* The planet in our solar system that is second-closest to the sun, often called the morning or evening star.

Verulamium (vĕr·yṳ·lā′mĭ·um) *n.* The old Roman name for a town in southeastern England, now called St. Albans.

vic′tȯ·ry *n.* The defeat of an enemy in battle; a conquest; a triumph.

Vĭ·en′nȧ *n.* The capital of Austria, on the Danube River.

vī·ō′lȧ *n.* A stringed musical instrument similar to a violin but a little larger and with a deeper tone.

vī·ȯ·lin′ *n.* A stringed musical instrument played with a bow; a fiddle.

Virgin of Guadalupe (vir′ġin of gwä·dȧ·lṳpe′) *n.* The patron saint of Mexico.

vĭ′ṣiȯn *n.* A dream.

Vĭ′vȧ The Spanish word meaning "long live."

wea′ry *adj.* Exhausted; fatigued; tired.

wid′ōwed *adj.* Having had one's husband die.

wis̱′dȯm *n.* The ability to use knowledge; sense.

witẖ′er *v.* To fade; to perish.

woṳnd *v.* To injure; to harm.

yam *n.* A vegetable similar to the sweet potato.